Studies on the Nature of War

Volume 2

WAR AND ETHNICITY

GLOBAL CONNECTIONS AND LOCAL VIOLENCE

Studies on the Nature of War

SERIES EDITOR: GIORGIO AUSENDA

In print:

Effects of War on Society

Forthcoming:

War and Games

WAR AND ETHNICITY

GLOBAL CONNECTIONS AND LOCAL VIOLENCE

Edited by

David Turton

UNIVERSITY OF ROCHESTER PRESS

Center for Interdisciplinary Research on Social Stress
San Marino (R.S.M.)

First published 1997

University of Rochester Press is an imprint of Boydell & Brewer, Inc.
PO Box 41026, Rochester, NY 14604-4126, USA
and of Boydell & Brewer Ltd.
PO Box 9, Woodbridge, Suffolk IP12 3DF, UK

This volume contains the papers presented at the second conference on "Studies on the Nature of War" organized by the Center for Interdisciplinary Research on Social Stress, which was held in San Marino from 20th March to 24th March 1994 under the auspices of the Department of Public Education and Culture of the Republic of San Marino.

Library of Congress Cataloging-in-Publication Data
War and ethnicity : global connections and local violence / edited by David Turton.
p. cm. -- (Studies on the nature of war ; vol. 2)
ISBN 1-878822-82-9 (alk, paper)
1. War. 2. War and society. 3. Ethnic relations. 4. Culture conflict.
I. Turton, David. II. Series.
U21.2.W352 1997
355.02'74--dc21 96-48994

A catalogue record for this book is available
from the British Library

Printed in the Republic of San Marino

CONTENTS

INTRODUCTION: WAR AND ETHNICITY

DAVID TURTON

Refugee Studies Programme, University of Oxford, Queen Elizabeth House, 21 St Giles, Oxford OX1 3LA

> They come armed with spades and picks to dig up the decomposing cadavers, carrying the remains into exile in tin coffins strapped to trailers and roof racks. It is a macabre and desperate act motivated by a deep-rooted attachment to ancestral land, a fear of desecration of burial plots and a measure of political expediency.
>
> The first exhumations were carried out on Friday in front of television cameras. The next day the order came from the rebel headquarters at Pale for the digging to stop while the Speaker of the Serb Assembly...held talks with Carl Bildt, the international community's high representative in Bosnia who is keen to prevent a Serb exodus.
>
> Western observers in Sarajevo believe the Serbs are using the prospect of mass exhumations to gain moral leverage on the international community.
>
> The threat [of the desecration of graves] posed by the Muslim Croat federation has been played up by a Serb leadership which has no interest in allowing the recreation of a multi-ethnic Sarajevo.
>
> ...Serbs phrase their claims to land in terms of the number of their dead kin buried there.
>
> A joke circulating in Sarajevo tells of a Croat, a Muslim and two Serbs arriving on the Moon. The Croat points at the lunar mountains and says 'Those are like the Dalmatian hills. This must be Croat land'. The Muslim argues the cratered surface resembles the shell-scarred roads of Sarajevo, 'so it must be Muslim'. One of the Serbs pulls a gun, shoots the other dead and says: 'A Serb has died here. This is Serb land'(*The Guardian*, 27 December 1995).

In this press report we see represented most of the key themes explored by the contributors to this book. First, there is the extreme fear and hatred that ethnic difference is capable of arousing in people who formerly lived together as neighbours. Second, there is the use of ethnicity by political leaders to mobilize their followers and manipulate the 'international community,' a strategy which is not only deliberate but also cynical, because it requires at least some degree of detachment from the collective emotions it plays upon. Third, there is the use of electronic media for the global dissemination of images of grief, suffering and destruction brought about by the 'ethnic enemy.' Fourth, there is the territorial imperative of ethnic nationalism: the appeal to a selectively remembered and 'invented' past to justify current claims to territory. And finally, the Serb who, in the joke, kills another Serb to establish a national claim to territory may be taken to represent the characteristic readiness of nationalist leaders everywhere to sacrifice the lives of their followers, supposedly to advance the cause of that abstract entity, 'the nation,' but in reality to extend and consolidate their own hold on political power.

The war in former Yugoslavia was, for obvious reasons, a major topic of debate during the conference which gave rise to this book. We met in San Marino, in March 1994, in conditions of calm reflection and personal comfort which could hardly have been further removed from the mayhem and misery then being experienced just a few hundred miles away, across the Adriatic. Apart from the Balkans, our discussions of ethnic violence ranged mainly over African and Asian countries—including Ethiopia, Somalia, Uganda and Sri Lanka. This geographical spread reflected two unmistakable characteristics of war in the contemporary world which provided the context and *raison d'être* of our meeting: most wars today take place within, rather than between, states and in the South rather than in the North. The evidence for this is set out in a later chapter by Klaus Jürgen Gantzel. His figures show a total of 184 wars between 1945 and 1993, with a steady annual increase from under 10 to 42 at the end of 1993.[1] Nearly a quarter of all wars that had taken place since 1945, therefore, were in progress in 1993. This increase in the incidence of war is accounted for almost entirely by an increase in the number and duration of 'internal' or intra-state wars in the Third World. Of the 184 wars counted by Gantzel since 1945, 122 (66 per cent) have been internal and 172 (93 per cent) have taken place in the Third World, most of them in Asia and Africa.[2] The most obvious consequence of this increase in internal war is the huge growth in the world total of refugees, from around 2 million in 1970 to over 16 million in 1995, with a further 20 to 30 million people displaced within their own national borders (U.S. Committee on Refugees 1993; International Federation of Red Cross and Red Crescent Societies 1996:131-5).

As Gantzel points out, and as we are only too well aware from the 'New World Disorder' that followed the end of the Cold War, internal wars are likely to be more intractable than inter-state wars because the international community does not have well developed procedures and mechanisms for settling them. A second key difference is that internal wars are characteristically fought with light weapons, small arms and landmines, now easily and cheaply available almost everywhere, rather than with expensive high technology weapons of mass destruction. A third difference is that internal wars are particularly destructive of the lives and livelihoods of civilians. It is true that high technology weapons, particularly those used in aerial bombardment, have caused millions of civilian deaths in inter-state

---

[1] Using a slightly broader definition of 'conflict' than Gantzel's, the *World Disasters Report* gives the number of conflicts in progress in 1993 as 47 (International Federation of Red Cross and Red Crescent Societies 1995:110). Using a more restricted definition than Gantzel's (including the criterion that casualties must exceed 1,000 persons) the Stockholm International Peace Research Institute arrives at a total of 34 wars in 1993 (Louise 1995:1).

[2] According to the *World Disasters Report*, none of the 47 conflicts it records for 1993 were between states and only 8 took place in Europe (1995:112).

wars during this century. But in today's internal wars civilians often become the targets rather than the bystanders of violence. Thus, while civilians accounted for 10 per cent of those killed during the First World War (Louise 1995:9), and 52 per cent of those killed during the Second, it has been estimated that they make up 90 per cent of contemporary war deaths (Summerfield 1996:1). And finally, the violence of internal war is not carried out at a distance, against anonymous and invisible victims, but in immediate physical confrontation with friends, neighbours and even relatives.

This, of course, is one of the most bewildering and disturbing aspects of today's wars, for those caught up in them no less than for those observing and trying to understand them. How is it possible for people who have been living together on the best of terms since childhood to behave towards each other with such awful cruelty and inhumanity as we have seen, for example, in Rwanda and former Yugoslavia? If we ask those who carry out and experience these atrocities, they frequently describe, explain and justify them in terms of a deep and ineradicable difference between 'them' and 'us.' And yet, it often appears that it is the atrocities themselves which have created, or at least raised the salience of, the differences described.[3] Here we meet the enigma of ethnicity. Ethnic sentiment can undoubtedly motivate people to acts of extreme violence against those whom they classify as 'other' but, when one attempts to examine the empirical basis of this sentiment, it recedes from view, like a mirage. Gantzel, for example, was able to find only three cases since 1945 of 'ethnic confrontations' acting as an 'original cause of war' and he is quick to point out that even the most striking of these (the Hutu/Tutsi conflict in Rwanda) was far more complex, on closer examination, than such a simple designation would suggest. As he points out, 'in many cases rivals for power make use of ethnic differences as a political resource, but the differences themselves are not responsible for war' (this book, p. 136, note 20).

It was taken for granted at the conference that ethnicity will not serve as a causal explanation of war. There seemed to be general agreement that competition for political power and the material resources to which such power gives access would do far better as a general explanation of the phenomena we were discussing. It was also taken for granted that ethnicity is not a thing in itself, even though its power to influence behaviour is largely the result of it being seen as a *natural* property of a group. It is, rather, a relational concept: it refers to the way cultural differences are communicated and is therefore created and maintained by contact, not by isolation (Barth 1969; Eriksen 1993:34-5). But although it is (to various degrees and in various ways) 'imagined' and 'invented,' ethnicity is not, as has often been pointed out, 'imaginary.' It is real in at least two senses. First,

[3] See the comment by a Bosnian Muslim quoted by Gallagher (this book, p. 63).

it is a subjective reality which has enormous potential to mobilize and motivate collective behaviour, and not only in war. Second, it does not emerge from nowhere but requires specific historical conditions in order to flourish. It is the special achievement of those who use it as a political resource that they are able to 'construct' an identity for their followers which, although based on a highly selective and distorted view of their collective past, has enough connection with that past to make it plausible and meaningful. Any discussion of the relationship between ethnicity and war must therefore include the following questions. First, if ethnic differences are not given in nature, in what historical circumstances do they typically become salient? Second, by what specific techniques do leaders seek to use ethnicity as a political resource? Third, how can we explain the special power and efficacy of ethnic ideas to move people to collective action, especially at times of extreme social disruption and change? Fourth, how are we to explain the increase in internal wars and localized violence in recent years and what does this trend imply for the future of the nation-state? And fifth, what can the international community of politicians, aid organizations, journalists and academics do to help prevent and mitigate the terrible consequences of internal war and politicized ethnicity? I shall now discuss each of these questions in turn, in the light of the chapters which follow.

The historical emergence of ethnicity

There is no doubt about the relatively recent emergence of the *word* ethnicity in academic and popular discourse.[4] The question is, are the *phenomena* it is used to designate new, in any significant respect, or is this just a new and more fashionable way of describing something that has been there all along? The deliberate and self-conscious substitution of the term 'ethnic group' for 'tribe' in anthropological writings over the past 20 years might seem to support the latter view. This substitution was desirable on at least two counts. First, it was a recognition that the term 'tribe' was associated with the unacceptable 'reification' of the anthropological unit of analysis into clearly bounded, self contained and historically permanent entities. Since the concept of ethnicity is, by definition, relational, it is meaningless to think of an ethnic group as having an existence apart from its interrelations with at least one other ethnic group and, since these interrelations occur over time, it is also meaningless to think of an ethnic group as having an unchanging 'essence.' Second, the substitution of 'ethnic

4 Readers who, at this point, would like to be reminded of the history of the term should turn to the Postscript, in which Giorgio Ausenda provides a comprehensive survey of various theoretical approaches to the study of ethnic phenomena.

group' for 'tribe' helped to break down the distance which anthropological writing (though not field research) has tended to place between the anthropologist (who, of course, never belongs to a tribe) and those whom he or she studies (Fabian 1983:33). But the substitution also has at least one potential drawback: it can divert attention from the possibility that there is something specifically modern about ethnicity in the contemporary world—or, to put it more strongly, that ethnicity is a specifically modern phenomenon.

This is an argument Richard Fardon has made in relation to his study of the 'ethnogenesis' of the Chamba, an ethnic group which straddles the border between Nigeria and Cameroon. According to Fardon, the Chamba did not exist in the nineteenth century, "not just because Chamba describes people whose origins, language and culture are diverse...but because ethnic entities which have the form of the modern Chamba ethnicity are modern inventions" (1987:182). Fardon's general point is that the otherwise wholly desirable dropping of the word 'tribe' from the anthropologist's vocabulary, in favour of 'ethnic group,' carries the risk that we will think of ethnicity as some kind of 'natural,' universal phenomenon for which we have simply found a new label and, consequently, that we will overlook the special, because historically conditioned, character of ethnic differences in the contemporary world. There *is* something universal about ethnicity, of course, and this something might be described as "the human need to belong, to identify and hence also to exclude" (Gellner 1964:149). But this 'need' can obviously be expressed and satisfied in many ways which we would not necessarily wish to include under the label 'ethnic.' If we ask "What is peculiar to *ethnic* discriminations?", moreover, we find it is impossible to give a definition that will unambiguously set aside ethnic from non-ethnic ways of expressing difference, identity and exclusion—a problem that, as Fardon notes, also attaches to the attempt to define 'nation' (Seton-Watson 1977:5). Not that this should worry us, since it is precisely the vagueness and ambiguity of the ethnic idea that explains both its huge popularity in academic and popular circles and its power to move individuals to collective action. A question we can hope to answer, on the other hand, by investigating particular cases, is "What, if anything, is peculiar to 'modern' ethnicity?" Clearly, if there is such an identifiable type of ethnicity, then it must have arisen in reaction to certain political and economic processes which we take to be characteristic of modernity.

Such an understanding of ethnicity has become virtually the current orthodoxy amongst Africanist historians and political scientists, for whom contemporary African ethnicities are not "primordial" relics of the distant past but, on the contrary, products of "the same world-historical process that has produced modern capitalism, wage labour and class structures" (O'Brien 1986:905 in Eriksen 1993:88). The argument rests on an analysis of the relationship between ethnicity and the nation-state. The export of this alien form of political organization to Africa had the effect of re-shaping existing ethnic identities and sometimes creating totally new ones, although not necessarily with the awareness, let alone conscious intent, of those who were the main actors in the process. Key factors here were the classifying of subject peoples into artificially bounded categories through the work of administrators, anthropologists and missionaries; the creation of territorially discrete administrative sub-divisions which made local ethnicities more fixed and less permeable than before; the unequal distribution of the economic, educational and other benefits of modernization, which meant that some regions and groups were favoured while others were marginalized; and the concentration of political power at the state's centre, which provided an 'arena' within which ethnic groups became, in effect, competing interest groups (Markakis 1994; Vail 1989; Young 1985:73-82). The result was a transition from a non-competitive to a competitive form of ethnicity or "political tribalism" (Lonsdale 1994).

Even the recent genocidal conflict between Hutu and Tutsi in Rwanda, which Gantzel found to be the most superficially obvious case of a genuinely 'ethnic' conflict since the end of the Second World War, cannot be explained in this way. This is not only because the genocide was deliberately planned by the Hutu élite of the Habyarimana government as a means of clinging on to power (de Heusch 1995:6; Prunier 1995; de Waal 1994) but also—and this is what concerns me in this section—because the ethnicity they played upon and orchestrated was largely a product of the recent colonial and post-colonial past. The point is not that Tutsi and Hutu identities were invented ab *initio* by the German and then Belgian authorities, nor that these authorities were aware of the consequences of their administrative decisions and policies. The point is that the system of indirect rule established in both Burundi and Rwanda made these identities "much more systematic and extensive classifications of the subject populace" (Young 1985:76). It was probably only in the central part of the pre-colonial kingdom of Rwanda that the key institution of traditional Tutsi domination, the 'cattle contract' between a pastoralist Tutsi 'patron' and an agriculturalist Hutu 'client,' was widespread (de Heusch 1995:3; Newbury 1995). But the colonial administration "absorbed the ideology of domination of the central Rwandan state, codified and rationalized it, and extended it throughout the domain" (Young 1985:76-7).

The policy of institutionalizing Tutsi domination and recruiting the indigenous élite almost entirely from the Tutsi 'aristocracy' (a classic case of the unequal distribution of the benefits of modernization referred to earlier) was legitimated by the theory that the Tutsi belonged to a superior Hamitic race,[5] with its origins in Ethiopia, to which the Bantu Hutu were considered to be self-evidently inferior. And then, a few years before independence was

5 "In the 1930s, the Belgians conducted a census and issued an identity card for each

proclaimed in 1962, the Belgian authorities did a *volte face* and proceeded to support a 'social revolution' of Hutu against the Tutsi minority which led, between 1959 and 1964, to the brutal killing of 10,000 Tutsi and the exodus of 150,000 Tutsi refugees, mainly to Uganda (de Heusch 1995). It was the sons and grandsons of these refugees who, as members of the Rwandan Patriotic Front, took part in the military campaign against the Hutu government of Rwanda, beginning with an invasion from Uganda in 1990. We must assume that their prolonged exile from a Rwandan "land of dreams" (A. D. Smith 1986:28) had as important an impact on their Tutsi identity as the experience of exile in Tanzania had for the identity of Hutu refugees who fled the genocidal massacres perpetrated by the Tutsi élite in Burundi in 1972 (Malkki 1992).

The particular ethnic materials, then, out of which the Hutu political and intellectual élite fashioned its policy of politicized ethnicity were a legacy of 50 years of Belgian colonial rule. The failure (or unwillingness) of the leaders of the international community to appreciate the extent to which Tutsi and Hutu ethnicities were a reaction to the experience of colonialism made it easier for them to portray the 1994 genocide in Rwanda as an eruption of ancient and irrational tribal antagonisms, rather than as the carefully planned, deliberately executed—and therefore preventable—operation it was.[6]

A story with clear similarities to this was told at the conference about the conflict in former Yugoslavia. Both Tom Gallagher, in his account of the techniques used to whip up ethnic hatred and violence by the Serb and Croat leadership and Stefan Troebst, in his equally valuable account of why the same process did not occur in Macedonia, criticize the popular view, propagated by intellectuals, politicians and journalists, that the conflicts that

---

individual, which specified whether they were Tutsi, Hutu or Twa. Such was the slender basis for the racial typology that the census takers were obliged to use ownership of cows as a criterion: those with ten or more were Tutsi, those with less were Hutu, in perpetuity. On the basis of a cow or two hinged the status of overlord or serf, and with it access to education and every other privilege bestowed by the administration. The cards still exist today—they are the means whereby the road-block militiamen know whom to kill and whom to spare" (de Waal 1994:3).

6 One of the main conclusions of an evaluation of emergency assistance in Rwanda by the London based Overseas Development Institute (ODI) was that "the failure of the international community to either prevent the genocide or do more to limit its spread was by far the most significant failing of the whole response" (ODI 1996:50). It is particularly ironic that French involvement in the crisis (sending military forces to assist the Habyarimana government and helping to train the Hutu militias which carried out the genocide) seems to have been motivated by the desire to protect "the great visionary project for a francophone African space" from the Anglo-Saxon threat represented by the English-speaking Rwanda Patriotic Front (de Heusch 1995:7; see also Prunier 1995, cited by Mitchell 1995).

erupted in the Balkans after 1989 were merely the result of the "clock of political life and culture in Eastern Europe" starting to "tick again" after it had been stopped by the Red Army in 1944 (Troebst, this book, p. 77). According to this view, the root cause of the conflicts was the endemic and atavistic tribal antagonism which has, allegedly, always been the hallmark of Balkan history but which had been 'deep frozen' under communism. Troebst points out that this is simply not good history. As part of the 'success story of communist nation building by modernization,' the countries of Eastern Europe underwent a profound transformation between 1944 and 1989.

> Urbanization, industrialization and secularization turned this overwhelmingly rural part of Europe into a heavily industrialized agglomeration of towns and town-like settlements inhabited by first-generation city-dwellers whose regional and ethnic identities and religious and other traditions were replaced from above by nationalism and the new class ideology (this book, p. 79).

Far from being 'deep frozen' during these years, identities of various kinds—national, regional, religious and ethnic—were also being transformed and were a key factor in the deliberations and calculations of the political and intellectual élite. Gallagher notes the parallel drawn by the Austrian historian Anton Bebler (1993) between the federal system adopted by Tito and the Soviet constitutional model of a union of theoretically sovereign and culturally autonomous national republics. The powerful central position given to Serbia in the Yugoslav federation was analogous to that of Russia in the USSR.[7] No federal district was created for Serbia, while Belgrade, the main Serb city, was preferred as the state capital to the multi-ethnic Sarajevo. The attempted decentralization of political power to the regions in the 1960s only served to promote intra-state national rivalries because, in the absence of genuine political pluralism and multi-party elections, it "had the effect of blocking any parties that transcended ethnic lines" (p. 50). Competition for the political and economic resources controlled by the Serb centre was, therefore, inevitably carried on through the idioms of ethnicity and nationality. During the discussion of his paper at the conference, Gallagher referred to the moderate reform party of the former Yugoslav President, Ante Markovich, a respected figure who tried to rise above an ethnic appeal. At the elections which took place on the eve of the conflict, however, his party had very little success. "People voted for ethnically based parties," said Gallagher, "because Tito had created a federalized political system and they gained their identity from the federal units."

---

[7] Gallagher also notes that the wartime struggle of the Partisans was used to give substance to the image of a collective Yugoslav identity. This is reminiscent of the use made of the so called 'Great Patriotic War' by Soviet propagandists in their efforts to integrate "minority nationalities" into the "broader entity of the Soviet Union" (H. Smith 1976:369, cited by Rudensky 1993:190).

It seems, then, that the break-up of the former Soviet Union and Yugoslavia along ethnic lines cannot be explained as the result of old ethnic divisions becoming 'defrosted' during the communist 'thaw.' Rather, the shape and salience of these divisions was a product of the federal political system adopted by Lenin, Stalin and Tito. According to Edward Friedman (1993), the fostering of "ethnic assertion against a state-centered group" is an essential feature of "the Leninist political system" which "leaves an extraordinarily deep imprint on identity politics" (1993:223).

> Local people are locked into regional poverty by Leninist controls that keep them from fleeing state-imposed, place-specific collectives, a system that also uses internal passports, region-specific food coupons, and police registration in hotels to prevent minorities enjoying the greater resources monopolized elsewhere by the dominant group. The system fosters a divisive process, privileging the dominant group, peripheralizing the minorities. Because a nation state is a shared space, this absolute geographical split fostered by Leninist structures threatens to split the nation itself. The logic of Leninism is de-nationalization (1993:226).

Crawford Young (1994) makes a similar point in commenting on the "appropriation of the [federalist] concept by Lenin and his heirs as a device for 'solving the national question.'"

> In the Soviet case, and subsequently the Yugoslav and Czech instances modelled upon it, territorial subdivisions based upon 'titular nationalities' were created.... It is striking that, in all three communist federations, the loss of ideological and political legitimacy by the regime resulted at once in the fragmentation of these states along the often gerrymandered lines of nationality divisions, which originally reflected the strategic ethno-political calculus of the center (1994:11-2).

The recent re-organization of the political system in Ethiopia should be mentioned here, both because of its relevance to Zitelman's discussion of Oromo ethno-nationalism (in a later chapter) and because it is an example of the introduction to Africa of the Soviet/Yugoslav constitutional model. The new system was introduced by the Tigray People's Liberation Front (TPLF) following its takeover of Ethiopia from the Mengistu government in 1991. The purpose was "...to maintain the continuity of the Ethiopian borders...while introducing a degree of regional and local autonomy and *preserving the hegemony of the TPLF*" (Zitelman, this book, p.106, my emphasis). The strategy was to set up an umbrella organization for the TPLF, called the Ethiopian Peoples' Revolutionary Democratic Front (EPRDF), divide the country into administrative territories based on ethno-linguistic criteria and create puppet 'People's Democratic Organizations' in order to sideline the existing ethnic political movements. The strategy worked brilliantly, at least in the short term: the EPRDF had a landslide victory in the supposedly democratic elections held in 1994, winning over 80 per cent of seats in the new national assembly. But the creation of ethnic federal units without genuine power sharing could well have disastrous long term consequences. According to Frederick Gamst, who was an international observer during the 1992 elections in southwestern Ethiopia,

> ...the EPRDF made a fundamental error in policy when it followed its outmoded Leninist ideology of using federated ethnicity...as the basis for the reconstruction of the polity. Reinforcement of nationalism—in the sense of ethnicity—and the divisiveness of ethnocentrism and sectarianism were the harvest to be reaped from the ideological seeds being sown by the EPRDF.... Perhaps the best that can be achieved is another ethnically seething India (Gamst 1995:5).

The failure, or refusal, of outside observers to recognize the impact of political and economic change on the development of ethnic and national sentiment, whether in Eastern Europe or Africa, has made it easier for these observers to ignore, or fail to give serious causal weight to, the role of "tiny political élites...in using ethnicity and religion to mobilize, polarize and radicalize larger target groups" (Troebst, this book, p. 81). It has also made it easier for the international community to stand aside while millions of people have been killed or made homeless,[8] on the grounds that, to intervene in such 'tribal' confrontations would be at best useless and at worst counter-productive. The assumption that the root causes of these wars lay in 'age old' tribal antagonisms not only had its political and diplomatic uses, therefore, but it also diverted attention from what really needed to be explained: how was it that these "tiny political élites" were able to arouse people who had been living for generations in multi-ethnic, multilingual and multi-religious communities to such extremes of ethnocentrism? One part of the explanation lies in the kind of historical conditions I have been discussing—conditions which are largely beyond the control of individual actors but which ensure that the necessary ethnic materials are ready to hand when needed. A second part of the explanation lies in the particular techniques and strategies which are deliberately employed by political leaders to turn these materials into a powerful resource for advancing nationalist territorial claims. This is the subject of the next section, after which I shall turn to a third part of the explanation, which lies in the particular mobilizing power of ethnic ideas and symbols, especially at times of rapid economic and political change and extreme social disruption.

Ethnicity and nationalism

One of the most striking characteristics of industrial and industrializing societies in the latter part of the twentieth century has been the unexpected

[8] According to one estimate, 230,000 people, most of them civilians, had been killed in Croatia and Bosnia-Hercegovina by 1994 and 2,000,000 refugees had been created (Nagan 1994:6). The genocide and civil war in Rwanda "caused the violent death of between 500,000 to 800,000 people, the movement of over 2 million Rwandese into neighbouring countries and the temporary displacement of well over one million people inside Rwanda" (ODI 1996:10).

resilience of ethnic identity as an idiom for the pursuit of political and economic interests. Both Marxist and liberal-capitalist interpretations of history predicted the opposite: in the case of Marxism, the expectation was that class would become the all-important form of social identification and, in the case of liberalism, the expectation was that 'primordial' differences between groups would simply wither away in the face of industrial, scientific and technological progress, universal education and mass communication (Dandeker 1993; Glazer & Moynihan 1979:31). What both sociological traditions appear to have missed was the possibility that a cultural, linguistic or religious difference might be defended and asserted not only as an end in itself but also as a means—and a particularly effective means—to economic and political advancement.

> ...whereas in the past religious conflicts were based on such issues as the free and public practice of a religion, today they are based—like the one which is tearing Northern Ireland apart—on the issue of which group shall gain benefits or hold power. Language conflicts—as in India—today have little to do with the rights to the public use of the language.... They have more to do with which linguistic group shall have the best opportunity to get which job.... [T]he weight has shifted from an emphasis on culture, language, religion as such, to an emphasis on the economic and social interests of the members of the linguistic or religious group (Glazer & Moynihan 1979:31-2).

According to Glazer and Moynihan, one important explanation for "the new salience of ethnicity" lies in the control of economic resources by the state, whether of the 'socialist' or 'welfare' type. Since these resources are finite, there is a competitive advantage to be gained from asserting claims on behalf of a group which is "small enough to make significant concessions possible" rather than on behalf of "large but loosely aggregated groups such as 'workers,' 'peasants,' 'white collar employees'" (1979:32). But the "strategic efficacy" (1979:33) of ethnicity in these circumstances cannot be explained simply on the grounds that the groups so mobilized are smaller than those mobilized on the basis of economic, or class, position. Paradoxically, ethnicity is an effective means of mobilizing groups around common material interests precisely because of its non-material, that is symbolic, content, which masks or 'mystifies' those interests for the group members themselves. In the words of Daniel Bell, quoted by Glazer and Moynihan, "Ethnicity has become more salient [than class] because it can combine an interest with an affective tie" (1979:38).

The analysis of ethnicity must therefore take account of both its 'instrumental' or material aspects *and* its 'primordial' or cultural aspects, since its very effectiveness, as a means of advancing group interests, depends on it being *seen* as 'primordial' by those who make claims in its name.[9] And, if ethnicity is to be analyzed in this way, we obviously have to

---

9 This is the subject of the next section.

pay particular attention to the role of political leaders and intellectuals who make the primordial claim credible. They do this by constructing a plausible history for the group—plausible because based on the re-ordering and selective interpretation of actual historical events—which clearly separates it from specific and significant others and establishes its right to some kind of special status, treatment or existence. This activity of constructing an historical narrative to legitimate ethnic claims becomes particularly evident when ethnicity is linked to nationalist or separatist politics, as it has been, especially in Europe, since the late nineteenth century (Hobsbawm 1992). This is because the "ethno-nationalist" has to use history to show not simply that "we" are different from "them" but that the difference is so great that we cannot be expected to share the same territory. The strategies employed by leaders and intellectuals to fill "the empty containers of nationalism" (Hobsbawm 1992:4) with ethnicity are described in greatest detail in this book by Gallagher and Zitelman. Although they deal with very different cases, both geographically and culturally, instructive comparisons can be made between Gallagher's account of how Serb and Croat nationalists in former Yugoslavia set out to "turn history into a contemporary political resource" and Zitelman's account of the attempt, largely by émigrés and refugees, to create an Oromo national self-consciousness in the Horn of Africa.

Before coming to these cases, however, it is worth remembering that, just as ethnic politics, and therefore ethnic conflict, does not have to be separatist or nationalist (as they are not in the USA for example), so nationalism, the doctrine that nations have the right to form territorial states, does not have to be ethnic. The distinction between 'ethnic nationalism' and 'liberal nationalism' is spelt out in detail by Jakob Rösel in a later chapter. Ethnic nationalism was a development of the late nineteenth century in Eastern and Central Europe, but the earlier liberal nationalism, which originated in Western Europe and the USA, was taken up by twentieth century anti-colonial liberation movements in Africa and elsewhere (Hobsbawm 1992:4). Liberal nationalism is based on 'civic' criteria, that is on the presumed equal participation of all citizens in a common economic, legal and educational system. It therefore conceives the nation as consisting

> ...of all those individuals who have lived together under a common system of law and who, as a result of political reform and revolutions, have acquired the right of democratic self-determination. It is the memory of having lived under a common rule of law, the existence of a democratic constitution and the constant practice of self-government which impart to these diverse individuals a common, a national identity (Rösel, this book, p. 148).

Ethnic (or ethno-) nationalism is based on ethnic or ethno-linguistic criteria, that is, on the presumed common ancestry, history, language and culture of all members of the group (A. D. Smith 1988:8-9; 1989). Although these distinctions are between types of nationalist doctrines or programs, not between nations as units of population,[10] the need to keep "the two concepts of nation" analytically separate is brought out with particular clarity and force by Rösel. This is not simply for the sake of historical accuracy, but because the liberal concept of the nation is a necessary condition for the successful acknowledgement and accommodation of ethnic groups in a multi-ethnic state. Katherine Verdery, with Eastern Europe specifically in mind, adds a third conception of the nation which she calls "socialist paternalism" and which,

> ...emphasized neither citizenship nor ethnicity but a quasi-familial dependency.... Instead of political rights or ethno-cultural similarity, it emphasized a moral tie linking subjects with the state through their rights to a share in the redistributed social product. Subjects were presumed to be...grateful recipients...of benefits their rulers decided upon for them (1992:8).

She also notes an "elective affinity" between socialist paternalism and ethno-nationalism. Both use kinship metaphors to describe the relationship between subject and state and both emphasize the collectivity over the individual.

The question that inevitably arises is, under what circumstances does ethnicity become, not just politicized, but politically separatist? Or, to put it another way, what turns ethnic politics into nationalist politics? Hobsbawm's answer, at least for the recent history of Eastern Europe, is in two parts. On the one hand, ethnicity is the ultimate guarantee, or "fall back position," for individuals who are experiencing the failure of once taken for granted economic and political structures and ideological certainties. On the other hand, ethnicity

> ...turns into separatist nationalism for much the same reason as colonial liberation movements established their states within the frontiers of the preceding colonial empires. They are the frontiers that exist. Only more so, for the Soviet constitution itself had divided the country into theoretically ethnic territorial sub-units, ranging from autonomous areas to full federal republics. Supposing the union fell to pieces, these were the fracture lines along which it would naturally break (1992:6).

A. D. Smith, writing ten years before the collapse of Soviet communism, stresses the role of discontented and frustrated intellectuals who turn to ethnic self-consciousness, the elaboration of a common group history and, ultimately, to political separatism as a route to "the status and power that had eluded them in the state of the dominant community" (1979:30). Both Hobsbawm's and Smith's insights are born out by Gallagher's and Zitelman's accounts of ethnic nationalism in former Yugoslavia and the Horn of Africa.

---

10 Smith, for example, would argue that all nations "are formed out of 'civic' and 'ethnic' components" and that "the modern nation, to become truly a 'nation' requires the unifying myths, symbols and memories of pre-modern *ethnie*" (1988:10-1).

Gallagher brings out clearly the huge importance of history, and therefore of historians, in the mobilization of ethno-nationalist territorial claims. This, of course, has often been stressed, from Renan's comment that "A heroic past, of great men, of glory...that is the social principle on which the national idea rests" (1882:26) to Hobsbawm's that "Historians are to nationalists what poppy-growers in Pakistan are to heroine-addicts: we supply the raw material for the market" (Hobsbawm 1992:3). But although individual historians "feed" the nationalist's "habit," history as an academic discipline must be the enemy of nationalism, in so far as it is dedicated to finding out what actually happened in the past rather than to supplying a "mythical charter" (Nadel 1957:206-8) to legitimate present political interests.[11] History, according to Gallagher, has played a vital part in the politicizing of Serb and Croat national identity, precisely because these two populations are *not* radically set apart from each other, either physically, historically or culturally. They speak the same language (though using different scripts) and have lived together in the same towns and villages for generations. The most salient difference between them appears to be that they belong to different traditions of Christianity—the 'Eastern' or Orthodox tradition in the case of Serbia and the 'Western' or Roman Catholic tradition in the case of Croatia. Historians and other 'intellectuals' had to work hard, therefore, to provide their respective political leaders (themselves often former intellectuals) with the means to draw "sharp battle lines in a blurred landscape" (Gallagher, this book, p. 54).[12] Gallagher describes how the past was "redefined" and "re-arranged" to show that people who had been neighbours since childhood could no longer live together in the same territory, how the ethnic "other" was demonized by the attribution of collective and hereditary guilt for past atrocities and, in the case of Serbia especially, how the image was propagated of a victimized and threatened population, fighting for its very survival. One of the most telling comments in this book on the outcome of such ethno-nationalist myth-making and of the violence it was used to generate and sustain comes from a Bosnian Muslim.

> I never thought of myself as a Muslim. I don't know how to pray. I never went to a mosque.... But now I have to think of myself as a Muslim, not in a religious way but as a member of a people. I have to understand what it is about me and my people they want to obliterate (Vulliamy 1994:65, quoted by Gallagher, this book, p. 63).

---

[11] In the same lecture, *Qu'est-ce qu'une nation?*, from which the above quotation is taken, Ernest Renan made the famous remark that "l'erreur historique" is vital to the creation of a nation.

[12] We should remember, however, Fredrik Barth's point that ethnic boundaries are maintained by interaction across them, rather than by the distinctiveness of the cultural "stuff" they enclose. It follows that there is no reason to expect a correlation between cultural similarity and "a reduction in the organizational relevance of ethnic identities, or a breakdown in boundary-maintaining processes" (1969:33).

There could hardly be a more succinct statement of the case for seeing ethnic sentiment as the result rather than the cause of war.

It is not difficult to understand the attractiveness of nationalist rhetoric to the political leaders of Eastern Europe in the wake of the collapse of communism. In these circumstances nationalism was, quite simply, the most effective means available of gaining and/or keeping a political following. In fact, Eastern European communist leaders had been turning to nationalism "to consolidate their shrinking legitimacy" (Troebst, this book, p. 79) well before 1989, the most notable case in point being Nicolae Ceausescu in Rumania. It was, for both leadership and people, an easy transition to make because of what Verdery calls the "elective affinity" between "socialist paternalism" and ethno-nationalism (see also Goluvbovic 1993:68, quoted by Gallagher, this book, p. 70), while a policy of unrestrained nationalism had the added and familiar advantage (for the leadership) of sidelining potentially troublesome issues of everyday domestic politics. Nor is it difficult to understand the attractiveness of the nationalist cause to "intellectuals frustrated by their lack of recognition and influence" (Gallagher, p. 66). That many of these should nevertheless have been émigrés[13] is a predictable irony, since it is difficult to reflect on and objectify your own culture unless you have, at least to some extent, escaped from it, gained a distance from it—even become a stranger to it.[14] Finally, it also comes as no surprise to learn of the important part played by electronic media—especially television—in disseminating nationalist propaganda in former Yugoslavia. The special emotive power of the visual image was, for example, exploited to the full in television coverage of "the cult of digging up decomposed bodies" (Gallagher, this book, p. 61), whether of Serb victims of the Nazi puppet state of Croatia during the second World War or of Croat victims of communist persecution since the war. Gallagher attributes great importance to television, "a new factor in Balkan nationalism" (p. 48), in explaining how nationalist leaders were able to turn ethnic sentiment into ethnic hatred with such success. Through their control of television, they provided their followers, especially those living in rural areas, with a constant diet of nationalist propaganda, which went virtually unchallenged by other sources of information coming from the outside world.[15]

---

13 Gallagher mentions particularly the advisers to the Croat President, Franjo Tudjman, many of whom were drawn from the Croat diaspora.

14 Cf. Gellner: "Genuine peasants or tribesmen, however proficient at folk-dancing, do not generally make good nationalists" (1964:162).

15 During the discussion of his paper at the conference, it was suggested to Gallagher that he was underestimating the extent to which people 'interact' with television messages, using and interpreting them in ways which the originators of the messages may not have intended or anticipated. He replied that the general tendency of television to "foreclose the

The Oromo case, described by Zitelman, provides an interesting comparison with former Yugoslavia. We see here the same linking of ethnicity and nationalism, the same prominence of émigré and refugee intellectuals in the nationalist myth-making élite; the same reliance on the historical reconstruction of a collective past to give substance to the assertion of a common cultural identity; and the same portrayal of this identity as threatened by a long-standing ethnic enemy—in this case the Amhara of Ethiopia's Christian, Semitic and imperial 'core.' But there are also important differences. The most obvious is that those elements of modernity which have generally been considered necessary for nationalism to flourish and which have long been present in Eastern Europe (a universal education system, widespread literacy, effective mass communications, etc.) are not available to help in the task of creating a pan-Oromo consciousness. The Oromo number approximately twice the combined Serb and Croat population of former Yugoslavia[16] and are widely distributed over one of the largest and least developed countries in Africa. They speak the same language but are made up of several formerly autonomous groups, such as the Arsi, Guji and Boran, with different subsistence economies ranging from intensive plough agriculture to camel and cattle herding. Most are Muslim, especially the lowland pastoralists, but the ancestors of many of the highland cultivators were converted to Orthodox Christianity after the Abyssinian conquest of the nineteenth century. In short, "Dispersion, adaptation to varied ecological conditions and mingling with other ethnic groups resulted in considerable differentiation among the numerous Oromo communities" (Markakis 1994:231).

The best known (at least in the West) movement for an independent Oromo state (Oromiya) is the "secular and modernist" Oromo Liberation Front (OLF) which was formed in 1974, the year in which the Emperor Haile Selassie was deposed (Zitelman, this book, p. 107).[17] The OLF has concentrated on developing "the idea of a reified, essentialist 'Oromo culture'" (p. 111), based on the image of an Oromo "golden age," in which "democracy was flourishing under the Gada system and Ethiopian

---

range of options" in political debate is compounded in former communist countries, where people have been "educated to be uncritical" of the "supposedly benevolent state."

16 Zitelman estimates the Oromo population as approximately 25 million. Nagan (1994:4) estimates the Serb population of former Yugoslavia at just over 8 million and the Croat population at just over 4 million.

17 It is one of the strengths of Zitelman's account that he does not ignore the existence of four other Oromo national movements, two of which have roots going back to the 1960s and strong links with Somalia, one of which broke away from the OLF in 1978 and adopted an Islamic agenda and one of which was set up by the Tigray People's Liberation Front (TPLF) when it took over the government of Ethiopia in 1991.

colonialism had not yet disturbed the peace of the green pastures" (pp. 113-4).[18] The OLF put great emphasis on literacy, using the Roman and not the Ethiopian syllabic script, and distributed its educational material amongst Oromo refugees living in camps in Somalia and Sudan. Zitelman notes the important role of "the international Oromo diaspora" (p. 112) in developing and defining the notion of a single Oromo cultural identity. As already noted for the Serb and Croat cases, it is not surprising to find émigré intellectuals deeply involved in the process of ethno-nationalist myth-making but, in the Oromo case, the distance between the myth-makers and the population the myth was intended to mobilize is particularly striking. It is not simply that there is a huge geographical, educational and cultural divide, between, say, a university graduate living in Toronto and a nomadic herder living in southern Ethiopia, even if they both speak dialects of the same language, but also that, as Zitelman remarks (p. 112), the Oromo identity fashioned by the diaspora communities was largely a reaction to their own experience of exile in various North American and European cities.

Two observations suggest themselves. The first is that the ethnic version of nationalism, especially the dogma that culturally defined units have, and should exercise, the right to self-determination, is a relatively recent European export to Africa,[19] and is as alien to African cultural traditions as the nineteenth century liberal version of nationalism which was taken up by the founders of the post-colonial states (Hobsbawm 1992:5). If the spread of ethno-nationalism to Africa is seen as part and parcel of 'globalization,' this merely reminds us that globalization is not a politically neutral process (see below, p. 25). The second observation is really a question: how far can we yet speak of an Oromo national consciousness, as opposed to a Boran, Guji or Arsi consciousness? Walker Connor has pointed out that national consciousness is a mass, not an élite phenomenon and that, on this basis, even contemporary European nations "emerged far more recently than has generally been recognized" (1990:95).

> ...the masses' view of group-self has often been indiscernible. Scholars have therefore been over-reliant upon the musings of élites whose generalizations concerning the existence of national consciousness are highly suspect (Connor 1990:97-8).

---

[18] Gada is the traditional but highly complex and varied generation-set system of the Oromo, based on eight-year cycles (Baxter 1978; 1994:180-1).

[19] Cf. E. Roosens (1989), writing of the Huron of Quebec, the Aymara of Bolivia and the Luba of Zaire: "The intentional instrumental use of the right to one's own 'objective culture' and of the right to continued experience as a people...[are] products of Western culture and particular relations between people on the world level...at least some leaders must have gone to the West via an acculturation process or an assimilation process before an ethnic struggle could occur in terms of the right to one's own culture" (1989:150-1, emphasis in original).

Evidence presented in a recent article by Gunther Schlee and Abdullahi A. Shongolo suggests that "the musings of élites" about an Oromo national consciousness, based on a common language and Gada symbolism, should indeed be treated with scepticism.

> The OLF with its nationalism may have had a long history elsewhere, in other parts of Ethiopia and in exile...but its ideology definitely had not made much progress in Boranland throughout the Mengistu period. The term 'Oromo' was simply unknown to many ordinary people. One was Boran or Garre or Gabra (1995:11).

But, as Connor also points out, "nation formation is a process, not an occurrence" (1990:100) and there is no doubt that the process of Oromo nation formation will continue. When the history of that process comes to be written, it will probably be found that a decisive moment—perhaps *the* decisive moment—in the development of mass Oromo consciousness was the setting up of an 'ethno-federal' political system by the EPRDF after the fall of Mengistu Haile Mariam in 1991. The new administrative region of Oromiya, with Oromo as its public language, has given the Oromo, "although not independent and although living under far from democratic conditions...a degree of cultural autonomy unknown since their inclusion in the Ethiopian Empire" (Zitelman, this book, p. 107).[20] This will surely make ethnicity a more effective—and potentially more lethal—weapon in the hands of future Oromo nationalists than it has been in the hands of the OLF.

The power of ethnic symbols

So far I have concentrated on the 'constructed' and 'instrumental' nature of ethnicity. I have assumed that it is not an 'objective' or 'essential' property of a group and that what needs to be explained, when considering the relationship between ethnicity and war, is why people are nevertheless prepared to carry out such ferocious acts of violence in its name. But, as I have also suggested, in order to answer this question, we need to understand not only (a) the historical trends and conditions that shape and give salience to ethnic identities, without anyone's deliberate intent and (b) the techniques of ethnic mobilization consciously employed by political and intellectual élites; but also (c) the special power of ethnicity to move human beings to collective action. I come now to this third point, which takes us from the instrumental towards the 'primordial' and into the field of ethnic symbols.

Neither the constructedness nor the instrumentality of ethnicity can be explained unless we are prepared to see it as an independent as well as a

[20] During the discussion of his paper at the conference, Zitelman pointed out that "nobody talked about Oromiya 20 years ago."

dependent variable in human affairs. This is a point which has been much insisted upon, although not precisely in these terms, by Anthony Smith in his various discussions of "primordialist" and "instrumentalist"[21] approaches to ethnic and national phenomena (e.g., 1988, 1991 and 1995). While not defining himself as a primordialist, Smith argues against what he calls the "broadly 'instrumentalist' spirit that pervades the various modern accounts of the nation" (1988:3). Citing B. Anderson (1983), Gellner (1983), Hobsbawm and Ranger (1983), and Kedourie (1960), he claims that instrumentalism

> ...prevents a proper recognition of the fundamental significance of pre-modern ethnic communities in providing a model and basis for the subsequent development of nations and nationalism (A. D. Smith 1988:8).

It is not necessary to accept the whole of Smith's thesis about the "ethnic origins of nations" (1986) in order to agree with him that "tradition always implies some continuity with the past" and that "The [past] acts as a constraint on invention. Though the past can be 'read' in different ways, it is not any past..." (1991:357-8). Stated in this way, the point seems obvious—indeed so obvious that one wonders whether even those whom Smith names as "instrumentalists" would wish to disagree with it. But it is nevertheless important because it draws attention to the constraints within which those who would use the past as a political resource have to work and, therefore, to the skill, knowledge and luck they presumably need in order to succeed. For they have to ensure that the past they 'invent' or, as Smith would prefer, "reconstruct" (1991:358), both serves the particular purpose they have in mind and appears to be a "natural" extension of existing historical memories and interpretations. These memories and interpretations, therefore, constrain the process of "invention" and, to this extent, the past is both "invented" *and* "given."

The "givenness" of the past is not, as Smith himself points out, simply a matter of the nationalist élite getting enough of the historical facts right to create a plausible narrative. Rather, it is a matter of the role of "memories, myths and traditions" in forming and sustaining the collective life of a community.

> It is not possible to appropriate or annexe the past of another community (French history by the British, or vice versa, despite the many interweavings of their pasts) in the construction of the modern nation. The reason is not just because the ideology of nationalism prizes historical authenticity, but because later generations of a particular community are formed in their collective life through the memories, myths and

---

[21] Whether 'primordialism' and 'instrumentalism' really do reflect empirically separable academic approaches to ethnicity is another matter. My suspicion is that, like the drawing of other academic boundaries which have been the subjects of continuous but unresolved debate, this is another example of 'the human need to belong, to identify and hence also to exclude' (Gellner 1964:149).

> traditions of the community into which they are born and educated (A. D. Smith 1991:358).

Smith does not go into the nature of these "memories, myths and traditions," nor does he analyze how they operate in practice, but what he appears to be referring to (whether he would put it in these terms or not) is the way members of a community represent and talk about their common past in symbolic terms, a process which Anthony Cohen has aptly described as the "symbolic construction of community"(1985). The analysis of ethnic symbolism has mainly been the preserve of social and cultural anthropologists (e.g., Abner Cohen 1974; Anthony Cohen 1985; Geertz 1975 [1963]; Kapferer 1988; Leach 1954; Turner 1969): sociologists, historians and political scientists have either ignored it or, like Smith in the passage just quoted, taken its importance for granted. Nor is it a central concern of any of the contributors to this book, which makes it all the more important to include a brief discussion of it here. The reason for doing so is not only to help explain how ethnicity can be used to move people to collective action in war, but also to bring out the broader and more positive significance of ethnicity. For it is by representing the past in symbolic terms that people are able to maintain a sense of the historical persistence and distinctiveness of their communities and, therefore, of their ethnic identities, even while their personal and social worlds are changing, sometimes radically, in response to new economic and political conditions. This symbolic representation of the past cannot normally be achieved without the help of political leaders,[22] but it need not, and in most cases does not, involve ethnic violence and war.

When we speak of identity, in any context, we take for granted the merging in a single entity of two processes that are in themselves logically opposed: persistence and change (Mackenzie 1978:114). We cannot talk about the world unless we assume that it is made up of objects that remain the same through time and yet, because time never "stands still," we know that no material thing persists without change. What is it, then, about the world, that persists? A quick, Kantian, answer would be that it is not the world but the knowing subject which persists. More precisely, it is our mental categories, the 'conditions' of our knowing anything at all, which make it possible for us to talk about the world *as though* it were open to our direct observation, but without our knowing, or needing to know, what it is 'really' like. When we speak of *ethnic* identity the matter is a little different, because here we take for granted the merging of persistence and change in a reality which has no existence beyond the 'imagining' of those who see themselves as sharing in it, or being part of it. This reality cannot be

---

[22] On the necessity of leaders, cf. W. Mackenzie: "...self-consciousness about common identity requires some structuring of the situation; the emergence of leaders...the use of a rhetoric of identity.... Without this kind of leadership and its language, it is scarcely possible to find 'common purpose' in a collectivity" (1978:117).

reflected upon and spoken about directly, in the way a material object can, not only because of its lack of materiality but also because it supposedly embraces "the whole person," classifying him or her in terms of a "basic, most general identity" (Barth 1969:13), which overrides all others.[23] Ethnicity purports to say so much about a person that it can only be known and spoken about metaphorically, that is, by means of ethnic (or national or community) *symbols*. In Anthony Cohen's words, "The reality of community in people's experience...inheres in their attachment or commitment to a common body of symbols" (1985:16).

A symbol is by definition ambiguous, flexible, "multivocal" and "multi-referential" (Turner 1967; 1969). Its meaning cannot be definitively stated, either by actor or observer, because the reality it stands for is more or less unknown—if it were not, of course, the symbol would be redundant.[24] Symbols, then, always stand ready for interpretation and re-interpretation and this is precisely wherein their social usefulness lies. On the relevance of this point to symbols of collective identity, I can do no better than quote again Anthony Cohen.

> By their very nature symbols permit interpretation and provide scope for interpretative manoeuvre by those who use them.... (1985:17-8).
>
> Symbols are effective because they are imprecise. Though obviously not contentless, part of their meaning is 'subjective.' They are, therefore, ideal media through which people can...behave in apparently similar ways...without subordinating themselves to a tyranny of orthodoxy. Individuality and commonality are thus reconcilable.... [T]he 'common' form of the symbol...unites them in their opposition both to each other, and to those 'outside.' It thereby constitutes, and gives reality to, the community's boundaries (1985:21).

To stress the importance of symbols in arousing and sustaining ethnic sentiments, then, is not to suppose that they hold people in an overpowering and coercive grip, even though they may be *experienced* as unconditional, inescapable and timeless. If they really were all of these things, or rather, if

---

[23] Cf. Anthony Cohen (1985) writing of the Norwegian Saami of Nuortabealli sii'da (a cooperative unit of several households), who mounted a protest against a hydroelectric project on the Alta River (Paine 1982): "Ethnicity...implies a degree of commonality sufficiently high to override intervening sectional interests.... To be a Norwegian is only to be different from Swedes or Danes. To be a Norwegian Saami is to have a range of interests which, in discriminating you from 'white' Norwegians paints a much fuller portrait. To be a Saami in the Nuortabealli sii'da is to say almost everything of social significance about yourself, for it encompasses your kinship, your friendship, your domicile, your modes of life, love and death; it is the whole person.... [P]eople assert community, whether in the form of ethnicity or locality, when they recognise in it the most adequate medium for the expression of their whole selves" (Anthony Cohen 1985:107).

[24] "A sign is an analogous or abbreviated expression of a relatively known thing. But a symbol is always the best possible expression of a relatively unknown fact" (Jung 1949:601, quoted by Turner 1967:26).

they could not be experienced as unconditional, etc., while also being open to opportunistic interpretation, it would be impossible to imagine how any change could take place in a community which was not a direct result of some more or less extreme external influence or event. Although not infinitely malleable—they cannot mean what anyone wants them to mean, since they would then mean nothing—they must, by their nature, allow some "scope for interpretative manoeuvre" and it is this, as Cohen points out, that gives people the chance to express their individuality or (as I take this to mean) pursue their individual interests, even as they assert a shared identity. This in turn explains how it is possible for a community to be continually changing, in an organic or processual sense, while its members experience their collective identity as a constant. It also explains how, at times of drastic, sudden or 'revolutionary' change, it is possible for political leaders to use that most potent (i.e. malleable) of ethnic symbols, the past (in Smith's phrase, "memories, myths and traditions"), to mobilize collective action in response to new conditions and in pursuit of radically new objectives.

Global connections and local violence

It was definitely not one of the aims of our conference to explain the world-wide occurrence of war as a universal social institution. It would be as futile to attempt this, given the huge cultural and historical variety of the phenomena one would have to attend to, as it would be to attempt to explain the world-wide 'occurrence' of, for example, marriage or religion. It comes as no surprise, then, to learn from Gantzel that "comparative research on the causes of war has achieved virtually no cumulative effects" and that the reasons for this "include ideological biases, different methodological premises and theoretical approaches, badly integrated levels of analysis and incompatible definitions and frames of reference" (this book, p. 138). But the empirical findings reported by Gantzel raise two important questions which we did attempt to answer and which I shall consider in this section, namely (a) why has war become a predominantly intra-state phenomenon over the past 50 years? and (b) what political and constitutional arrangements might be employed to ensure the successful accommodation of ethnic and other forms of cultural diversity within the boundaries of a single state? Gantzel himself addresses the first question, while Jakob Rösel and Harry Goulbourne address the second.

In outlining his own "general theoretical approach," Gantzel is concerned to account not only for the predominantly intra-state nature of today's wars but also for the strong positive correlation his statistics reveal between war and underdevelopment. His approach may be summarized in the following propositions. (1)The peace which has been enjoyed by the "highly industrialized societies" since the end of World War II is the end result of a violent and bloody process of "creating the conditions for capitalism" which began in the early Middle Ages. (2) Although this process is, by its very nature, violent, capitalism itself is not. This is because violence is counter-productive to the economic and political interests of advanced capitalist societies. (3) The process of capitalist transformation which is taking place today in the "peripheral societies" of the Third World is fundamentally the same as that from which the highly industrialized societies have only recently emerged. It is therefore predictably violent. (4) With decolonization, furthermore, capitalist development ceased to be "coercively imposed" on the "peripheral societies" and became instead "mainly an internal matter." Hence war too is now very much an internal affair of the Third World. (5) Despite the fundamental similarity between the capitalist transformation taking place today in the Third World and that which took place earlier in Europe, there are a number of characteristics which are peculiar to Third World states and which explain why most wars since 1945 have been internal: their administrative apparatuses are weak; they lack a strong middle class; they face a world market which is dominated by the industrialized nations; and, because levels of material prosperity are low, political mobilization takes place on the basis of ethnic, religious and other cultural criteria rather than on the basis of "rational common interests."

It is not difficult to understand Gantzel's conviction that the inexorable spread of capitalism (or perhaps better liberal-democracy) from its European "core," culminating in the recent collapse of its only modern rival, communism, is all we have to go on in order to understand the direction of world history. As he put it in discussion, "There is nothing else but capitalist history." This view gains support from Fukuyama's thesis about the 'end' of history:

> While there are a variety of routes societies can take to get to the end of history, there are few versions of modernity other than the capitalist liberal-democratic one that look like they are going concerns (Fukuyama 1992:133, quoted by Kumar 1995:197).

This argument has, of course, been the subject of recent debate,[25] but the question that concerns me here is the more limited one of whether capitalism "tends to non-violent forms of conflict" (Gantzel this book, p. 140), a proposition over which there was predictable disagreement during the conference. My own view is that it is difficult to accept it without considerable qualification, for two main reasons.

The first concerns the significance we should attach to the fact that the highly industrialized countries of Europe and North America have been at peace with each other since the end of World War II. Leaving on one side

---

[25] See, for example, P. Anderson (1994).

the possibility that "the largest reason for the long peace [in Europe] since 1945 has been preparation for absolute war" (Hall 1992:361), one has to ask why the violent and bloody process of "creating the conditions for capitalism," which has been in progress for almost a thousand years (Ganztel this book, p. 140), should happen to have reached its fulfillment during the last fifty. Since capitalism is by nature dynamic, expansionist and growth oriented, it seems contradictory to think of it ever reaching an end state. But the essence of the problem here is empirical, not logical: how are we to distinguish *in practice* between the violent 'becoming' and the peaceful 'being' of capitalism, other than tautologically—by arguing that, since region X has experienced an extended period of peace, then capitalism must have reached its full 'being' there?[26] Is it not easy to imagine a European observer, writing at the turn of the last century, coming to the conclusion that capitalism had made peace not only possible but *necessary* in Europe—even though the European powers had yet to unleash the two most destructive wars of all time? And finally, even if it is accepted—as perhaps it should be—that war *between* the highly industrialized states is a present and future impossibility, the same degree of confidence cannot be entertained that they will not be troubled by internal violence.

There is another and more compelling reason to be sceptical about the proposition that capitalism "tends to non-violent forms of conflict." This relates to Gantzel's representation of capitalist development in the Third World, following decolonization, as an "internal matter." He treats this as self-evident, and yet it contradicts the more commonly held view that center and periphery are bound together in a *single* "world system" (Wallerstein 1974) or, as Kumar puts it, "The old division of the world into Three Worlds is now obsolete. There is only One World, the world of global capitalism" (1995:195). On this basis, it is an artificial exercise to separate out the advanced capitalist countries from the 'less advanced,' as though they each formed a separate, self-contained system. On the contrary, a convincing case can be made that the economic and political problems being experienced by Third World states are a direct result of their interrelations with the states of the advanced, capitalist 'core' and its international political and financial institutions. There is, for example, a net transfer of capital from the periphery to the core through debt and interest repayments (Africa, for example, repays the West more in interest repayments each year than it receives in aid) which helps to keep per capita income low in the periphery and high at the core. The pessimistic scenario this opens up is one of increasing poverty, environmental degradation and violent competition for

[26] In the discussion after his paper, Gantzel included the following countries in "the capitalist, dynamic and dominating core of Europe": Benelux, Sweden, France, Germany, Italy, Sweden and the United Kingdom. Spain ("now catching up") and Hungary were not included.

diminishing economic resources within the periphery, while the rich states of the capitalist core engage in non-violent competition for the raw materials and agricultural products of the periphery (Reyna 1991). Nor should we forget the involvement of the major industrial powers in the arms trade.[27] According to Louise, the estimated 23 million people who have been killed in the developing world as a result of war since World War II have been killed with weapons provided, for the most part, by the five permanent members of the UN Security Council (1995:7-9). According to this scenario then, capitalism—at least, the particular brand of free-market capitalism that appears to be carrying all before it today (UNRISD 1995:25-6)—is very much part of the problem, not the solution.

Gantzel has undoubtedly identified some of the most important *proximate* causes of war in the Third World. I find his 'general approach' unconvincing, however, mainly because he fails to treat center and periphery as two parts of a single system. This prevents him from addressing the indirect but crucial involvement of the advanced capitalist countries in Third World war and forces him to make difficult empirical discriminations between countries that do and do not qualify for 'advanced' status. These problems do not arise if we widen the context of our enquiry, in accordance with the Clausewitzian paradox that to understand violence one must see it as continuous with non-violent forms of action (Kloos 1993/94:14). That is, we should see intra-state war in the context of a *world-wide* trend towards the politicized, but not necessarily violent or separatist, assertion of ethnic and other local identities (see Glazer & Moynihan's discussion of "the new salience of ethnicity," referred to above, p. 11). It is true that this trend has, up to now, taken a violent and separatist form more often in the Third World than in the highly industrialized countries, and that the political and economic weaknesses of Third World countries noted by Gantzel help to explain why this should be so. But, as just noted, there are good grounds for attributing these weaknesses to the operation of "advanced capitalism" and, as Gallagher pointed out during our discussion of former Yugoslavia, economic decline is not a *sine qua non* of political mobilization along ethnic lines.[28]

One of the most frequently remarked upon characteristics of the contemporary world is that growing political, economic and cultural uniformity—'globalization'—has been accompanied by the proliferation of local, cultural and ethnic differences—'localization.' This is not an accident

---

27 Cf. P. Doughty, referring to Boutwell *et al.* (1995): "...the United States controls 70 percent of the 31.9 billion dollar world commerce in armaments... American weaponry supplies the punch in...39 of the 48 regional wars and armed conflicts underway at the start of this year" (1995:1-2).

28 He gave the example of "the Sikh insurgency in India, when the local economy was flourishing."

of history, of course, even though it was not predicted by either the Marxist or liberal traditions in social theory. Globalization and localization are inextricably linked, but they are not simply reflexes of one another: globalization is a *precondition* of localization. This is true both formally and empirically. One cannot 'think' locally unless one already has an idea of a global context in which localities can co-exist. One cannot assert a right to local identity and self-determination except by appealing to some general principles. To make such a claim, then, is also to assert a global identity. Here I follow Ernesto Laclau (1995), who explains the matter very clearly:

> ...the assertion of any particular identity involves, as one of its dimensions, the affirmation of the right to a separate existence. But it is here that the difficult questions start, because the separation—or better, the right to difference—has to be asserted within a global community—that is, within a space in which that particular group has to coexist with other groups. Now, how could that coexistence be possible without some shared universal values, without a sense of belonging to a community larger than each of the particular groups in question? (Laclau 1995:105).

Empirically, the impact of globalization is seen in virtually every sphere of modern life, from the operation of supra-national political, economic and financial institutions, to multi-national corporations, satellite TV and the Internet. To refer to all this by the neutral-sounding term 'globalization' gives the comforting impression that we are talking about the culmination of a natural process from which all countries and regions benefit equally. In fact, of course, we are talking about the spread of capitalism and economic liberalism, an essentially Western project which creates losers as well as winners and which is "shaped by, and continues to follow the contours of, existing international power relations" (UNRISD 1995:35). It is the globalization of capital, therefore, which serves as the best overall model for the spawning of the local by the global.

> The free flow of capital across the surface of the globe... places strong emphasis upon the particular qualities of the spaces to which that capital might be attracted. The shrinkage of space that brings diverse communities across the globe into competition with each other implies localised competitive strategies and a heightened sense of awareness of what makes a place special and gives it a competitive advantage (Harvey 1989:271).

Formally, if ethnicity is defined as a relational concept and if ethnic identities are therefore seen as the product of contact rather than of isolation, it is easy to see that the proliferation of sub-national ethnic differences and separatist movements is another symptom of this "shrinkage of space." Two features of the global economy were frequently mentioned at the conference as particularly relevant to the proliferation of ethnic and other forms of intra-state violence. These were the instant diffusion of information and ideas—including the terminology of ethnicity and 'ethnic cleansing' itself—through mass media of communication and the spread and easy availability of light weapons, including landmines and small arms, including especially the AK47. Lethal, durable, simple to operate and maintain and, above all, cheap, the AK47 has played a key part in sustaining increased levels of intra-state violence and 'low intensity' warfare in Eastern Europe and Africa. It is estimated that, since it was first introduced into the Soviet army in 1947, around 55 million copies have been sold (Louise 1995:10). Even if governments wished to control the spread of such weapons, their ability to do so has been much reduced by the existence of 'transnational' financial and commercial institutions.

> Universal militarization has been part of the globalizing process. The diffusion of weapons has been facilitated by technological advances, the emergence of global networks, communication, transportation and rapid advances in trade practices. This contraction of the world into a single arena has created a market-place for all commodities, and the development of a sophisticated global black market has facilitated the delivery of illegal goods anywhere in the world (Louise 1995:19).

The dual process of globalization and localization has had serious and sometimes frightening (for example in Bosnia, Liberia and Somalia) consequences for the political viability and moral legitimacy of the nation-state. Being caught in a kind of pincer movement between globalizing and localizing forces, the state has become both "too small and too big at the same time" (Kloos 1993/94:9)—too small to act as an autonomous and independent political and economic entity and too big to satisfy the aspirations and claims of its ethnic and other minorities. The sub-title of Crawford Young's edited collection *Cultural Pluralism: The Nation-State at Bay?* (1993) reflects a widespread recognition that the nation-state is increasingly redundant in many areas of political, economic and cultural life and that "national unity," in the sense of cultural homogeneity, is no longer a feasible objective. Young locates the hey-day of the nation-state in the 1950s and 1960s, when "A vocation to nationhood was implicit in statehood" and

> ...national unity was universally believed to be indispensable to modernity, which imposed upon all states, especially newly independent ones, an imperative of 'nation building'.... The dominant value framework for conceiving the challenge of ethnic diversity was 'national integration.' Particularly in the early phases of this epoch, the tensions born of communal difference were believed to be difficulties of transition, destined to diminish and even ultimately disappear with the progressive achievement of modernity (Young 1995:2).

Today, however, "'National integration' and 'nation-building' have all but vanished from the repertory of progressive statecraft" (Young 1993:14). At the same time, huge numbers of people have been on the move, individually and collectively, since 1945, with the result that "More than 200 million persons now live in countries in which they were not born" (1993:16). The control of these movements is one area in which the nation-state can still hope to exert considerable muscle, but even the highly industrialized countries, including those of 'Fortress Europe,' are bound to become more, rather than less, ethnically and culturally diverse in the future (whether or not they succeed in reversing net immigration) because of the localizing impetus of globalization. In the words of Glazer and Moynihan, "the strategic efficacy of ethnicity as a basis for asserting claims against government" (1979:33) will not go away in the foreseeable future, whether in the highly developed or less developed countries. There follows from this the single most important question to arise from the consideration of war and ethnicity: if national unity based on cultural homogeneity is no longer an option (at least for 'progressive statecraft'), by what political means can ethnicity be accommodated, within a multi-ethnic state, so that it does not become a vehicle for the *violent* assertion of political and economic self-interest?

This question rests on a number of premises. The most fundamental is that ethnicity only becomes a 'problem' when it is used by political leaders to dehumanize the ethnic 'other,' as Gallagher describes for former Yugoslavia. The atrocities that have been committed there and elsewhere in the name of ethnicity should not be seen "as tragic confrontations between primordial groups but as the result of bad politics" and therefore as "amenable to prevention, negotiation or control" (Rösel, this book, p. 156). Another premise is that the doctrine of self-determination, which played such an important part in the anti-colonial struggle after World War II[29] and which has received new impetus since 1991 from events in the former Soviet Union and Eastern Europe, does not provide a satisfactory general principle for accommodating ethnic diversity. Or rather, it could only do so if there existed generally agreed upon criteria (agreed, that is, beyond the group seeking independence) for deciding which particular units of population have this right and which do not. The task of drawing up such criteria would, of course, be hopelessly impractical. It follows that there will always be the potential for new identities to become salient (since ethnicity is a relational, not an essentialist, concept) and to provide the basis for new and apparently legitimate demands for self-determination, *ad infinitum*.[30] Paradoxically, then, for self-determination to work as a general principle, some claims made in its name must be disallowed, which means that the

---

[29] Article 1 of the 1960 UN Declaration on the Granting of Independence to Colonial Countries and Peoples (UN Resolution 1514 [XV]) states that, "All peoples have the right to self-determination; by virtue of that right they freely determine their political status and freely pursue their economic, social and cultural development" (quoted by Young 1993:20).

[30] Cf. Young: "Self-determination as an international norm...needs to evolve beyond assertion of imprescriptible sovereignty rights by all self-identified 'peoples.' Its constant invocation in everyday ethnic interactions formulates differences in categories which are all too often unresolvable. Although in extreme cases the break-up of existing state units may be inevitable, secession cannot be a general formula for accommodation of diversity" (1994:34).

problem of how to accommodate ethnic diversity within a single political and territorial space will remain. A third premise is that the success of a policy to accommodate ethnic diversity should be judged by its capacity to limit the political mobilization of ethnic identity to non-violent forms of action, not by its capacity to prevent such mobilization altogether.

> Conflict—class, interest and ethnic—is a natural aspect of social existence; the heart of the matter is that it be conducted by civil process, by equitable rules, through dialogue and bargaining, in a framework of governance facilitating co-operation and reconciliation (Young 1994:4).

A fourth premise is that this "framework of governance" will, for the foreseeable future, be supplied by the nation-state. This is more a comment on the rudimentary development of international systems for protecting human rights and safeguarding minorities (witness, for example, the policy failures of the international community in Rwanda and Bosnia) than on the continuing political and economic vitality of the nation-state, or the "sociological necessity" of nationalism (A. D. Smith 1993). A fifth premise is that the accommodation of ethnic diversity requires power-sharing and therefore a reasonably balanced representation of ethnic groups in governmental and other national institutions. As Rösel points out, it is a "depressing fact" that this calls for a degree of enlightened self-interest, on the part of those groups (or their representatives) who are in a position to maximize their short-term hold on power, which may only come about through "sheer exhaustion and desperation following a protracted civil war" (this book p. 158).

The constitutional strategies described by Rösel for acknowledging and/or accommodating ethnic diversity are "consociationalism" (government by a coalition of proportionately represented groups), "ethnic syncretism" (allowing ethnic groups cultural but not political expression) and "federalism" (the spatial dispersion of power to regional centres). Although clearly based on different principles, it seems that two or more of these strategies are likely to be combined in actual cases. In discussion, Rösel described the new Spanish constitution as a combination of federalism (the granting of "regional autonomies" has helped to control separatist movements) and "ethnic syncretism" (the "celebration" of the diverse cultures of Spain). India, with its "linguistic" states, strong state governments and ideology of "unity in diversity," is another example of the combination of these two strategies (which demonstrates, incidentally, the wide variation that can be found in different cases which exemplify the same formal strategy or strategies). Although the territorial dispersion of political power can be used to "undercut ethnic boundaries" (Rösel, p. 159) and although "Most contemporary federations are not explicitly constructed on an ethnic basis" (Young 1994:12), the regional units are "often, in reality, ethnic groups" (Rösel, p. 158). One recent example of ethnic identity being adopted as the explicit organizing principle of a federal system is the new Ethiopian constitution which, as noted earlier, bears uncomfortable comparison with the Leninist model of the former Soviet Union and Yugoslavia in its capacity for encouraging, rather than "down-grading" the politicization of ethnicity. [31]

A necessary precondition for the long-term success of all three strategies is the "liberal concept of the open and democratic nation" but, in the short-term, their implementation within a democratic framework gives groups based on ethnic identification "a new official status, a new respectability and a new arena for their ambitions" (Rösel, p. 159). For this reason, Rösel admits to "considerable unease" in putting forward the proposition that democracy is a "prerequisite for the regulation of ethnic conflict" (p. 160) but he sees this as a dilemma from which there is no escape, not least because "democratic systems of government are gradually acquiring a near-universal prevalence and legitimacy. We are thus forced to work out strategies for the prevention and control of these conflicts in democracies" (p. 170). We should note here that the global transition to democracy raises a more fundamental dilemma. In his discussion of democratization in southern Africa, W. van Binsbergen (1995) asks whether, in adopting democracy, Africans are tying themselves to a culturally alien (i.e., North Atlantic) political doctrine, disguised as a "universal heritage of mankind," and thereby becoming "more effectively subjugated...to unequal global power relations under northern hegemony." Is this, he goes on to ask, "the hidden agenda of the democratization process?" (van Binsbergen 1995:4-5).[32]

The Western European democracies have evolved through the long (but far from peaceful)[33] implementation of what has been called a 'dominant nation' strategy for the accommodation of ethnic diversity, within a framework of legal equality and civil rights. The legitimacy of these long-established constitutional arrangements has, however, been increasingly and successfully challenged by ethno-nationalist movements in recent years in Spain (resulting in regional autonomy for Catalans and Basques), Belgium (resulting in a consociational federation for Walloons and Flemings) and

---

[31] Cf. J. Markakis (1995): "According to Ethiopia's current rulers, empowering ethnicity is the only way to secure peace and stability in that country. Whether this holds true only time will tell. It should be kept in mind that while ethnicity's effectiveness in opposition to post-colonial regimes is proved, its effectiveness as an instrument of government is not" (1995:6).

[32] See also Chatterjee: "History, it would seem, has decreed that we, in the post-colonial world, shall only be perpetual consumers of modernity. Europe and the Americas, the only true subjects of history, have thought out on our behalf not only the script of colonial enlightenment and exploitation, but also that of our anti-colonial resistance and post-colonial misery. Even our imaginations must remain forever colonised" (1991:512).

[33] Wales and Scotland, for example, were integrated into the United Kingdom only through military force and the suppression of attempts at rebellion.

Britain (resulting in a commitment from the Labour Party, to introduce regional parliaments for Scotland and Wales). A parallel development in the ethnic politics of Western Europe has been the growth of the so-called 'multi-cultural society,' due to the influx of non-European immigrants after World War II.

The consequences of this development for Britain are discussed in a later chapter by Harry Goulbourne.

> Britain has become, since 1948, a society characterized by both European and non-European cultural patterns and rich in the variety of colour tones, religions and languages. [In 1991] people with backgrounds in Africa, Asia and the Caribbean accounted for 3,006,500 or 5.5 per cent [of the population] (Goulbourne, this book, p. 172).

The resultant cultural diversity has been interpreted as a threat to the 'British way of life' by political leaders of the far right, who have not hesitated (whether cynically or not it is hard to say) to mobilize majority ethnic feeling against ethnic minorities for their electoral advantage. The complaint they make is that, unlike earlier waves of immigrants, these relatively recent arrivals (easily distinguishable, of course, by skin colour) are "resistant to absorption, some defiantly claiming a right to superimpose their culture, even their law, upon the host community" (Tebbit 1990:78, quoted by Goulbourne, this book, p. 174). These same politicians have been amongst the most vociferous opponents of closer political and economic integration of Britain with the European Union, on the grounds that this would result in an unacceptable diminution of national sovereignty, and amongst the most vociferous opponents of the dispersal of political authority from Westminster to elected assemblies in Scotland and Wales, on the grounds that this would herald the break-up of the United Kingdom. It is an extraordinary irony, not to say contradiction, that the fervour with which these politicians have defended British national sovereignty and the integrity of the United Kingdom is matched only by the fervour with which they have embraced the consequences of economic liberalism and the globalization of capital (including, for example, the sale of British companies to foreign buyers), and sought to reduce, at almost any cost, the role of the nation-state in the life of the citizen, through the privatization and deregulation of public services, institutions and utilities.[34] But, as Goulbourne rightly comments, there is also a contradiction at the heart of more liberal minded calls (such as

[34] This undermining of state institutions has spread from the highly industrialized to the developing countries through the 'structural adjustment' programmes of the World Bank and the International Monetary Fund and through the channelling of increased proportions of foreign aid through NGOs rather than through government bodies.

that of the 1985 Swann Report, *Education for All*) for a multi-cultural society in which, on the one hand, ethnic minorities would be encouraged and assisted to maintain their distinct identities and, on the other, in which all citizens would share "common aims, attributes and values" (p. 175). Goulbourne's response to this dilemma is, like Rösel, to put his trust in democracy, with the proviso that "The state should seek neither to preserve extant cultures nor to privilege any one cultural group over another" (p.175).

The international response

Having discussed the characteristics and possible causes of recent internal wars, it seems logical to go on to discuss the "response" of the international community to the "stimulus" of these events, as though we were dealing with two analytically and empirically separable sets of data. This is an artificial separation, however, dictated more by the requirements of narrative exposition than by the phenomena themselves. The response of the international community to the events in, for example, Somalia and Bosnia, cannot be understood, any more than the events themselves can be understood, except within the context of a particular set of power relations existing within the international political system. We come back to the point that globalization is not a politically neutral process and that it is the precondition for localization. The international community—meaning by this a global political structure consisting of relations between states of unequal political and economic power—is the context and precondition for internal war, including the extreme examples of it which have led to the complete disintegration of former nation-states, as in Somalia, Yugoslavia and the Soviet Union. The way the international community responds to internal war is simply another manifestation, of this global political structure. We should not be surprised to discover, then, that international intervention in internal wars is prone to sustain and institutionalize the very behaviour it is intended to combat and control.[35]

When we speak of the international community in this context we are, above all, speaking of the countries which, because of their economic power and political influence, dominate the existing global political structure and have most to gain from its continuance. It is inevitable, therefore, that the political élites of those countries will respond to the problem of internal war, both in their public pronouncements and in the actions they take to intervene

[35] For a more detailed survey of current issues in humanitarian intervention, particularly where they affect Non-Governmental Organizations, see Giorgio Ausenda's Postscript to this book.

in it, in ways that support rather than call into question the legitimacy of that structure. This must go a long way to explain the startling paucity[36] and superficiality of the analyses offered by Western politicians and diplomats of recent events in Rwanda, Somalia and the former Yugoslavia.

These analyses have been variations on the 'ancient tribal antagonism' theme and have therefore reflected and supported the views and interpretations of local extremists and radicals rather than of those dedicated to compromise and coexistence. Gallagher notes, for former Yugoslavia, that,

> At different times politicians like the British Foreign Secretary Douglas Hurd...have made statements about the atavistic and endemic nature of conflicts in the region which suggest that they share the views of radicals that conflict and division...is the normal mode of existence in the Balkans (this book, p. 69).

And here is the US Secretary of State, Warren Christopher, speaking at a news conference in February 1993:

> The death of President Tito and the end of communist domination of the former Yugoslavia raised the lid on the cauldron of ancient ethnic hatreds. This is the land where at least three religions and a half-dozen ethnic groups have vied across the centuries. It was the birthplace of World War I. It has long been a cradle of European conflict, and it remains so today (1993:81, quoted by Roberts 1995:8).

What this seems to be saying is that we should accept it as perfectly normal for people of different religions to murder each other—if they happen to live in the Balkans. Warren Christopher's rhetoric, like all political rhetoric, is designed to persuade with imagery and metaphor rather than to convince with logic and evidence. It, therefore, conveniently ignores the "extensive ethnic coexistence (including widespread intermarriage)" which has been a feature of Balkan society for generations (Roberts 1995:9). It also fails to acknowledge and support those individuals—such as Serb religious figures—who have stood out against the actions of the Belgrade government and the thousands of people (especially in Sarajevo) who have refused to succumb to the principle of separation on ethnic grounds (Gallagher, this book, pp. 68-9). Statements like these are not just bad history and worse social analysis: they contribute, even if indirectly, to the very horrors and atrocities they simultaneously condemn, because they accept and therefore give legitimacy to the world view of local leaders who use supposedly, 'ancient' ethnic hatreds to mobilize support for their policies.

---

36 Roberts, writing of former Yugoslavia, notes that "There have been short statements and sound-bites galore, but no Western political leader has made a major statement analyzing in depth the causes and character of the war, and the policy options for outside powers" (1995:6).

The logic of the 'ancient tribal antagonism' hypothesis is that the most sensible policy would be one of non-interference. In the age of instant television coverage of the world's 'disaster spots,' however, inaction is not a viable policy for a democratically elected leader with even one eye on the next election. Hence, perhaps, the attempt to gain political advantage from high profile humanitarian interventions which simultaneously divert the attention of the public from the underlying causes of the crisis. It was media coverage of the suffering in Somalia, for example, which was responsible for

> ...catapulting the Somali crisis dramatically up the international political agenda to join Yugoslavia at the top. This even jolted the British Foreign Secretary and his EU colleagues into making a hasty visit to Mogadishu...joining the throng of international dignitaries and film stars who touched down briefly on photo-opportunity missions (Lewis, this book, p. 187).

Here we notice a kind of unholy, although not deliberate, alliance between the media and the politicians, who conspire between them to present such events as those in Somalia and former Yugoslavia as dramatic and short-term emergencies rather than as the outcome of long-term structural processes.

Television news particularly, with its penchant for images of death and destruction and for easily digestible explanations which reinforce the taken for granted assumptions of the audience, plays into the hands of politicians who wish to divert attention (their own included) from the underlying structural causes of internal war. Duffield argues in a later chapter that the response of the international community to "complex political emergencies" continues to be based on what he calls the "natural disaster model," according to which all that is required to re-establish the 'normal' state of social progress and well being is the short-term delivery of basic relief commodities.[37] Since the 1980s, expenditure by the major donors on emergency relief has increased significantly as a proportion of development aid. This is no doubt due in part to increased need but the possibility cannot be ruled out that some donor governments are deliberately increasing their expenditure on relief, with maximum media coverage in mind, because this 'plays' better with their electorates than lower-profile, longer term development activities (Borton 1993:190). What cannot be doubted is that this preoccupation with emergency assistance helps to distract attention from

---

[37] It should be noted that the definition of a disaster as the temporary disturbance of 'normal' life by an unforeseen physical event is nowadays increasingly discredited within the field of disaster studies itself despite (or perhaps partly because of) the highly 'tech fix' approach adopted by those who designed the current UN "International Decade for Natural Disaster Reduction." See Blaikie *et al.* (1993) for a good introduction to the 'vulnerability' approach to disasters.

the examination of underlying causes and the search for long-term solutions. Even more worrying has been what Duffield calls the "growing politicization of 'neutral' relief aid" (this book, p. 210).

This has come about because of the preparedness of the UN, following the end of the Cold War, to intervene in situations of unresolved military conflict and because of the consequent emergence of 'military humanitarianism.' The 'peace-keeping' activities of the UN have expanded greatly in recent years,[38] both in their number and in the scale of individual operations, but their main impact has been on the delivery and distribution of humanitarian aid. The UN Protection Force (UNPROFOR) in former Yugoslavia, for example, was the largest peace-keeping operation ever mounted by the UN. It was set up in February 1992 "to create the conditions of peace and security required for the negotiation of an overall settlement of the Yugoslav crisis"[39] but "Its most effective performance has been in humanitarian assistance, including to besieged areas" (Roberts 1995:17).

> This role in itself poses problems: it requires forces to be widely dispersed, and to operate with the permission of the dominant forces in the area.... Hence it becomes very difficult for the UN...to take, or encourage, tough action against the parties. Indeed, critics argue that...a peacekeeping and humanitarian role tend to buttress the military status quo (Roberts 1995:32).

One such critic is Duffield, who argues that military humanitarianism, with its "corridors of tranquillity" and "negotiated access," far from bringing warring parties together as was naively hoped, has actually helped to make humanitarian aid an integral part of "the political economy of internal war" (this book, p. 210). It has done this by, among other ways, giving recognition and legitimacy to the military protagonists, sidelining local leaders and undermining local, culturally specific, institutions for the resolution of conflict.

Ioan Lewis's account of the impact of UN intervention in southern Somalia gives strong support to these criticisms. He draws a striking contrast between the impact of the massive UN military, economic and humanitarian intervention in the south and the situation in the north where local clan groups were largely left alone to engage in a slow, laborious but ultimately successful process of indigenous peace-making. The UN leadership in Mogadishu, with "the usual Eurocentric preoccupation with hierarchical political structures" (p. 190) focused its efforts at reconciliation on the very leaders who had a vested interest in pursuing the conflict—the rival war lords, Generals Aideed and Morgan—and on other faction leaders

---

[38] "Between 1987 and 1992...there were 13 UN peacekeeping missions, the same number as in the previous 40 years" (Duffield, this book, p. 209).

[39] UN Security Council Resolution 743, 21 February 1992, quoted by Roberts 1995:32.

who were selected as Somali "representatives" by UN officials who had little knowledge or experience of Somali conditions. The position of local extremists and military leaders was thereby bolstered, while the opportunity was lost to engage with indigenous political structures and to "tap into" their peacemaking and conflict resolving capabilities. This was partly the result of the familiar shortcomings of the UN bureaucracy and its unsatisfactory recruitment policies; and partly the result of the sheer complexity and scale of the UN operation which made it ill suited to "local Somali timetables and processes" (p. 198). The forced exit from the scene, after only seven months, of the Secretary General's special envoy, Mohamed Sahnoun, who had a good understanding of the Horn of Africa and who had attempted to deal with a wide cross-section of Somali society, indicates a deep-seated institutional incapacity on the part of the UN to engage in what Lewis calls the "slow cradling that Somalia ideally needs" (p. 196). Gallagher pointed out, during the discussion of Lewis's paper, that the UN had a similar record in former Yugoslavia. It did not, either locally or in higher level negotiation processes such as the Vance-Owen talks, make use of those who, like religious leaders, were willing and able to play conciliatory and placatory roles, "It empowered the radicals...but it disempowered the representatives of those who were committed to some kind of common existence."

The response of the international community to internal war, then, is very much part of the problem it is attempting to solve. I am not making here the familiar point that humanitarian aid is delivered in inefficient and inappropriate ways. The point, rather, is that the response and the problem are mutually reinforcing because they are products of the same global structure of power relations. In fact, there have been huge improvements, over the past 20 years, in the way aid is delivered and countless lives have been saved by the prompt, energetic and dedicated efforts of international and non-governmental organizations. There are doubtless many practical improvements still to be made but the overwhelming impression to be gained from the international response to internal war over the past few years—in Rwanda, Somalia and former Yugoslavia—is that the key failure has been one of policy, not practice.[40] The many shortcomings of the international response, and those of the UN itself, have only been touched upon here and are by no means exhausted in the chapters by Lewis and Duffield. Perhaps the most important conclusion we can draw, not only from their chapters but also from the book as a whole, is the one insisted upon by Duffield: that the leaders of the international community "display a serious

40 One of the main findings of the 'Joint Evaluation of Emergency Assistance to Rwanda' was that "the number who died as a result of causes that could be considered avoidable (had the humanitarian response been more effective), was several times lower than those who died as a result of the genocide and conflict. The critical failings in the international community's overall response, therefore, lay within the political, diplomatic and military domains rather than the humanitarian domain" (ODI 1996:10).

predilection not to examine the underlying causes of conflict" (p. 212). This, of course, is a "predilection" they share with those other leaders, some of whom they have described as war criminals, who have used ethnicity as a resource to further their political ends, motivating their followers in the process to carry out the most atrocious acts of violence against former neighbours. Although sincerely deploring these acts, Western leaders appear to accept the reasoning of their perpetrators that ethnic hatred is a 'natural' human attribute and that ethnic and cultural pluralism is therefore a recipe for conflict. We who spend our lives in, and gain our livelihoods from, academic enquiry should recognize that 'intellectuals' have frequently played a key role in whipping up murderous ethnic sentiments amongst their fellow citizens and that, whether we like it or not, our disciplines—especially, perhaps, history and anthropology—provide what Hobsbawm calls the "raw material" of nationalist and ethnic ideologies. This should make us all the more determined to go on insisting, as we do in this book, that ethnicity is socially constructed, that it does not erupt suddenly and spontaneously but only in specific historical circumstances and that it is unlikely to become a lethal force in human affairs except through the deliberate calculation of political élites.

The chapters

In the next chapter, Tom Gallagher gives a detailed account of the techniques used by the Serbian and Croatian political and intellectual élites to whip up ethnic hatred and violence in former Yugoslavia. These techniques included the assertion of 'inalienable historical rights,' the cultivation of a persecution complex by reminding people of past wrongs committed by ethnic opponents and an insistence that guilt for such wrongs is both hereditary and collective. During the final years of peace in Yugoslavia, communist leaders turned to ethno-nationalism as a means of bolstering their shrinking authority and history was manipulated to emphasize differences and popularize an ethnocentric outlook. Gallagher describes the groups which sought to turn history into a contemporary political resource and the sections of the population to whom they appealed. He points out that, by presenting the violence as 'atavistic' and 'endemic,' Western leaders merely reflected the combatants' own views that conflict rather than co-existence is the normal mode of existence in the Balkans.

Despite its reputation as a 'powder keg' of the Balkans, the Macedonian state was alone among the former Yugoslav republics in escaping unharmed from the post-Yugoslav imbroglio. Stefan Troebst considers various predicted scenarios of ethnic violence in Macedonia and shows why each one failed to materialize. The main argument of his chapter is that, in analyzing ethnic conflict in Eastern Europe, one should turn to empirical evidence and fresh data, rather than rely on historical analogies and stereotypes. In particular, the so-called 'deep freeze' explanation of internal war in Eastern Europe (i.e., the post-Cold War thawing of ethnic sentiment and nationalist xenophobia which had been frozen under communism) is thoroughly a-historical, since it ignores the impact of massive economic and political changes that had taken place in these countries since World War II.

Thomas Zitelman focuses on the efforts of various 'liberation' movements to create a national consciousness among the Oromo of the Horn of Africa. Focusing on the symbolic and cultural elements in the formation of an ethnic identity, rather than on competition for scarce material resources, he describes the history and origin of various Oromo movements, the best known of which is the secular and modernist Oromo Liberation Front (OLF). Members of the Oromo diaspora, living in such cities as Toronto, London and Berlin, were deeply involved in the process of ethno-nationalist myth-making. The identity they fashioned was largely a reaction to their experience of exile in these European and North American cities. The new administrative region of Oromiya, set up as part of the new ethnic-federal political system in Ethiopia, has given the Oromo a degree of cultural autonomy unknown since their inclusion in the Ethiopian Empire.

Klaus Jürgen Gantzel presents statistical information generated by his long running research programme into the causes of war at the University of Hamburg. Nearly a quarter of all wars that have taken place since 1945 were in progress in 1993. This increase in the incidence of wars is accounted for almost entirely by an increase in internal or intra-state wars and over 90 per cent of wars since 1945 have taken place in the Third World. Gantzel goes on to suggest that these findings can be explained by the process of capitalist transformation which is taking place today in the Third World and which is essentially the same as that from which the highly industrialized and now peaceful societies have only recently emerged. The process is inherently violent, even though it 'tends towards peace.' A number of characteristics of Third World states (weak political and economic structures, lack of a strong middle class, lack of control over the international market, low levels of material prosperity and political mobilization based on ethnicity) explain why most wars since 1945 have been internal wars.

Jakob Rösel is concerned with the search for political solutions for what are, essentially, political conflicts. He insists on the need to distinguish between two mutually incompatible concepts of the nation: an 'open' and liberal/democratic one and a 'closed' and ethnic one. Although difficult to disentangle empirically, the two must be kept analytically separate because they have opposite implications for the containment and control of ethnic conflict. Ethnic nationalism leads inevitably to conflict and civil war but these are not the unavoidable consequences of the liberal concept of the nation. Three constitutional strategies are described for acknowledging and accommodating ethnic diversity ('consociationalism,' 'ethnic syncretism' and 'federalism') each of which presupposes a democratic form of government. Democracy is thus a precondition for the regulation of ethnic conflict, even though it may in the short run give salience to ethnic differences and create opportunities for ethnic mobilization.

An important element in the ethnic politics of Western Europe since World War II has been the growth of the so-called 'multi-cultural society.' In Harry Goulbourne discusses this phenomenon in Britain, where people with African, Asian and Caribbean backgrounds account for well over 5 per cent of the population. The resultant cultural diversity has been interpreted as a threat to the 'British way of life' by right-wing political leaders who have not hesitated to mobilize majority ethnic feeling against ethnic minorities for electoral advantage. On the other hand, more liberal minded calls for a society in which cultural diversity co-exists with common national aims and values contain a fundamental contradiction. The important point stressed by Goulbourne is that cultural interaction is a dynamic process from which identities do not emerge unchanged. The state should not, therefore, take deliberate action to assist ethnic minorities to maintain their 'distinct identities,' since this would be to misunderstand the nature of cultural interaction. The role of the state should be to guarantee the freedoms and liberties of the individual.

Ioan Lewis describes the impact of the massive UN military, economic and humanitarian intervention in southern Somalia—the first unilateral UN military intervention in a (theoretically) sovereign state. He draws a striking contrast between the political and economic chaos created in the south of the country and the situation in the north where local clan groups were left largely alone to engage in a slow, laborious but ultimately successful process of indigenous peacemaking. The UN leadership in Mogadishu focused its efforts at reconciliation on the local war lords, thus giving them added legitimacy and credibility. The position of local extremists was thus bolstered, while the opportunity was lost to engage with indigenous political structures and traditional leaders. This was the result of the familiar shortcomings of the UN bureaucracy and its unsatisfactory recruitment policies (UN officials had little knowledge or experience of Somali conditions) and the complexity and scale of the UN operation which made it unsuited to the local Somali timetable and political processes.

Since the 1980s, expenditure by the major donors on emergency relief in so-called 'complex political emergencies' has increased significantly as a proportion of development aid. Mark Duffield argues that the response of the international community to these emergencies continues to be based on the 'natural disaster model,' according to which all that is required to re-establish the 'normal' state of social progress and well-being is the short term delivery of basic relief commodities. Preoccupation with short term assistance serves to distract attention from the examination of underlying causes and the search for long-term solutions, while so called 'military humanitarianism' has helped to make humanitarian aid an integral part of the political economy of internal war. It has done this by giving recognition to the military protagonists, sidelining local leaders and undermining local institutions for the resolution of conflict. The long term solution to internal war must encompass reform of the global economy and underlying causes should not be ignored in the rush to provide emergency relief.

In the first part of the Postscript, Giorgio Ausenda surveys various definitions of ethnicity and related concepts (class, caste, race, and nation) and discusses the most important theoretical approaches to the understanding of ethnic phenomena. He also lists a number of questions concerning the relationship between war and ethnicity as suggestions for further research. In the second part of the chapter he discusses the role and functions of governmental and non-governmental organizations in the changed 'operating environment' of the post-Cold War world. The overriding concern to emerge from this discussion is that humanitarian intervention in situations of unresolved conflict, including the use of military forces, may actually contribute to the cause of the problem. While admitting that the short-term future of humanitarian intervention is not bright, Ausenda points to a number of steps that could be taken to improve matters—such as stronger leadership from the UN, greater accountability to both donors and beneficiaries and the effective implementation of decisions to use force. The chapter ends with a list of questions for further research on humanitarian intervention.

References

Anderson, B.

1985 *Imagined Communities: Reflections on the Origins and Spread of Nationalism.* London: Verso.

1994 *The Ends of History.* London: Verso.

Barth, F.

1969 Introduction. In *Ethnic Groups and Boundaries: The Social Organization of Culture Difference.* F. Barth (ed.), pp. 9-38. Boston: Little, Brown & Co.

Baxter, P. T. W.

1978 Borana age-sets and generation-sets: Gada, a puzzle or a maze? In *Age, Generation and Time: Studies in East African Age Organisation.* P. T. W. Baxter & U. Almagor (eds.), pp. 151-182. London: Hurst.

1994 Ethnic Boundaries and Development: Speculation on the Oromo Case. In *Inventions and Boundaries: Historical and Anthropological Approaches to the Study of Ethnicity and Nationalism.* P. Kaarsholm & J. Hultin (eds.), pp. 247-260. Occasional Paper No. 11, International Development Studies, Roskilde University, Roskilde (Denmark)

Bebler, A.
1993 Yugoslavia's variety of Communist Federalism and her demise. *Communist and Post-Communist Studies* 26 (1): 72-86.

Blaikie, P., I. Davis, T. Cannon & B. Wisner
1993 *At Risk: Natural Hazards, People's Vulnerability and Disasters.* London: Routledge & Kegan Paul.

Borton, J.
1993 Recent trends in the international relief system. *Disasters* 17 (3): 187-201.

Boutwell, J., M. T. Klane & L. W. Reed
1995 *Lethal Commerce: The Global Trade in Small Arms and Light Weapons.* Cambridge, MA: American Academy of Arts and Sciences.

Chatterjee, P.
1991 Whose Imagined Community? *Millennium: Journal of International Studies* 20 (3): 521-525.

Christopher, W.
1993 New steps towards conflict resolution in the former Yugoslavia. (Opening statement at a news conference, Washington DC, 10 February 1993). Published in *US Department of State Despatch* 4 (7): 81.

Cohen, Abner
1974 *Two Dimensional Man.* London: Tavistock.

Cohen, Anthony
1985 *The Symbolic Construction of Community.* Chichester/London: Ellis Horwood/Tavistock.

Connor, W.
1990 When is a Nation? *Ethnic and Racial Studies* 13 (1): 92-103.

Dandeker, C.
1993 The Causes of War and the History of Modern Sociological Theory. In *Effects of War on Society.* G. Ausenda (ed.), pp. 37-58. San Marino (R.S.M.): AIEP Editore for CIROSS.

Doughty, P.
1995 Commentary: Power and Ethnic Conflict. *Human Peace* 10 (3): 1-2. (Newsletter of the Commission on the Study of Peace, International Union of Anthropological and Ethnological Sciences).

Erikson, T. H.
1993 *Ethnicity and Nationalism: Anthropological Perspectives.* London/Boulder: Pluto Press.

Fabian, J.
1993 *Time and the Other.* New York: Columbia University Press.

Fardon, R.
1987 'African Ethnogenesis': Limits to the Comparability of Ethnic Phenomena. In *Comparative Anthropology.* L. Holy (ed.), pp. 169-188. Oxford: Basil Blackwell.

Friedman, L.
1993 Ethnic Identity and the De-Nationalization and Democratization of Leninist States. In *The Rising Tide of Cultural Pluralism: The Nation State at Bay?* C. Young (ed.), pp. 222-241. Madison: University of Wisconsin Press.

Fukuyama, F.
1992 *The End of History and the Last Man.* London: Penguin Books.

Gamst, F.
1995 Experiential Reflections on the 1992 Elections in Southwest Ethiopia. *Human Peace* (Newsletter of the Commission for the Study of Peace, International Union of Anthropological and Ethnological Sciences) 10 (3): 3-8.

Geertz, C.
1963 The Integrative Revolution: Primordial Sentiments and Civil Politics in the New States. In C. Geertz, *The Interpretation of Culture,* pp. 255-310. New York: Basic Books.

Gellner, E.
1964 *Thought and Change.* London: Weidenfeld & Nicholson.
1983 *Nations and Nationalism.* Oxford: Blackwell.

Glazer, N., & D. P. Moynihan
1979 Why Ethnicity? In *America and the New Ethnicity.* D. R. Colburn & G. E. Pozzatta (eds.), pp. 29-42. Port Washington, N.Y./London: National University Publications, Kennikat Press.

Goluvbovic, Z.
1993 Nationalism and Democracy: The Yugoslav Case. *Journal of Area Studies* 3: 65-77.

Hall, J. A.
1992 Peace, peace at last? In *Transition to Modernity: Essays on Power, Wealth and Belief.* J. A. Hall & I. C. Jarvie (eds.), pp. 342-367. Cambridge: Cambridge University Press.

Harvey, D.
1989 *The Condition of Postmodernity: An Enquiry into the Origins of Cultural Change.* Oxford: Basil Blackwell.

de Heusch, L.
1995 Rwanda: Responsibilities for a Genocide. *Anthropology Today* 11 (4): 3-7.

Hobsbawm, E.
1992 Ethnicity and Nationalism in Europe Today. *Anthropology Today* 8 (1): 3-8.

Hobsbawm, E., & T. Ranger
1983 *The Invention of Tradition.* Cambridge: Cambridge University Press.

International Federation of Red Cross and Red Crescent Societies
1995 *World Disasters Report.* Dordrecht (The Netherlands): Martinus Nijhoff.
1996 *World Disasters Report.* Oxford: Oxford University Press.

Jung, C.
1949 *Psychological Types.* London: Routlegde & Kegan Paul.

Kapferer, B.
1988 *Legends of People, Myths of State: Violence, Intolerance and Political Culture in Sri Lanka and Australia.* Washington, DC: Smithsonian Institution Press.

Kedourie, E.
1960 *Nationalism.* London: Hutchinson.

Kloos, P.
1993 Globalization and Localized Violence. *Volk* 35: 5-18.

Kumar, K.
1995 *From Post-Industrial to Post-Modern Society: New Theories of the Contemporary World.* Oxford: Blackwell.

Laclau, E.
1995 Universalism, Particularism and the Question of Identity. In *The Identity in Question.* J. Ratchmann (ed.), pp. 93-108. New York and London: Routlegde & Kegan Paul.

Leach, E.
1954 *Political Systems of Highland Burma.* London: Athlone Press.

Lonsdale, J.
1994 Moral Ethnicity and Political Tribalism. In *Invention and Boundaries: Historical and Anthropological Approaches to the Study of Ethnicity and Nationalism.* P. Kaarshelm and J. Hultin (eds.), pp. 131-150. Occasional paper No. 11, International Development Studies, Roskilde University, Roskilde, Denmark.

Louise, C.
1995 *The Social Impact of Light Weapon Availability and Proliferation.* UNRISD Discussion Paper 59. Geneva: UNRISD.

Mackenzie, W. J. M.
1978 *Political Identity.* Manchester: Manchester University Press.

Malkki, L.
1992 National Geographic: The Rooting of Peoples and the Territorialization of National Identity among Scholars and Refugees. *Cultural Anthropology* 7 (1): 24-44.

Markakis, J.
1994 Ethnic Conflict and the State in the Horn of Africa. In *Ethnicity and Conflict in the Horn of Africa.* J. Markakis & K. Fukui (eds.), pp. 217-237. London: James Currey.

1995 The Political Challenge of Ethnicity. Conference on 'Ethnicity in Africa: Roots, Meanings and Implications,' Edinburgh University, 24-26 May.

Mitchell, P.
1995 Genocide in our time. *Times Higher Educational Supplement*, 29 December.

Nadel, S. F.
1957 Malinowski on Science and Religion. In *Man and Culture: An Evaluation of the Work of Malinowski.* R. Firth (ed.), pp. 189-208. London: Routledge & Kegan Paul.

Nagan, W. P.
1994 Towards unpacking the war in former Yugoslavia: an international lawyer's perspective. *Human Peace* 10 (2): 3-7 (International Union of Anthropological and Ethnological Sciences).

Newbury, C.
1995 *The Cohesion of Oppression.* New York: Columbia University Press.

O'Brien, J.
1986 Toward a reconstitution of ethnicity: capitalist expansion and cultural dynamics. *American Anthropologist* 88 (3): 898-906.

ODI (Overseas Development Institute, London)
1996 The International Response to Conflict and Genocide. Lessons from the Rwanda Experience, *Humanitarian Aid and Effects.* Study 3, Steering Committee of the Joint Evaluation of Emergency Assistance to Rwanda. Copenhagen: Danish Ministry of Foreign Affairs.

Paine, R.
1982 *Dam a river, damn a people.* IWGIA Document 45, Copenhagen: IWGIA.

Prunier, G.
1995 *The Rwanda Crisis: 1959-94. History of Genocide.* London: Hurst.

Ranger, T.
1994 The invention of tradition revisited: the case of colonial Africa. In *Inventions and Boundaries: Historical and Anthropological Approaches to the Study of Ethnicity and Nationalism.* P. Kaarsholm & J. Hultin (eds.), pp. 9-50. Occasional Paper No. 11, International Development Studies, Roskilde University, Roskilde, Denmark.

Renan, E.
1982 *Qu'est-ce qu'une nation?* Paris: Calmann-Levy.

Reyna, S. P.
1991 What is to be done? An historical structural approach to warfare and famine. In *The Political Economy of African Famine.* R. E. Downs, D. O. Kenner & S. P. Reyna (eds.), pp. 339-371. Philadelphia: Gordon & Breach.

Roberts, A.
1995 Communal conflict as a challenge to international organization. Conference on *The Third World After the Cold War: Ideology, Economic Development and Politics*, Queen Elizabeth House, Oxford, 5-8 July.

Roosens, E.
1989 *Creating Ethnicity.* London: Sage.

Rudensky, N.
1993 War as a factor of ethnic conflict and stability in the USSR. In *Effects of War on Society.* G. Ausenda (ed.), pp. 181-192. San Marino (R.S.M.): AIEP Editore for CIROSS.

Schlee, G., & A. Shongolo
1995 Local war and its impact on ethnic and religious identification in Southern Ethiopia. *Geo Journal* 36 (1): 7-17.

Seton-Watson, M. H.
1977 *Nations and States.* London: Methuen.

Smith, A. D.
1979 Towards a theory of ethnic separatism. *Ethnic and Racial Studies* 2 (1): 21-37.

1986 *The Ethnic Origins of Nations.* Oxford: Blackwell.

1988 The myth of the 'modern nation' and the myths of nations. *Ethnic and Racial Studies* 11: 1-25.

1989 The origins of nations. *Ethnic and Racial Studies* 12 (3): 340-367.

Smith, A. D. *(cont.)*

1991 The nation: invented, imagined, reconstructed? *Millennium: Journal of International Studies* 20 (3): 353-368.

1993 Ties that bind. *L. S. E. Magazine* 1993 (Spring): 8-11.

Smith, H.

1976 *The Russians*. London: Sphere Books Ltd.

Summerfield, D. A.

1996 *The Impact of War and Atrocity on Civilian Populations: Basic Principles for NGO Interventions and a Critique of Psychosocial Trauma Projects*. London: Overseas Development Institute.

Tebbit, N.

1990 Fanfare of being British. *The Field* (May): 78-79.

Turner, V.

1967 *The Forest of Symbols*. Ithaca, N.Y.: Cornell University Press.

1969 *The Ritual Process: Structure and Anti-structure*. Chicago: Aldine.

UNRISD

1995 *States of Disarray: The Social Effects of Globalization*. An UNRISD report for the World Summit for Social Development. London: Banson.

Vail, L. (ed.)

1989 *The Creation of Tribalism in Southern Africa*. London: James Currey.

Van Binsbergen, W.

1995 Aspects of Democracy and Democratisation in Zambia and Botswana: Exploring African Political Culture at the Grass Roots. *Journal of Contemporary African Studies* 13 (1): 3-31.

Verdery, K.

1992 Comment: Hobsbawm in the East. *Anthropology Today* 8 (1): 8-10.

Vulliamy, E.

1994 *Seasons in Hell: Understanding Bosnia*. London: Simon & Schuster.

de Waal, A.

1994 The genocidal state: Hutu extremism and the origins of the 'final solution' in Rwanda. *Times Literary Supplement*, 1 July: pp. 3-4.

Wallerstein, E.

1974 *The Modern World System: Capitalist Agriculture and the Origins of the European World Economy in the Sixteenth Century*. New York: Academic Press.

Young, C.

1985 Ethnicity and the colonial and post-colonial state in Africa. In *Ethnic Groups and the State*. P. R. Brass (ed.), pp. 57-93. London & Sydney: Croom Helm.

1993 The dialectics of cultural pluralism: concept and reality. In *The Rising Tide of Cultural Pluralism: The Nation State at Bay?* C. Young (ed.), pp. 3-35. Madison: University of Wisconsin Press.

1994 Ethnic Diversity and Public Policy: *An Overview*. Occasional Paper No. 8, World Summit for Social Development. Geneva: UNRISD.

MY NEIGHBOUR, MY ENEMY: THE MANIPULATION OF ETHNIC IDENTITY AND THE ORIGINS AND CONDUCT OF WAR IN YUGOSLAVIA

TOM GALLAGHER

Department of Peace Studies, University of Bradford, Bradford, West Yorks BD7 1DP

The different elements making up Yugoslavia always had to cope with a difficult historical inheritance. The legacy of conflicting imperialisms, arbitrarily-drawn boundaries, differing political cultures, and the incompatible hopes and fears of major groups in society enormously complicated the task of creating a united federation of South Slav Peoples (Remington 1993:365). Ultimately, the attempt to eradicate divisive historical memories so as to prevent competing nationalist visions destroying the federal system were unsuccessful and Yugoslavia slid into civil war in the middle of 1991.

Historians already disagree over whether the Yugoslav experiment was destined to fail or whether a different political approach to handling problems of ethnic diversity might have yielded up more successful governing arrangements. But it is clear that rival visions of Yugoslavia held by the Croats and the Serbs, the two largest South Slav peoples united by language and shared ancestry but placed apart by religion and contrasting political experiences, have been the major source of internal discord since Yugoslavia (the word means land of the South Slavs) was created in 1918.[1] The Croat-Serb confrontation which led to the breakdown of the first Yugoslav state was controlled but not eradicated after the state's second incarnation in 1945. Different conceptions of Yugoslavia and what the role of Serbs and Croats should be were never far from the surface in a federal Marxist-Leninist state whose rallying-cry was "Brotherhood and Unity." Despite guaranteeing over a generation of peace, Marshal Tito's political system failed to create an enduring consensus or find ways of managing conflict.

The retention of an authoritarian system of government, along with a complex system of decentralized decision-making, created mounting disagreements. After Tito, regional élites competed for influence until an attempt to recentralize the political system by traditionally dominant Serbia plunged the whole federation into crisis in the second half of the 1980s. Nationalism was embraced and institutionalized by communist élites in order to ensure their survival. This was taken furthest in Serbia and a counter-mobilization ensued in Croatia when competitive elections were

1 For the best short historical account of the political sub-divisions of South Slav ethnicity see Lederer 1969.

permitted in 1990. Pan-Yugoslav consciousness existed and there is evidence that it was growing in the 1980s but it proved too weak to stem the ethnic tide.

The final years of peace in Yugoslavia saw history being manipulated to emphasize differences and popularize an ethnocentric outlook. In this paper I will identify the groups seeking to turn history into a contemporary political resource and the sections of the population to whom they appealed. I will investigate the techniques used to whip up passions over the past. These include the emphasis on asserting 'inalienable historical rights'; the cultivation of a persecution complex by reminding citizens of past wrongs done by ethnic opponents; an insistence that people carry hereditary and collective guilt for such wrongs even though most were not born when they were committed; and, finally, the stress on conspiracies from within and without, all pointing to the fact that the nation has never known a greater historic peril.

I also argue that the successful manipulation of historic grievances and present-day fears created the image of a collective enemy, one that removed the restraints on political differences being settled by violent means. The role of the electronic media, a new factor in Balkan nationalism, then allowed the conflict to become increasingly indiscriminate.

Despite their rival territorial claims which in the early 1990s were being settled on the battlefield, Serbia and Croatia evolved in a parallel direction thanks to the political conditioning of the late 1980s. Citizens were instructed that the only sure means of survival stemmed from the subordination of everything to the nation and those able to interpret the collective national will. Both countries were led by individuals who claimed to be uniquely gifted to interpret the national will, right past wrongs, and prepare the way for a glorious future.

Yugoslavia 1945-91: the failure of conflict resolution

Whatever the outcome of the conflict in different parts of the territory once known as Yugoslavia, the controversial role of Josip Tito is bound to absorb the energies of historians for a long time to come. He commanded both respect and affection and was a symbol of political legitimacy for many Yugoslavs grateful for the 35 years of internal peace and improving living standards that coincided with his span of rule (1945-80). In the early 1990s his portrait still adorned shops and offices in Sarajevo and Skopje, capitals of the republics of Bosnia-Herzegovina and Macedonia, which were created in one case to remove a territory from the ambit of Serb-Croat rivalry and, in another, to widen the neutral space from which a common 'Yugoslav' identity might emerge. There are many Yugoslavs prepared to admit that while Tito indulged both his ego and his taste for luxurious living, he was at least prepared to share the good life with his own people and that the benefits of his long rule (compared with what came after) will cause history to judge him kindly. Perhaps, as time elapses, Tito's ability to balance competing ethnic and ideological interests in the wake of a savage civil-war fought in the shadow of German and Italian military occupation, will seem an increasingly remarkable feat.

Tito was of course able to bend currently irreconcilable foes to his will and emerge as a supreme arbiter because of the prestige he had earned in the Second World War. No other east European communist movement had succeeded in pushing foreign occupiers from the national territory without needing the 'fraternal' help of the Soviet Red Army. The feeling that Yugoslavia had accomplished a popular revolution as fundamental as the one within the communist motherland, Russia, (and in circumstances no less adverse), gave the Yugoslav communists the confidence and strength to defy Stalin's edict of excommunication in 1948 and plot their own distinctive course as a non-aligned Marxist state.

The ideology of Tito's regime was eclectic, drawing upon Marxism's more democratic and humane instincts and also importing various capitalistic socio-economic principles (Cohen 1992:2). Writers who take a less benevolent view of Tito and link features of his rule and key decisions taken by him with the catastrophe that engulfed much of his country in the 1990s, argue that he could have used a strengthening international and internal position to create a more enduring political system able to absorb inter-ethnic rivalries and centrifugal tendencies.

The Austrian historian, Anton Bebler, criticizes Tito for adopting as a political blueprint the Soviet constitutional model, one destined to be a failure in the USSR itself. He reckons that Tito was repeating the mistake of the post-1918 monarchist Yugoslav élite which copied another foreign, and for Yugoslavia, inappropriate model of national integration, that of post-1789 centralist France (Bebler 1993:75); the post-war state was created "not with the requirements of conflict prevention in mind" (Bebler 1993:77). The division of the state into federal units was carried out by small groups of senior communist officials in closed sessions and, in many cases, without the consent of the populations concerned (Bebler 1993:77). Bebler argues that, following the Soviet example, a powerful central position was given to Serbia (similar to that of Russia in the USSR), no federal district being created. Calls to site a federal capital in an ethnically-mixed city like Sarajevo went unheeded and Tito chose instead to make Serbia's main city, Belgrade, the Yugoslav capital.

The different republics were given fictional sovereignty fully complemented by cultural and political institutions; in return they ceded political power to Tito and the communist party (Doder 1993:11). The party was the main pillar of state authority, the other two being the military and the political police. The last two were dominated by officers from Serbia which led to various degrees of resentment elsewhere, above all in Croatia.

It is difficult for such an authoritarian system to include effective instruments for national conflict prevention and control. Instruments in which political disputes could have been resolved by negotiation and compromise, such as the federal presidency, were left politically powerless. The media were prevented from discussing conflicts of interest. Exploration of past events when South Slav brotherhood had collapsed into fratricidal conflict, were taboo. The example of France shows that the exploration of memories of internal schism and conflict, such as those of the Second World War, can prove painful and divisive. But efforts to come to terms with the past can sometimes prove cathartic provided they are handled with care and sensitivity (e.g. the Spanish civil war after Franco's death and the restoration of democracy). Despite serenely claiming that the communist revolution had solved the national question once and for all, Tito never felt confident enough to allow even a controlled re-examination of the turbulent events which had preceded the formation of communist Yugoslavia.

A common Yugoslav identity was promoted by stressing a number of images and experiences, the main ones being the wartime Partisan struggle, Yugoslavia's system of 'economic self-management,' her role as founder-leader of the non-aligned movement, and not least Tito's own personality cult. But Titoism ultimately proved to be a technique of government rather than an enduring ideology capable of securing the legitimacy of the state. According to Sabrina Petra Ramet, Tito tried to build a sense of common identity around an empty core: ultimately it was clear what the content of 'Slovenianism,' 'Croatianism' and 'Serbianism' was in each case, but "Yugoslavianism had no content except the sum of its parts" (Ramet 1991:251).

An innovation that could have replaced paternalistic autocracy with a more genuinely self-regulating system was the attempt in the 1960s to decentralize the communist party and transfer political power to the regions. But the decentralization of power to regional communist élites was not accompanied by genuine political pluralism, encapsulated by multi-party elections. Tito may have been prompted to embark upon decentralization by evidence that a Yugoslav identity was becoming a real, as opposed to a synthetic aspect of national life: intermarriage by people belonging to different ethnic groups was on the increase, growing numbers of citizens identified themselves in census returns as 'Yugoslavs,' and the country was internally at peace with inter-group violence conspicuous by its absence despite the high-levels of violence seen in the early 1940s. But regionalism without genuine pluralism had the effect of blocking any parties that transcended ethnic lines, something which had fateful consequences when genuine competition was finally allowed in the midst of mounting inter-ethnic distrust at the end of the 1980s.

The constitution of 1974 was meant to preserve Tito's vision of a communist and federal Yugoslavia after its creator's death. It invested each Yugoslav republic and province with theoretical 'statehood' and created "a semi-confederative political structure in which powerful sectional leaderships from the single-party competed for influence and support at the top level of the system" (Cohen 1992:33). The federal government determined the broad direction of policy, but the emphasis on achieving unanimity among all republics and provinces meant that decision-making was cumbersome. A policy-making process that moved at a snail's pace after elaborate consultations and consensus-seeking procedures was ill-suited to grapple with the difficult legacy left by Tito, especially in the economic sphere. Living standards began to fall in the 1980s and regional economic differences started to widen as the foreign loans, which had compensated for the inefficiency and corruption of the 'economic self-management' system, started to dry up.

The welfare state, established in previous decades, arguably restrained inter-ethnic rivalries and, with its partial dismantlement, it became less easy to disguise these. But it was at élite level, rather than at the base of society, that economic disputes first spillt over into inter-ethnic, or regional rivalry.

Complaints from Slovenia and Croatia about the amount of revenue being directed to prop up inefficient heavy industries in the south-eastern republics, revealed unhappiness with Tito's commitment to an equalization of economic development as a means of easing inter-ethnic tensions; some highly-placed Serbs chose not to remain silent when complaints about the massive expenditure devoted to a military-industrial complex disproportionately staffed by Serbs, reached their ears.[2]

In 1986, some of Serbia's leading intellectuals, grouped in the Serbian Academy of Arts and Sciences, published a 70-page memorandum which described the Serbs as "the most persecuted people in Yugoslavia" and accused Tito of having sought to "destroy Serbia" (Andrejevich 1993b:18-9, n.12; Ramet 1991:220). It would be ethnically-conscious intellectuals, a group which in Eastern Europe has long been encouraged to regard itself as the guardian of national values and which publicly voiced ethnocentric views that, in less than five years, would push Yugoslavia over the abyss to civil-war.

Tito may not have allowed intellectuals to revive the historical grievances which, elsewhere in communist Eastern Europe, had exacerbated majority-minority relations in some countries, (reviving longstanding inter-state disputes in others), but his regionalization of political authority had prevented intellectuals emerging as a force promoting a common

---

2 60-70 per cent of the military general staff consisted of Serbs and Montenegrans and in 1989, 57 per cent of the federal budget was allocated to the Yugoslav Federal Army (JNA) (Ramet 1991:251).

Yugoslav identity. Cultural affairs were the exclusive responsibility of individual republics and most intellectuals and creative artists were preoccupied with their own national cultures (Klaic 1993). It was far from unknown for Eastern European intellectuals seeking state protection and state patronage to exploit nationalism in order to advance personal or group interests. The economically insolvent and territorially fragile states of inter-war Eastern Europe provide numerous examples (Seton-Watson 1945:140-5). But Yugoslav national rivalries were being openly pursued in a dangerous political vacuum with the federal government increasingly unable to play the role of rule-enforcer. The lack of political trust and co-operation among members of the regionally-divided policy élites prevented effective reforms and allowed expressions of group intransigence which, in Tito's time, would have been suppressed.

The political stalemate was broken in 1987 with the emergence of a Serb politician prepared boldly to assert Serb interests and depart radically from Titoist methods for the management of the national question (Cohen 1992:53-4). Slobodan Milosevic owed his rise to growing Serbian bitterness about their declining demographic position in the province of Kosovo, seen as a cradle of Serb nationhood. On a visit to Kosovo in April 1987, he gave reassurance to anxious Serbs who had been pushed around by the local police: "No one will be allowed to beat you! No one will be allowed to beat you!" (Cohen 1993:52). It is not clear whether Milosevic (a 43-year-old communist banking official with no previous record as a nationalist) stumbled as if by accident on the emotive power of nationalism, or whether he had already been preparing the ground for a power-grab based on advancing Serb interests within the Yugoslav federation. By 28 June 1989, the 600th anniversary of the battle of Kosovo Polje when the Serbs suffered a crucial defeat at the hands of the Ottoman Turks, Milosevic had evolved into a populist nationalist who emphasized trust in his own personality rather than in political institutions. At a huge rally commemorating the battle, Milosevic promised his audience that never again would Islam subjugate the Serbs (Vulliamy 1994:57). By now severe measures were being taken against the Albanians of Kosovo which placed their province, hitherto a relatively autonomous unit attached to Serbia, under direct rule from Belgrade. Pro-Serb leaderships had also been installed in Voivodina and Montenegro. These changes gave Milosevic effective control over 4 of the 8 regional leaderships represented in the collective state presidency, the most important executive body in the country (Burg 1993:360). Critics of Milosevic (not all of them to be found outside Serbia) viewed what had happened as the opening move of an attempt to recentralize the whole country around Serbia. Indeed, when the new Serbian leadership chose to discuss their plans, their preference for a unitary state with no federal borders, and with a strong federal president who could control defence, security and foreign policy, struck fear in all the other republics outside

Belgrade's orbit (Cohen 1993; Ramet 1991). Milosevic was viewed by his opponents as a dangerous demagogue who coveted the job of all-powerful President of a Yugoslavia shorn of institutionalized checks and balances.

The menacing nature of developments in Serbia hastened attempts by local communist élites in Slovenia and Croatia to acquire greater legitimacy from their own populations by holding competitive elections. For the reform-minded Slovene communists, identification with Slovene interests proved a successful survival strategy and their leader Milan Kucic was elected his country's first President in 1990. It is worth recalling that Croatia had already witnessed a communist-led nationalist movement seeking better terms within the Yugoslav federation in 1971. Then, unlike the late 1980s, the center had been able to impose order on a wayward regional leadership with politically inconvenient ideas. No Croatian 'Milosevic' emerged, at least from communist ranks, but the 1990 election resulted in the triumph of a movement dominated by former communists and nationalistic Croat emigrés who preached a language of national assertion and avenging past wrongs committed against the Croat nation, not dissimilar to that being heard in Serbia.

Dr. Franjo Tudjman, a former general who was purged for his connections with the Croatian national upsurge of the late 1970s, emerged as Croatia's leader in 1990 after his Croatian Democratic Alliance won 42 per cent of the vote in competitive elections. He claimed to be "part of the Christian Democratic fraternity of Western Europe" (Vulliamy 1994:58). But ethnicity was promoted as the governing principle of the new state. The 1990 constitution defined Croatia as "the national state of the Croat nation." The first section contains a history of Croatia from the seventh century and is mainly an argument in favour of uninterrupted Croat statehood irrespective of long periods in which the territory was shared by others. Minorities are recognized as citizens but, in a 'nation-state,' minorities are bound to feel in an uncomfortable position and little was done to prevent this happening (Dimitrijevic 1993:50).

With increasing regularity Tudjman chose to direct attention to the cultural differences between Serbs and Croats. He and his colleagues frequently employed anti-Serbian rhetoric even though Serbs made up 12 per cent of Croatia's population (Cohen 1992:131). Tudjman failed to put a brake on such insensitive statements, even though he must have known their possible effect on a Serb minority which had vivid memories of wartime persecutions at the hands of extremist Croats in alliance with Nazi Germany. In 1990 he declared that "according to our traditions we are closely linked with Central Europe and with Germany...Croatia will have closer ties with Germany than with any other country" (Cohen 1992:97). In 1990, he also echoed Milosevic's call for a Greater Serbia by suggesting that the Croats and Muslims (in his view mainly Islamicised Croats) living in Bosnia-Herzegovina ought to be part of a new affirmation of Croatian sovereignty (Cohen 1993:97).

Tudjman and Milosevic were the two most powerful men in Yugoslavia during its final months as a common political unit. Both had conflicting visions of what Yugoslavia should be, Tudjman preferring a loose confederation as the only acceptable alternative to Croatia's existence as a separate state, Milosevic making clear his preference for a centralized state. They showed a propensity to agree over the partition of Bosnia in 1990 and in 1993, but the future of Serb-inhabited areas of Croatia placed the leaders of two race-conscious élites on a collision course that spilled over into war after Slovenia successfully declared its independence in June 1991. The warfare made it easy to overlook important similarities between the political systems hammered out by Milosevic and Tudjman: the plebiscitary style of democracy, the preference for measures designed to silence or intimidate their opponents (especially in the media), a refusal to tolerate meaningful minority rights, a messianic leadership style and, as time would show, a determination to pursue risky and intransigent policies even when they caused enormous suffering to their own people.

History as ethnic manipulation

Whenever a society enters a period of turbulence and profound re-examination, when one political epoch may be giving way to another that remains ill-defined, it is normal for the past to be re-assessed sometimes with great intensity in order to shed light on what the future might hold. In the post-Tito years it was clear to many that Yugoslavia had entered such a period of political transition, even while its constituent parts were still at peace with one another. The reluctance of the political authorities to allow the recent past to be analyzed in ways that challenged official orthodoxy meant that past events became of paramount importance to groups and individuals with strong views that they had been unable to express openly before. Amidst mounting political disagreements, contentious episodes from Yugoslavia's post-1918 history were re-evaluated, often with the intention of emphasizing differences between contemporary ethnic groups. History became politics projected onto the past. Since no distinct physical characteristics distinguished those south Slavs in disagreement about the future of Yugoslavia, it is perhaps inevitable that historical differences were magnified in order to create sharp battle-lines in a blurred landscape.

The South Slavs had had separate histories until 1918. They had never shared a common homeland and, after the creation of a Yugoslav state, they still found themselves, to a greater or lesser extent, divided by cultural tradition (Byzantine, Ottoman, and Catholic Central European) as well as by religion (Orthodox, Muslim, Catholic). Those cleavages were seized upon in the late 1980s by intellectuals who insisted that history had not ordained the South Slav peoples to enjoy a common existence and that an exclusive path was the only just historical outcome. Such historical determinism was frequently advanced by arguably the two most successful intellectuals-turned-politicians: Franjo Tudjman, a historian and former Yugoslav partisan and army officer under whom Croatia declared its independence in 1991; and Dobrica Cosic, the foremost living Serb writer whose historical novels have been compared with Tolstoy's in their scale and in the way that they evoke the spirit of endurance of the Serbian people. Both men issued statements about the incompatibility of the Serbs and Croats which were expressed in remarkably similar language.

Tudjman told one interviewer in 1991:

> Croats belong to a different culture - a different civilization from the Serbs. Croats are people of western Europe, part of the Mediterranean tradition. Long before Shakespeare and Molière, our writers were translated into European languages. The Serbs belong to the east. They are eastern people like the Turks and the Albanians. They belong to the Byzantine culture.... Despite similarities in language, we cannot be together (Cohen 1992:208).

Dobrica Cosic was equally judgmental in an interview he gave shortly after being elected President of Serbia in 1992:

> The foundation of their [Croat] nationalism has been religious, ever since the mid-nineteenth century. So the Croat is a Catholic even more than a nationalist. Catholicism in Croatia has the role of an outright constitutional principle. Hence the Croat's profound hostility towards the Serb, guilty in his eyes of two capital sins - both an Orthodox or an atheist and a Communist! ...And behind Croatian nationalism there lies...hatred of diversity. This ideology subsequently became part of the...people's unconscious, exacerbating antagonism and antipathy, to the extent of mutual hatred and the desire to fight. The tragedy of Serb and Croat is exactly that of Cain and Abel (Cohen 1992:282).

As historic events which extolled Croat or Serb sectionalism began to be celebrated after being delegitimized in Tito's era, both national communities proved highly sensitive to each other's symbols and anniversaries. Those that served to consolidate the cultural identity and pride of one group, could give offence to, or even instill a sense of alienation in, the other. Often little care was taken to prevent this happening.

One community which proved to be very sensitive to the public uses historic symbolism was put to, were the Serbs of Krajina, a region belonging to the Yugoslav republic of Croatia and which independent Croatia claimed as its own. The Krajina stands on one of the main religious frontiers criss-crossing Europe. Misha Glenny has pointed out that as well as "...forming the border between the empires of Islam and Christendom for three centuries, it is also the line of fissure between...the Roman Catholic and Orthodox Christian faiths (Glenny 1992:6). Many of the original Serb inhabitants had migrated to the region to escape Ottoman persecution and they had been recruited to serve as border guards in a region that constituted the Austrian Military Frontier, one that had long served (1578-1881) as a defensive buffer against further Ottoman expansion in the Balkans (Glenny 1992:5-6). The Serbs of Krajina had suffered fierce persecution at the hands of the Croatian Ustashe rulers of the Nazi puppet state of Croatia (1941-45). Given that many could recall friends and relatives who had been massacred during this time, it is not surprising that the decision of the Tudjman government to revive insignia used by the Ustasha, to rename streets after ministers in the wartime government, and to express a desire to change the currency to the *kuna*, last in circulation between 1941 and 1945, should strengthen the resolve of many Serbs to resist incorporation in a revived Croatian state (Traynor 1993b). Perhaps Tudjman's willingness to risk international opprobium by borrowing from the tainted Ustasha legacy only serves to betray how poor a quarry the Croat past was for a state busy seeking new legitimating symbols; it also may reveal the derivative and even second-rate quality of the nationalist intellectuals in Croatia (and in other east European countries treading the same path) that they proved unable to find more original and inspiring symbols to grace the new state.[3]

In 1991 Serbs and Croats were controlled by race-conscious élites which claimed to be completing the historic process of the *narod*, the Slavonic word that means 'people' and 'nation' at the same time (Vulliamy 1994:5). Historians were at the heart of this process, striving to "provide nations with a sense of historical identity, contemporary respectability and future legitimacy" (Pearson 1987:36). The re-definition—and sometimes the re-arrangement—of the past witnessed in the early 1990s was a continuation of the practice first seriously employed by historians writing the histories of the new states that emerged from the defeated empires of east-central Europe after 1918. The historian, Raymond Pearson, has described the process in the following way.

> Often the historical exigencies of nationalism carried academics far beyond the traditional confines of their discipline. No nationality would admit to 'newness'; all solemnly subscribed to the concept of national 'revival.'
>
> ...Factual accuracy was an early casualty in the competition for long historical pedigrees. With the Dark Ages being lit up by the garish beams of historical scholarship, historians were soon reduced to operatives in nationalist myth-making factories. It became easy to identify with Renan's jaundiced judgment that "to forget - and I venture to say - to get one's history wrong, are essential factors in the making of a nation" (Pearson 1987:36, 37).

Strenuous attempts were made in both Serbia and Croatia to deny and conceal persistent evidence of cultural diversity within the respective Serb

---

3 Slovakia's wartime leader, Monsignor Jozef Tiso has become a symbol of inspiration for nationalists under whom Slovakia became a self-governing state on 1st January 1993, despite his regime having been a puppet of the Nazis, to whom Slovakia's Jewish population were handed over.

and Croat national communities. Vuk Karadzic, the intellectual giant of nineteenth century Serbia, recognized vast cultural differences between the Serbs and the Habsburg Monarchy and those of the Ottoman Empire (Banac 1992:ix). Strong cultural differences are to be found among the Croats, those of the Istrian peninsula and Dalmatian coast often feeling remote from Zagreb, (a sense of apartness reflected in 1993 local election results).[4] The emphasis on shrill displays of unity may, in part, address real fears of fragmentation on the part of politicians well aware that Serbs and Croats are not as homogeneous, nor as separated from one another, as the official propaganda reaching the rest of the world strenuously insists.

Insecurity about the strength of national consciousness means that those who initiate dialogue across the ethnic boundaries in order to preserve a common living space are regarded as suspect by many 'on their own side.' Marshal Tito, who exemplified cultural pluralism, has become a subversive spectre for nationalists seeking to delegitimize the Yugoslav experience. The Croatian state barely acknowledges that Tito was a son of Croatia and that history is likely to recall him as an outstanding Croat influence on European history on account of his military and state-building achievements in the 1940s (Drakulich 1993). As long as the Serbia of Slobodan Milosevic claims to be the successor of the Yugoslav state, no full attack on Tito's political legacy will be launched in Belgrade, but the mausoleum where his remains are interred was a deserted spot in 1992, the centenary of Tito's birth.

Bosnia, Kosovo and the 'historic rights' of Serbs and Croats

The Yugoslav ideal proved most enduring in Bosnia-Herzegovina owing to the high percentage of mixed marriages in the area and the larger than average percentage of citizens who classified themselves as 'Yugoslavs' in census returns, especially in the cities.[5] Bosnia's geographical location at the center of Yugoslavia, the interspersion of ethno-religious groups throughout the republic and the region's traditional role as a meeting ground and contested territory for Serbs and Croats meant that it was bound to be seriously affected if the Yugoslav state began to unravel.

4 President Tudjman showed his abhorrence of ideas contrary to the ideal of the unitary state in a speech made not long after his party was rejected by the Istrian population in local elections: "It is with Croatia that Istria will finally become part of Europe. And only a sovereign and independent Croatia can guarantee that never again will Istria become someone else's turf and be subjected to foreign occupation." He went on to warn that "...preaching about Istria as a trans-national, trans-regional community of the Croatian, Slovene and Italian parts of Istria is nothing but explicit flirtation with plans for Croatian Istria's separation from the state of Croatia" (BBC 1993).

5 Bosnia is permissible shorthand for the whole territory (Vulliamy 1994:29).

Even before the start of the war, the two main antagonists showed a readiness to make a deal to divide Bosnia, irrespective of what other issues might separate them. In March 1991 Milosevic and Tudjman met on the border of their two republics and reached a general agreement about partitioning Bosnia between them (Glenny 1992:148; Hayden 1993a:6).

Both Serb and Croat leaders have described Bosnia-Herzegovina as an artificial nation which Tito created to contain Serb-Croat conflict and which was later used to serve the cause of Yugoslav non-alignment in the Middle east (Remington 1993:365). The emergence of a viable Bosnian state would have been a standing rebuke to the exclusive nationalist projects being hatched in both Belgrade and Zagreb: for many in Yugoslavia Bosnia was still seen as 'little Yugoslavia' because it embraced the federal project in miniature. Sarajevo, its capital, was a crossroads between Europe and the Orient, where the concept of *narod* lacked meaning (Vulliamy 1994:78).

The partition of Bosnia would enable the architects of renewed and expanded Serbian and Croatian states to join together separated brethren (such as the Serbs of Krajina and the Croats of western Herzegovina) with the motherland. Geography and enduring patterns of human settlement had paid scant respect to the concept of homogeneous nation-states which fuelled the 'historic missions' of both Serbia and Croatia. But religion had fortuitously intervened in the 1980s when, as the Croatian national revival was getting underway, the Holy Mother of God made an appearance to a group of children in Medjugorije, not in Croatia but in Bosnia-Herzegovina. The Madonna's appearance, according to Tudjman, "had heralded the re-awakening of the Croatian nation" as well as reminding the world of Croatia's role as a rampart of western Christendom (Vulliamy 1994:61).

The intellectuals responsible for creating Croatian national consciousness had long stressed Croatia's role as a defender of Catholic Europe and its civilization. Tudjman paraded his Christian European credentials and, when engaged in offensive action against the beleagured Bosnian government, he was careful to describe himself as "part of the Christian Democratic fraternity of Europe" (Vulliamy 1994:58).[6] To many Croat nationalists, the Bosnian Muslims were 'Islamicized Croats.' Given their reluctance to accept the Muslim faith which Bosnians had adhered to for half a millenium, it is not surprising that Croat as well as Serb nationalist fighters saw the need to destroy symbols of the Islamic presence in the western Balkans. The oldest mosque in the Balkans, the Ustikolina, was levelled during the Serb offensive in eastern Bosnia; the town of Banja Luka has seen its mosques levelled in 1992-93 as its large Muslim population has been systematically

---

6 The Croatian authorities have denied involvement in the Bosnian war but a report to the European Union in February 1993 established that regular Croatian troops were being deployed in support of the forces of 'Herzog Bosna' which are commanded by Matei Boban, who leads Tudjman's party in Bosnia-Herzegovina (Black 1994).

driven out by terror and intimidation; the high-arched limestone bridge in Mostar built in 1566 was blown up by Croat artillery shells in November 1993; meanwhile in besieged Sarajevo, one of the worst acts of cultural vandalism was the shelling of the Oriental Institute and the destruction of 22,000 manuscripts, some of which were 900 years old (Traynor 1993c). A claim to sacred historical ownership of territory becomes less compelling if there is physical evidence of different civilizations which reveals a mixed, rather than an exclusive, heritage.

Often, those prepared to be most insistent in enforcing the historic rights of one *narod* or another proved to be outsiders. Thus in eastern Slavonia, scene of a Serbian push in 1991 which culminated in the siege of the Danubian city of Vukovar, it was immigrants transferred here from other parts of Yugoslavia following the removal of the large German community who took the lead in the fighting; meanwhile longer-established villages of Slavonian Serbs were able to live in peace with adjacent old Croat communities, even after the war started (Glenny 1992:107-8).

It was probably no coincidence that the insistence on Croatia's historic rights in Bosnia came from Croat emigrés in the Americas and in Australia, whose contact with the Croat homeland had often been tenuous until the end of the 1980s. Extreme nationalism had flourished among them and maps showing a greater Croatia had been published which suddenly ceased to appear a distant fantasy after emigrés carved out a leading role in Croatian politics. In 1990 it was the money of Croat emigrés, many from western Herzegovina, which helped secure an election victory for Tudjman. He has since surrounded himself with advisers from the Croatian diaspora who see a chance of bringing into reality the 'imagined community' of a Croatia encompassing the mountains of Herzegovina which many of them hail from. However, the emphasis on acquiring territory has been at the cost of destroying Croat communities in central Bosnia which became the subject of Muslim attacks in 1993 following the start of the Croat expansionary drive. By helping itself to part of a neighbouring, allied, and internationally recognized, state, Bosnia-Herzegovina, Croatia gravely weakened its own case for the restoration of its territorial integrity (one-third of Croatia had been occupied by pro-Belgrade forces in 1991). But the affirmation of 'historic rights' often means that the present is negated for a mythical or 'imagined' past. The Croat experience shows how efforts to breathe life into imagined communities can lead to the sure destruction of actually existing ones.

The territory which undoubtedly has dominated the Serb imagination before all others is Kosovo, the largely Albanian-inhabited province which is seen as the fulcrum of Serbian myth and legend. Demographic pressure from the Albanians once more allowed the spectre of Serbian extinction to be raised. The Serbian sense of martyrdom stems from a battle fought at

Kosovo Polje in 1389 which led to four centuries of Ottoman rule. It went down in Serbian legend as a supreme sacrifice in defence of the nation, Christendom, and European civilization. The emphasis on honouring the sacrifice of ancestors was powerfully conveyed at a special gathering of the Serbian Association of Writers in March 1989 to which gathering, its president, Matijin Beckovic declared that "...there is so much Serbian blood and so many sacred relics that Kosovo will remain Serbian land even if not a single Serb remains there" (Ramet 1991:243). Already, the disinterred bones of King Lazar, the fallen hero of the 1389 battle, were being hawked around the country in what one foreign journalist described "as a mass indulgence of self-pity" (Traynor 1993b). When the 600th anniversary fell in 1989, government leaders promised both revenge for a battle lost and resurrection.

Albanians and Bosnians had fought alongside Serbs in 1389. But historical accuracy was beside the point. The aim was incitement of ethnic hatred and revenge against the modern equivalent of the Ottoman Turk—in this case the Albanians who later converted to Islam (Traynor 1993b). For many Serbs, Albanians have become 'terrorists,' 'secessionists,' or 'tourists' (Barber 1993). By denying the individuality of the Albanians and viewing them as threatening objects, it was easier to take indiscriminate action against them; in 1989-90 the last remaining vestiges of Albanian autonomy in Kosovo had been eradicated and the territory became a police state where the Albanian majority have been subject to systematic economic and political victimization.

The preoccupation of Serbian nationalists with a defeat of historic magnitude still puzzles some observers. But it does make contemporary sense. State propaganda depicts the Serbs not as triumphant conquerors but as threatened innocents, potential victims of enemies ranged on all sides. Since at least 1989, the enormously influential state broadcasting services have attempted to inculcate in their viewers the image of a nation in mortal peril, fighting for survival and badly misunderstood (Barber 1993). Promotion of a sense of threat makes it easier for the government to insist on unity and to delegitimize its opponents; it also justifies the use of ruthless tactics against those who are seen as denying Serbia's right to exist.

Collective and hereditary guilt

For all the inventiveness used by historians and others to devise the image of Serbs as a victim nation, the high number of Serb dead in the main European wars of this century gives the sense of martyrdom a popular resonance. Politicians attempted to place the sense of martyrdom at the service of an expansionary Serbia even before the present conflict. Having endured so much, there were many Serbs in 1918 who could be persuaded that they were the rightful leaders of the Yugoslav state formed in that year. The new country had a Serb monarch, a Serbian-led army, and a Serb-dominated political system. Having seen themselves as the Piedmontese of the Balkans, who had liberated the South Slavs from Austria-Hungary and Turkish rule and who warranted the leading role in the new state, Serbian politicians made the mistake of failing to appreciate the historic sensitivities of other national groups (Djuric 1991:479). It was one Tito sought to avoid by dividing power among the Yugoslav nationalities and strengthening the identity of the weaker ones.[7] Denied their status of first among equals, nationally-minded Serbs were angered.

The image of the Serbs as a persecuted people whose trials matched those faced by the Jews, became a well-known metaphor in the last years of Yugoslavia (Ramet 1991:200).[8] Official restraints on the discussion of wartime fratricidal conflict were removed. Both Serbs and Croats became involved in the cult of digging up decomposed bodies—Serb victims of fascist Croatia, Croat victims of communist persecution, often subject to blanket television coverage (Harris 1992; Vulliamy 1994:7). The emphasis upon recent wrongs enabled the wall of mutual distrust to rise even higher and speculation is likely to rage about whether it was part of a planned process for the war that followed. The use of television to raise emotions about wartime experiences undoubtedly went furthest of all in Serbia but it was assisted by insensitive actions of the Tudjman government which enabled Belgrade to argue that a new martyrdom of Serbia was in prospect. Besides the adoption of controversial symbolism dating from the 1940s, Croatia's leader went to great pains to minimize the number of wartime casualties in a book called *Wasteland: Historic Truths*. The controversy centred around Jasenovac camp where hundreds of thousands of Serbs, Jews, Muslims, Gypsies and dissident Croats had been murdered. By 1993 a monument in memory of the 1500 Jews executed at Jasenovac had been demolished and the museum had been closed (Chazan 1993b; Vulliamy 1994:24-5).

Such insensitive actions make it easier for Serb radicals to argue not only that Croats never properly paid for wartime cruelty but that guilt for the massacres is collective and hereditary. Images of historic wrongs were also used to justify the Serbian offensive against Muslim-inhabited areas of eastern and northern Bosnia after April 1992. General Ratko Mladic, the commander of the forces which drove out, sometimes killing, 200,000 Muslims in eastern Bosnia to link up Serb-populated areas, used historic

---

7 An example of the latter was the decision to commission a well-known Harvard Slavicist, Horace Landt, to create a grammar for the Macedonian language (Doder 1993:11, note 7).

8 Vuk Draskovic, leader of the Serbian Renewal Party often proclaimed the Serbs to be "the Jews of modern times."

metaphors to justify his actions: "Serbian mothers watched children taken away by Mussulmans to become Sultan's slaves, to be sold as slaves" (Gowing 1993). If a commander succeeds in convincing his men that their opponents bear the stain of hereditary guilt, then it is easier for indiscriminate tactics to be used against them. The enemy become dehumanized; they are viewed as a collective scourge rather than as individuals who happen to be on the opposite side.

The Bosnian conflict in its most harrowing early phases was essentially a war directed against civilians. They were not merely in the way of competing armies but were the chief target in what was a relentless drive to secure territory 'cleansed' of its previous inhabitants. Mass flight was induced by terror tactics, the best known of which was the rape of Muslim women. There was also a strong element of collective guilt in the minds of the perpetrators, according to *Amnesty International*. It noted that women have often been "...singled out...as a form of retribution because of the perpetrators' presumptions of the actions or intentions of the women's male relatives" (*Amnesty International* 1993:6). There is further evidence that in order to persuade their men to rape Muslim women, Serb commanders employed historical arguments: "...they convinced their troops that the reason for their suffering stemmed from the heritage of the Ottoman Empire. Hence mass rape could be justified on historic grounds" (Enloe 1993). It is no coincidence that some of the marauding militias in eastern Bosnia called themselves Hajduks, in memory of the anti-Muslim brigands of the seventeenth century.[9]

The impact on the ordinary foot soldier of the propaganda depicting an ethnic 'enemy' who carried collective and hereditary guilt, was revealed in the court testimony and media interviews of Borislav Herak, a Sarajevo Serb sentenced to death in March 1993 by the Bosnian government for multiple murder and rape. A journalist described how a factory-worker who had never nursed hatred of his fellow Muslims and Croats with whom he had grown up, changed upon getting caught up in the war:

> Once he joined up with the Serbian fighters, the exercises involved slitting pigs' throats as practice for killing Muslims. He was told that the 'Islamic' government would stigmatise the Serbs, as the Nazis did the Jews, that Serbian babies were being slaughtered and Serbian girls held in brothels, and that the Muslims had killed his father. They had not. After his father visited him in prison, he realised he had been lied to (Traynor 1993b).

Contemporary as well as historical images were used to demonize the Muslims. General Mladic claimed that the Serbs were in danger of being outbred by Bosnia's Muslims, the prospect of becoming outnumbered by an

---

9 The number of rape victims is a matter of considerable dispute. Estimates range as high as 20,000 (European Community figure) to 50,000 (the Sarajevo State Commission for Investigation of War Crimes) (Vulliamy 1994:32; cf. Jones 1994:117).

ethnic foe being a traumatic one that breeds intransigence as evidence from numerous inter-ethnic conflicts might show: "...the Islamic world does not have the atomic bomb, but it does have a demographic bomb. Atomic bombs are under some kind of control. Their enormous reproduction is not under any kind of control" (Gowing 1993).

An aide to Radovan Karadzic, the Bosnian Serb leader, when talking to journalists above the besieged city of Sarajevo, insisted that "...down there they are fighting for a single land that will stretch from here to Teheran, where our women will wear shawls, where there is bigamy..." (Vulliamy 1994:49). The fact that attendance at mosques in pre-war Bosnia had been under 3 per cent (leading one journalist to describe the Bosnians as "the world's most rotten Muslims") was overlooked by the besiegers of Sarajevo who sought to depersonalize their victims by turning them into a collective conspiracy in the heart of Europe (Vulliamy 1994:63). The Serbian *narod*, bludgeoned by Turks and Croats, mistreated by atheistic communists, was now threatened by an Islamic holy war.[10]

The Muslims had been recognized as a national group by Tito's Yugoslavia in 1972. Twenty years later there were signs that some of the leaders of the Bosnian state were ready to use the Islamic faith as a symbol to rally the Muslim majority and perhaps win support from the Arab world.[11] In the midst of war it is not unknown, even for secular and revolutionary regimes to use religion to rally patriotic pride. Stalin, for example, made a successful appeal to Russian Orthodox sentiment in the Second World War. But it is unusual for a struggling nation to be so dependent on religion as a pillar of national identity. The dilemma was well summed up by one Bosnian, Emir Tica, in charge of transport for the Bosnian army in Travnik, the old capital of Ottoman Bosnia.

> I never thought of myself as a Muslim. I don't know how to pray. I never went to a mosque. I'm European like you. I don't want the Arab world to help us, I want Europe to help us. But now I have to think of myself as a Muslim, not in a religious way, but as a member of a people. Now we are faced with obliteration, I have to understand what it is about me and my people they wish to obliterate (Vulliamy 1994:65).

The Islamic threat was by no means the only conspiracy felt to be directed against Serbia. In 1991-92, when the main military front had been in Croatia, the emphasis had been on the danger that Germany posed to Serbia.

---

10 Serb and Croat nationalists opposed to an independent Bosnia often cite a thesis on an Islamic state written by Bosnian President Ali Izetbegovic in 1970 as proof of his Muslim fundamentalism. But less partisan commentators have viewed it as a tortured attempt to devise a political manifesto for European Islam compatible with modern political systems (Tanner 1993; Vulliamy 1994:66-7).

11 The Bosnian parliament was preparing to revive the old Ottoman word, 'Bosnjak' as a name for Bosnian Muslims which it feared might lead to the forging of a new Bosnian identity that excluded non-Muslims (Thompson 1993).

Mihailo Markovic, a prominent philosopher and vice-president of the ruling Socialist Party, believed in 1991 that a "...4th Reich was uniting against Serbia":

> ...one grows suspicious when one sees that it is Germany, Austria and Hungary that want to recognise Croatian independence. It is the old direction of German penetration into the south-east to drive for access to the Adriatic (Hockenos 1991).

Those who saw the manipulative hand of organized religion in Balkan affairs included the Vatican in the circle of foreign enemies while General Mladic was prepared to speak of an 'infernal' Western plan to disunite and destroy the Orthodox world, with the next target after Serbia being Russia.[12]

The imposition of economic sanctions against Serbia in 1992 was seen as confirmation of the suspicion that the outside world's disposition towards it was one of unbending hostility. It reinforced a siege mentality which Milosevic's party was able to exploit electorally. An externally-orientated Serb like the millionaire businessman Milan Panic who returned from the USA to serve briefly as Prime Minister in the second half of 1992, proved unable to convince a majority of Serbs that the West was ready to show greater understanding if voters turned their backs on xenophobic and aggressive politicians seeking to grab territory by unlawful means. Just as states like Germany and world centers of faith like the Vatican were irredeamably hostile to Serbia, so countries like Greece and Russia were treated as 'brother nations' on account of religious ties and past assistance rendered to South Slavdom. Historical facts were manufactured or re-arranged to lend credence to the view that Serbia was fighting an age-old conspiracy against its right to exist. Enemies were created and then de-humanized to strengthen the conspiracy image and licence the ruthless measures needed for it to be kept at bay.

The nation as a collective individual

The prevalence of conspiracies, the emphasis on avenging past wrongs and asserting historic rights, and stereotypical images of neighbouring peoples, made it much easier for Serbia's rulers to popularize the view that the only means to guarantee ethnic survival was to subordinate all to the nation. Slobodan Milosevic was not the first politician, nor will he be the last who recognized that a politics dominated by nationalism blocks the emergence of normal issues of political discourse, such as contests over values, the quality of government and the allocation of resources. A politician's record is subject to much less critical scrutiny when such core matters can be overlooked. His power can stretch far beyond normal bounds if he is able to

---

12 *Borba*, (Belgrade daily), May 9 1993, quoted in Andrejevich 1993b.

convince enough citizens that he has the ability to interpret and defend the collective national will.

In a political system where national values reign unchallenged, ethnocentric attitudes (whereby the culture, customs, language and even the right to exist of other groups, are deemed wrong), can easily spread. The English philosopher, John Stuart Mill, one year after the 1848 revolutions had collapsed into ethnocentric strife, warned that the elevation of nationalism in this way, makes men indifferent to the rights and interests "...of any portion of the human species, save that which is called by the same name and speaks the same language as themselves" (Kohn 1965:51). History would need to evolve a little further before it became apparent, in the second quarter of this century, that men, in or out of uniform, can lose all inhibitions about committing violence on behalf of the state if the state's aims are clothed in nationalist terminology: fascism successfully stressed the authority and absolute precedence of the national community over the individual and the need for a ruthless and disciplined vanguard to take action on its behalf. One does not need to brand the Serbian state (nor its pale imitator, Croatia) as fascist to recognize that nationalism was being elevated to a core organizing principle as the values of democracy and freedom of thought were being pushed to the margins.

Whether or not they were true believers, intellectuals were to the fore in promoting nationalism almost as a secular religion. The fact that intellectuals in Zagreb and Belgrade who insist that Serb and Croat are different languages (when most international authorities see them as a single language) may have a vested interest in taking such an uncompromising line, was not lost on observers. Lenart Cohen believes that "many Serb intellectuals" tended to opportunistically view Milosevic's advocacy of Serb nationalism as "a new avenue to influence political affairs" (Cohen 1992:54). The view is quite commonly held that nationalism is incidental to Milosevic, being just an instrument to gratify a mammoth urge for power.[13] Milosevic would not be the first powerful European figure to appeal to nationalists while not himself being a true believer.[14]

Napoleon, the first real popularizer of modern nationalism, appealed first to French nationalism and then to the desire for self-rule of subject peoples whose foreign rulers were temporarily cast down by his armies, while his real goals were to found an empire and a dynasty. History has yet to deliver a definitive judgment on whether Milosevic (who never publicly espoused

[13] This view was well put by Dessa Trevisan, the veteran Belgrade correspondent of *The Times* on Britain's Channel 4 on August 1 1993.

[14] Milos Vasic, an indefatigible proponent of free speech in Belgrade and editor of the weekly Vreme believes that Milosevic succeeded in tricking both the 'communists' and 'nationalists' in Serbia: "the communists believed that he was only pretending to be a nationalist and the nationalists that he was only pretending to be a communist" (quoted in Cohen 1992:54).

nationalism until the mid-1990s) was using it as a means to an end, whether it be personal power or the preservation of a particular economic and political system, or a combination of both, and perhaps it never will. As for Tudjman he has all the hallmarks of the true nationalist believer, someone whose writings on nationalism make him view the nation as a sort of collective individual, against whom physical individuals have no standing (Hayden 1993b:665). This kind of formulation makes him as dangerous to his own people as to neighbouring ones but, being twenty years older than Milosevic, he has less opportunity to gratify power urges based on nationalism.

The revenge of the outsider

Nationalist conflicts were revived in Yugoslavia not as a result of pressures from below but owing to the actions of disaffected members of the communist élite and to intellectuals frustrated by their lack of recognition or influence. The nationalist appeal would not have been successfully made, but for the existence of social groups receptive to an ethnocentric message. The content of this message has already been examined. To see which groups proved most receptive to it, it is necessary to examine briefly changing patterns of settlement in Bosnia.

While many Bosnian towns and cities confirmed the existence of a harmonious multi-ethnic community, in the countryside Serbs, Croats, and Muslims were far more insular. Memories of wartime internecine conflict did not become blurred or forgotten as in the cities owing to the fact that the rhythm of life continued without the changes associated with urban modernization. Weapons in use during the Second World War were retained, particularly by Serbs (Vulliamy 1994:39). Intermarriage was far less frequent and, indeed, contact with other communities could often be rare. Dusan Makavejev, a Belgrade film director, has described "...a life without neighbours" in the upland areas of Yugoslavia where it is not terribly hard to turn people's thoughts to violence by manipulating images of the ethnic enemy. He identified a parochial and patriarchal rural culture, ethnically "pure," "fearful of urban energy," prepared to "take up arms against cities as mythical places of affluence and sin."[15]

It is an exaggeration, but perhaps only a slight one, to describe nationality conflicts in Eastern Europe after 1900 as comprising a struggle for dominance between urban communities able to tolerate cultural diversity and the rural hinterland where appeals to nationalist uniformity often found a warmer response. In certain places, such as Serbia and Rumania, bourgeois nationalists and, later, nationalist-inclined communists, obtained some

[15] *The Times*, London: August 8, 1993.

popular acquiescence for fundamentalist politics by mobilizing the countryside against the cities. State-controlled television was often the only source of information about the outside world reaching rural communities; if it transmitted a diet of fundamentalist nationalism, as happened in Serbia after 1987, television undoubtedly succeeded in turning ethnic suspicions into hatreds, giving ultra-nationalists a dangerous new weapon none of their predecessors had acquired. In addition, rural elements have gained influence in politics as urban moderates have been swept aside: Milosevic has built up a well-armed police force (which rivals the Serbian army in size) composed of rural Serbs from Croatia, Bosnia and Kosovo who have little love for Belgrade's anti-war intellectuals or patience with the opposition politics of the city (Tanner 1993a:10). He has licensed and rewarded irregular militias led and staffed by marginal social types, some of whom have criminal records, the best-known being Zeljko Raznjatovic, known as 'Arkan' and wanted on serious charges in several European countries.[16] The ascendancy of Croat extremists from rural Herzegovina who enjoy influential positions in the government, the ruling party, and the army of Croatia shows that parallel influences are at work there (Block 1993:9).

In Bosnia separate and conflicting urban and rural cultures have given rise to two words, *raja* and *papak*: the former is taken to mean the tolerant folk of the city, regardless of creed, the latter describes the country folk "...among whom old hatreds are kept alive by aggressive nationalist sentimentality"; according to journalist Ed Vulliamy, "...people in Sarajevo will tell you this is a war between *raja* and *papak*" (Vulliamy 1994:46).

The post-war years of rapid industrialization witnessed an influx of rural peasants into the city. It was a phenomenon witnessed all over Eastern Europe as the communist authorities made determined efforts to make the working-class the dominant social group in previously rural societies. In Bosnia rural Serbs moved to Sarajevo from nearby mountainous areas; Croatians from the bleak Highlands of Herzegovina came to the city of Mostar which, until 1950, had been shared principally between Muslims and Serbs; meanwhile Serbs from the rural Bosnian 'Krajina' settled in Banja Luka. Many of those newcomers were slow to adapt to an urban lifestyle, one "...either loyal to Tito's republic or apathetic towards both socialism and the *narod*" (Vulliamy 1994:40). Transplanted peasants clung stubbornly to rural attitudes and prejudices in many parts of Eastern Europe, especially where they had to live in proximity with people of a different ethnic background who might have been there much longer than they. The sense of dislocation that peasants might feel in the urban milieu, especially if they faced uncertain economic prospects, meant that they

16 Arkan was elected a deputy for Kosovo on a platform calling for the removal of the majority Albanian population (Vulliamy 1994:87-8).

could be appealed to by nationalist populists who offered them the category of nationalism in order to give their lives a social value.

It might not be altogether coincidental that the leader of the Bosnian Serbs was himself the classic outsider: Karadzic was born in Montenegro and only arrived in Sarajevo as a teenager (*The Independent* 1993). After his forces began the siege of Sarajevo in 1992, 60,000 of the city's 150,000 Serb inhabitants left the city. It is reckoned that most of those who stayed behind to endure the siege with Muslims and Croats had families there for generations: "...of those who left...almost all were from families which had arrived only years before" (Vulliamy 1994:40).

Muslims driven from their villages in the fighting of 1992-93 have converged on cities like Sarajevo and Tuzla still held by the Bosnian government. In 1993 commentators feared that "victims of ethnic cleansing, burning with a desire for revenge and unaccustomed to city life," would upset the delicate ethnic balance in these places. In Tuzla, where refugees comprising poorly-educated peasants made up one-third of the population by August 1993, locals expressed fears that these people might be used by Muslim activists radicalized by the failure of Europe to stop Serb militias butchering thousands of Muslims at the start of the war (Chazan 1993a:9).

Tolerance in the midst of conflict

The wars in the different parts of the former Yugoslavia had shown that once a political dispute with ethnic overtones had become violent, it is difficult to prevent the image of the 'ethnic enemy' becoming a generalized one. A heartening aspect of the conflict in Bosnia is that many who have death and terror visited upon them regularly, have nevertheless resisted separation on an ethnic basis. This is above all true of Sarajevo, 360,000 of its 526,000 inhabitants choosing to remain in the city up till October 1993 (Chazan 1993a:9). Large numbers are Serbs, 200,000 of Bosnia's 1.3 million Serbs remaining in areas controlled by the Sarajevo government (*The Guardian* 1994:21).

Vinko Puljic, the Roman Catholic bishop of Sarajevo, has remained in the city throughout the two-year siege and the support of the Croatian church authorities for an integral and multi-confessional Bosnia has placed them on a collision course with the political authorities in Zagreb (Magas 1993). Leading Serb religious figures have been even more outspoken in their criticism of the Belgrade authorities (although this criticism does not extend to the state's behaviour in Kosovo whose religious shrines are seen as a wellspring of Serbian Orthodox heritage). In November 1991 leading Serb theologians denounced with a clear voice the destruction of the city of Vukovar which fell in that month to Serb forces (Magas 1993). At a Whitsun service in 1992, Patriarch Pavle, head of the Serbian Orthodox Church, begged forgiveness for Serbia's part in the slaughter seen in Bosnia and Croatia: "...the domestic evil is the most dangerous enemy," he warned, a clear rejection of the government view that Serbia's most dangerous foes were to be found outside the country (Traynor 1992:24).

The moderation of religious leaders is important not least because religion is the most obvious cultural element that differentiates Serbs, Croats, and Muslims from each other. It is unfortunate that international religious bodies have not thrown their weight behind local religious forces committed to peaceful solutions to the conflict (Siegman 1994). The reluctance of influential Western decision-makers to recognize that the extremism of political and military leaders and those who obey their orders is unrepresentative of very large sections of the Bosnian population, is also unfortunate. At different times politicians, like the British Foreign Secretary Douglas Hurd (who has helped to shape the low-key western European response to the Yugoslav disaster), have made statements about the atavistic and endemic nature of conflicts in the region which suggest that they share the views of radicals that conflict and division, rather than co-existence, is the normal mode of existence in the Balkans.[17]

In 1993 the peace plan for Bosnia, devised by the UN/EC negotiators Lord Owen and Cyrus Vance, involved partitioning the region into ethnic units known as cantons, a solution which included no provisions for the tens of thousands of mixed families in Bosnia who were not consulted during the protracted negotiations. This plan proposed to divide up Bosnia into a series of ethnic units which was seen by its many critics as recognizing ethnic cleansing by punishing the victims and rewarding aggression against unarmed civilians.[18] Citizens of mixed marriage are reckoned to have made up 40 per cent of Sarajevo's peacetime population and 8 per cent of Bosnia's population, but the plan held out little for them. Nor did it offer security to the not inconsiderable number of Serbs and Croats who have remained loyal to the Bosnian government. For instance, the 40,000 Serbs in the city of Tuzla, awarded to the Muslims under Owen-Vance, were left with an unsavoury choice. At no small risk to themselves, many had defied ethnic

---

[17] Mr. Hurd has consistently argued that "the horrors" of Bosnia "cannot in fact be ended from outside" (Young 1993). The view that a country like Britain had no responsibility to stop the killing in Bosnia was elegantly put by a senior figure in the British establishment, Lord Blake, a retired Oxford historian. He wrote in 1992: "...there is no...British interest in the Balkans today. No one can stop these tribes slaughtering one another, except by military intervention on a scale that public opinion would never tolerate. There may be a case of using troops in a limited role of humanitarian relief. Even that is doubtful. Bismarck declared that Germany had no interest in the Balkans 'that was worth the healthy bones of a single Pomeranian musketeer.' Britain today is in exactly the same position" Blake (1992).

[18] Among the most perceptive press analyses of the Owen-Vance plan were: Black 1993; Eyal 1993; Savill & Elgood 1993; Woollacott 1993.

particularism and supported the ideal of an ethnically-integrated state. But they could either stay in an overcrowded Muslim canton where a religious identity was bound to increase, "...or else migrate to Serb cantons to face the wrath of those whose prejudices they had denied" (Sugich 1993).

Conclusion

I have attempted to explore the propaganda images which prepared the ground for the Serbs and the Croats, the two largest Slav peoples in what was Yugoslavia to settle political differences by means of conflict. I have shown that rival leaderships, at odds over territory, nevertheless, used very similar devices to impose their political will and ideology on their respective populations.

Nationalism became the core political value and organizing principle in both Serbia and Croatia. Leaders who insisted that they were able to interpret and defend the popular will of the nation gained control. Their nationalism denied individualism and disempowered intermediate institutions which were designed to set limits on what the state could do to citizens and, instead, the nation came to be seen as the collective individual. Citizens hitherto defined by jobs, education, character, ideas as well as nationality, were increasingly reduced to one dimension as the climate of insecurity turned nationalism into a state religion. The strength of this nationalist mobilization partly stemmed from the experience of communism. Tito's regime may have been eclectic and reform-orientated in part, but like the other communist systems it enhanced the super-collectivity above the individual.

One of the reasons why it has been possible for communists plausibly to recycle themselves as nationalists is that the distance between the communist collectivist ideology based on such concepts as 'the working class,' 'the class interest,' and 'the class enemy,' and the nationalistic collective ideology based on such concepts as the 'nation,' the 'national interest' and 'the national enemy' is much shorter than the distance between communism and democracy (Milic 1993:110). The Yugoslav social scientist, Zagorka Goluvbovic, has put it another way:

> The shift from communist to nationalist ideology was possible because both had significant features in common. Both ideologies a) are directed towards a destruction of society's autonomy vis-à-vis the state, b) adopt a missionary role promising salvation in an 'ideal order', c) are anti-individualistic and collectivist, d) are characterised by charismatic leadership, and e) are characteristic of societies which, when confronted with a modernisation crisis, offer a messianic solution (Goluvbovic 1993:68).

Intransigent political élites promoted a climate of insecurity in order to insist upon political uniformity and a suspension of meaningful opposition to their entric attitudes, whereby the culture, language, customs and t to exist of other ethnic groups are questioned, were promoted via official state channels, this being above all true of Serbia.

A crucial device in creating ethnic polarization which had fateful consequences in areas of mixed population like Bosnia, was the manipulation of history. In the absence of racial and linguistic differences between the competing élites promoting South Slav ethnicity, manipulation of the past may have been the obvious route to take for élites intent on widening group differences. The past was turned into a contemporary political resource by reviving old conspiracies or inventing new ones, emphasizing past wrongs, asserting historic rights, and promoting stereotypical images of neighboring peoples. The view that people carry collective and hereditary guilt for past wrongs committed by the nation they belong to, was popularized. The electronic media proved to be an influential device which enabled ultra-nationalists to entrench enemy images in parts of the popular imagination.

Once hostilities erupted after June 1991, the dehumanization of non-ethnics which the distortion of the past has accomplished, enabled the conflict to become an indiscriminate one. Those of mixed parentage or marriage and Serbs and Croats who desired no part in the conflict, have often been forced to take sides in conflict zones, something which is above all true of Bosnia-Herzegovina where much of the fighting in the 32-month war (June 1991-February 1994), has been concentrated. There are also groups exposed to propaganda about ethnic enemies who have participated with varying degrees of enthusiasm in a war mainly directed against civilians. Rural-dwellers have been more susceptible to this appeal than urban dwellers and it is not difficult to imagine its effect on individuals isolated from humanizing influences, such as full-time soldiers.

The ethnocentric message has been rejected by important groups in the population, evidence being presented by the ability of Sarajevans to resist ethnic hatred even in the midst of an unnerving siege and also by the strength of the anti-war movement in Belgrade. But in a war-dominated society, even if an overwhelming majority rejected ethnic polarization, it would make little difference given the power exercised by powerful and well-organized ethnic élites.

The destruction of Yugoslavia poses huge questions for agencies concerned with upholding standards of human conduct in political conflict situations. It will be a colossal error if the Yugoslav war is seen as a conflict whose brutal nature is determined by the troubled geo-political context in which it is being waged. International organizations with peace-keeping functions and European bodies like the Council of Europe and the Conference for Security and Co-operation in Europe will need to pay serious attention to the manipulation of ethnic tensions as a tool for making war. Much thought needs to be given about possible approaches that can be used to discourage politicians from adopting such methods. Progress in this area will not be easy as long as some Western policy-makers view the conflict in terms not dissimilar to those of hardliners in Belgrade and Zagreb. Ethnic conflict is viewed as a normal condition in the region; the Tito era as an artificial period of enforced co-existence that went against the grain of history. The separation of ethnic communities, however mixed they might be, is regarded as the only way to guarantee even an uneasy peace, this being the rationale behind the 1993 partition scheme for Bosnia drawn up by the UN negotiators, Lord Owen and Cyrus Vance.

Partition schemes generate huge movements of population and, in no small measure, contribute to international disorder. Overall, the Yugoslav tragedy raises disturbing questions about the ease with which lethal firearms can be poured into a conflict zone in the middle of Europe and the way that the modern media lends itself to spreading the image of 'the ethnic enemy.' To prevent the Yugoslav conflict becoming a dress-rehearsal for something much bigger, serious thought needs to be given to devising mechanisms, early warning-systems, and collective security measures that can reduce the chances of a society with Yugoslavia's many qualities being so comprehensively destroyed.

References

Amnesty International

1993 Bosnia-Herzegovina: rape and sexual abuse by armed forces. *Amnesty International* 1993: 1-13.

Andrejevich, M.

1993a The Radicalization of Serbian Politics. *RFE-RL Research Report* 2 (11), March 26: 14-22.

1993b Serbia's Bosnian Dilemma. *RFE-RL Research Report* 2 (23) June 4: 14-20.

Banac, I.

1992 Foreword. In *Balkan Babel, Politics, Culture and Religion in Yugoslavia.* S. P. Ramet (ed.), pp. ix-iv. Colorado: Westview Press.

Barber, T.

1993 What makes the Serbs the way they are. *The Independent* May 9: p.10.

BBC

1993 Survey of World Broadcasts, Eastern Europe, 1804 C/7, C/9, September 27 1993, Croatian Radio, 25 September, 1993.

Bebler, A.

1993 Yugoslavia's variety of Communist Federalism and her demise. *Communist and Post-Communist Studies* 26 (1): 72-86.

Black, I.

1993 Epitaph for a peace plan that wasn't. *The Guardian* 18 June: p. 11.

1994 Split deepens over Croatian sanctions. *The Guardian* 5 February: p. 8.

Blake, R.
1992 Steer Clear of the Balkans. *The Independent* 24 August: p.16.

Block, R.
1993 Tudjman losing support for carve-up of country. *The Independent* 30 July: p. 9.

Burg, S. L.
1993 Why Yugoslavia Fell Apart. *Current History* November: 357-363.

Chazan, Y.
1993a Tolerant Tuzla fears divisions will breed extremism. *The Guardian* 23 August: p. 9.
1993b Jews urge Zagreb to halt whitewash of wartime regime. *The Guardian* 18 November: p. 8.

Cohen, L.
1993 Broken Bonds: *The Disintegration of Yugoslavia.* Colorado: Westview Press.

Dimitrijevic, V.
1993 Ethnonationalism and the constitution: the apotheosis of the nation-state. *Journal of Area Studies* 3: 50-56.

Djuric, I.
1991 The Historical Roots of the Serb-Croat Conflict. *The Month* November: pp. 477-482.

Doder, D.
1993 Yugoslavia: New war, old hatreds. *Foreign Policy* 91 (Summer): 3-23.

Drakulic, S.
1993 Interview. *The Independent* 15 July: p. 16.

Enloe, C.
1993 Gender, ethnicity and war: Serbian rape of Muslim women. Paper presented at the 3rd ASEN conference on 'Race and Nation,' 14 May, London School of Economics.

Eyal, J.
1993 Peace, or myth wrapped in folly. *The Independent* 4 May: p. 16.

Glenny, M.
1992 *The Fall of Yugoslavia.* Harmondsworth: Penguin.

Goluvbovic, Z.
1993 Nationalism and democracy: The Yugoslav case. *Journal of Area Studies* 3: 65-77.

Gowing, N.
1993 Hatred of a general who plays games with death. *The Guardian* 2 August: p. 12.

The Guardian
1993a The other Serbs (editorial). *The Guardian* 26 May: p. 21.

Harris, P.
1992 Into the fire. *Scotland On Sunday* 16 August: p. 13.

Hayden, R.
1993a The Partition of B-H, 1990-1993. *RFE-RL Research Report* 2 (22) 28 May: pp. 1-14.
1993b Constitutional nationalism in the former Yugoslav republics. *Slavic Review* 53 (4): 654-673.

Hockenos, P.
1991 Yugoslav praxis school suffers identity crisis. *In These Times.* New York, 25 October: p. 14.

The Independent
1993a Profile: Radovan Karadzic, doctor, poet, monster. *The Independent* 9 January: p. 10.

Jones, A.
1994 Gender and Ethnic Conflict in ex-Yugoslavia. *Ethnic and Racial Studies* 17 (1): 115-134.

Klaic, D.
1993 Creators played their part in destruction. *The Independent* 26 August: p. 15.

Kohn, H.
1965 *Nationalism: Its Meaning and History.* New York: Van Nostrand.

Lederer, I.
1969 Nationalism and the Yugoslavs. In *Nationalism in Eastern Europe.* P. Sugar & I. Lederer (eds.), pp. 396-438. Washington: University of Washington Press.

Magas, B.
1993 Croat Catholics divided. *The Tablet* 17 July: pp. 908-909.

Milic, A.
1993 Women and Nationalism in the Former Yugoslavia. In *Gender Politics and Post-Communism.* N. Funk & M. Mueller (eds.), pp. 109-121. London: Routledge.

Pearson, R.
1987 *National Minorities in Eastern Europe.* London: Macmillan.

Ramet, S. P.
1991 *Nationalism and Federalism in Yugoslavia, 1962-91.* Indiana: Indiana University Press.

Remington, R. A.
1993 Bosnia: the tangled web. *Current History* November: 364-369.

Savill, A., & G. Elgood
1993 Lord Owen admits his peace plan has failed. *The Independent* 18 June: p. 8.

Seton-Watson, H.
1945 *Eastern Europe 1918-1941.* Cambridge: Cambridge University Press.

Siegman, H.
1994 Bosnia's holocaust puts the Churches to shame. *International Herald Tribune* 5 January: p. 4.

Sugich, M.
1993 Letter. *The Guardian* 5 May: p. 27.

Tanner, M.
1993a *The Independent* 4 July.
1993b Milosevic crushes his parliamentary rivals. *The Independent* 3 June: p. 10.

Thompson, M.
1993 Bosnian élite on the brink. *The New Statesman and Society* 12 December: p. 7.

Traynor, I.
1992 Church puts pressure on Milosevic. *The Guardian* 15 June: p. 24
1993a Sovereignty must not be used as a cover for abuses. *The Guardian* 16 June: p. 11.
1993b Serbs against the world. *The Guardian* 3 July: pp. 1-11.
1993c Cultural warriors. *The Guardian* 25 November: p. 13.

Vulliamy, E.
1994 *Seasons In Hell, Understanding Bosnia.* London: Simon & Schuster.

Woollacott, M.
1993 Bad Peace follows bad war. *The Guardian* 13 January: p. 26.

Young, H.
1993 When leadership fails in the face of Hitlerism. *The Guardian* 15 April: p. 26.

AN ETHNIC WAR THAT DID NOT TAKE PLACE: MACEDONIA, ITS MINORITIES AND ITS NEIGHBOURS IN THE 1990s

STEFAN TROEBST

European Centre for Minority Issues (ECMI), Kompagnietor Building, Schiffbrücke 12, D-24939 Flensburg

The crumbling of Soviet hegemony over Russia and Eastern Europe in 1989 resulted not only in the establishment of democracy, constitutionalism and the market economy, though at a slow pace, but also in a vociferous nationalism and several ethnic conflicts—a parallel development for which the Russian historian Vladimir K. Volkov has coined the apt term 'ethnocracy' (Wolkow 1991:34).[1] These tendencies have been seen by many observers as an indication that the clock of political life and culture in Eastern Europe, which was halted by the Red Army in 1944, has started to tick again. This explicitly historicist interpretation took a particularly popular form in the 'deep freeze metaphor' used by political analysts and social scientists to describe the results of the *Wende*:[2] nationalist and xenophobic sentiment, quickfrozen by internationalist communism, was said to be now defrosted by democracy (e.g. Elwert 1991:318n; Glotz 1990:39; Rupnik 1990). Even after the first outbreak of ethnic conflict in the then Soviet Union and the former Council for Mutual Economic Assistance (COMECON) area, apocalyptic visions of the whole region drowning in endless ethnic wars (and thus producing huge waves of refugees moving towards the EU countries) were cultivated by Western European politicians, journalists, scholars, and other writers (e.g. Enzensberger 1992, 1993). The Armeno-Azeri conflict over Arzakh (Nagornyj Karabakh) and the Serbian attacks on Slovenia and Croatia were taken as final proof of this dark scenario. The historical record of Eastern Europe in the nineteenth and twentieth centuries was systematically trawled for ethnic tensions which might flare up again, and with reeling heads the many newcomers among the area specialists soon compiled a list of several hundred ethnic trouble spots between the Aegean and the Baltic (e.g. Boden 1993; Bugajski 1994; Götz *et al.* 1992; Mark 1993; Oswald 1993).

Among the most prominent of these was what was termed, in the late nineteenth century, the 'Macedonian Question': the struggle for domination of the formerly Ottoman central Balkan region of Macedonia, divided since

---

1 This chapter is based partly on information gathered while I was serving as a member of the CSCE Spillover Monitor Mission to Macedonia in 1992 and 1993.

2 The great change which took place in Eastern Europe in 1989.

1913 among Yugoslavia, Bulgaria, Greece, and Albania.[3] To Western diplomats, academics and the media, the news that this 'perennial apple of discord' and 'powder keg of the Balkans' had, in the wake of the break-up of Yugoslavia, mutated into an independent state, the Republic of Macedonia,[4] meant war—inter-state war, civil war, and inter-ethnic war. Since 1991, two completely separate developments have taken place. On the one hand, the initial horror scenario—a forced incorporation of Macedonia into Greater Serbia and/or a partition among two, three or all four of its neighbours—has been considerably elaborated. Particularly popular in the international security community has been a 'domino theory,' according to which (a) a spillover from the Bosnian war theatre and/or the Kosovo into Macedonia is imminent, and (b) war in Macedonia will draw in Albania, Bulgaria, Greece and finally Turkey.[5] Furthermore, it is conventional wisdom that Macedonia has the "enormous potential to create a fireball through southeastern Europe, one which might pull in parts of Central and Eastern Europe" (Gow & Pettifer 1993:387).

On the other hand, however, the new Macedonian state, alone among the former Yugoslav republics, managed to escape unharmed from the post-Yugoslav imbroglio by easing the Yugoslav National Army (YNA) peacefully out of its territory. Its leadership handled several severe economic crises, caused by Greek blockades of transit traffic and by the UN embargo against rump Yugoslavia. And by restructuring a planned economy in a satisfactory way, it even stabilized its new currency. It succeeded, furthermore, in lowering ethnic tensions between its large Albanian minority and its titular nation,[6] and it gained international recognition despite the hostile attitude of most of its immediate neighbours. Even the catastrophic security situation of the country (the new Army of the Republic of Macedonia consists of 10,000 soldiers, three quarters of them conscripts and, although equipped with four Second World War T 34 tanks, it has neither heavy artillery nor an aircraft) has been improved by President Kiro Gligorov's careful diplomacy. He succeeded in calling a UN 'blue helmet' troop of 800 United Nations Protection Force (UNPROFOR) and 300 US soldiers into the country. While Macedonia was still very vulnerable, the

---

3 Even before 1989 the prominence of the 'Macedonian question' in the social sciences was considerable (cf. Weiner 1971).

4 In this chapter I have followed the lead of the American economist Michael Wyzan who stated in a paper on the Macedonian economy: "The country in question will henceforth be referred to simply as 'Macedonia.' No apologies are offered or implied to any parties who feel themselves offended" (Wyzan 1992).

5 For one example among many of this theory, see *The Economist* 25th December 1993: no. 52, pp. 17-20; for contradicting views see Troebst 1994a, 1994b.

6 'Titular nation' refers to the ethnic group after which a state is named.

political price of aggression now increased considerably. The international presence in Skopje was also enhanced by smaller civil missions of other international organizations like CSCE, EU, UNHCR, UNESCO and a large Sanctions Assistance Mission (SAM) set up jointly by the EU and CSCE (Troebst 1994c).

Before turning to the question of how this discrepancy between horror scenario from the outside and relative stability inside is to be explained, two more introductory remarks have to be made, one concerning the influence of historical, religious and ethnic stereotypes on those social and political sciences focusing on Eastern Europe, and the other concerning the 'deep freeze metaphor.' I shall start with the latter.

Notwithstanding its historicist disguise, this explanation is in fact a thoroughly a-historical one. This is because it implicitly assumes that the key to understanding post-1989 developments is to be sought in the pre-1944 era, thereby overlooking two highly significant phenomena. Firstly, the societies of Eastern Europe were transformed between 1944 and 1989. Urbanization, industrialization and secularization turned this overwhelmingly rural part of Europe into a heavily industrialized agglomeration of towns and town-like settlements, inhabited by first-generation city-dwellers whose regional and ethnic identities and religious and other traditions were replaced from above by nationalism and the new class ideology.[7] Transforming peasants into urban workers and thereby simultaneously turning them into Bielorussians, Slovaks, or Bulgarians was the success story of communist 'nation-building by modernization' in the twentieth century. Secondly the 'deep-freeze metaphor' ignores the forceful rehabilitation of Eastern European nationalism staged by the communist leaderships long before 1989, in order to consolidate their shrinking legitimacy.[8] Rumania's Nicolae Ceausescu is an extreme example of a communist party leader who expoused rabid nationalism. Serbia's Slobodan Milosevic, Ukraine's Leonid Kravchuk, Slovakia's Vladimír Meciar, Slovenia's Milan Kucan and Russia's Boris Yeltsin have followed the same path. Their careers as politicians all started

---

7 Concerning the "labyrinth of ethnoterminology," as J. Lador-Lederer called it (1986), I stick to the definitions given by G. Elwert: (1) "*As nationalism* I perceive social movements with common communicative and ideological or economically relevant features, which refer to the construction, consolidation or defence of a separate nation according to commonly acknowledged definition"; (2) "As a nation I perceive a—loose or solid—social organisation, which declares itself to be perennial, which is treated by the majority of its members as an—imagined—community and which refers to a common state-apparatus"; (3) "Ethnic Groups/Ethnies are cross-family and family groups, which ascribe to themselves a—sometimes exclusive—collective identity, with variable criteria for drawing the outer borderline" (Elwert 1989:446, 447, 449; cf. Connor 1978; Ganzer 1990; Heckmann 1992; Lador-Lederer 1986; Reiterer 1992; Stark 1988).

8 On Rumania see Verdery 1991; on Bulgaria see Troebst 1983.

in the Central Committee apparatuses of their respective countries and republics and they have all relied on nationalist rethoric in shifting their power bases from the membership of the now defunct communist parties to broader strata of society. Thus, never—particularly not between 1944 and 1989—has nationalism in Eastern Europe been inoperative. It was always there, and it has always, and successfully, been used to mobilize, radicalize and weld together titular nations and national minorities alike. A particularly striking example of this is, again, Macedonia which was officially ruled between 1944 and 1990 by the Yugoslav Communist Party but actually by the Macedonian League of Communists. At no point during their rule was this nationalist impetus outweighed by their ideological determination. A British liaison officer to the Tito partisans in Macedonia observed in 1944:

> The Macedonian partisan movement is primarily nationalistic and secondly communistic. In their propaganda the emphasis is all the time on Macedonian National Independence (Macdonald 1944).

This state of affairs did not change in any way up to 1990. What has changed since then—and not only in Macedonia—is that the former élites partly lost their political influence and thereby also lost control of the direction of nationalist sentiment. Like Goethe's sorcerer's apprentice, the former communists witnessed nationalism turning into a dangerous competitor. At the same time, however, nationalism has provided the ideological background for alliances between former communists and the new rightist parties.

The second remark I wish to make concerns the predominance of negative historical, religious and ethnic biases in the analyses of ethnic conflicts in Eastern Europe by academics, diplomats and the media. In particular, Western observers overlook the 'historical trap' set by the official national historiographies of the countries of Eastern Europe which depict the history of their own nations more often than not as an endless series of wars, occupations and genocidal attempts by ethnically alien foes (cf. Höpken 1993). Consequently, the history of Eastern Europe is perceived by many analysts as the sum of the national histories of its major peoples, all of them engaging in 'age-old' fights for territory and hegemony. The result of this distorted perspective is the resigned conclusion that little can be done about such atavistic behaviour and that the combatants should be left alone to solve their problems in their own way—by ethnic cleansing, mass murder, expulsion or forced assimilation. What a British ambassador to a Balkan country wrote home in the 1920s is still the typical view of the majority of Western observers:

> I hold no brief for the Macedonians, the Bulgarians, or any of the other semi-civilised races inhabitating the Balkan peninsula. Sentiment is out of place in dealing with those races, but all history appears to me to show that such inveterate conspirators and agitators as the Macedonians will never be either coerced or cajoled into the

> abandonment of their aspirations, and that to oppose them is merely to prolong the friction which has existed for generations and to repeat the errors of policy mentioned above (Sperling 1928).

What has changed is the role of the Macedonians, as this chapter will show, whereas the general Western attitude towards 'those races' is basically unchanged.

Particular misperceptions exist concerning the Eastern Orthodox variant of Christianity, to whose leadership and followers alike a predilection for 'Cesaro-papism' is airily imputed. For example, a long-standing German scholar of Eastern European politics wrote the following as late as 1992.

> A transnational comparison shows that to implement democracy will be harder for the Greek-Orthodox countries with their tradition of Cesaro-Papism and their lack of a routine division of power between church and state, party-church and state, leaders and society, than for countries like Lithuania or Hungary, where the Catholic church functioned for ages as a counterweight to the state (von Beyme 1992:166. My trans.)

Similar sweeping judgements are made concerning Muslims in the Commonwealth of Independent States (CIS), especially in the Caucasus, and in the Balkans. They are generally depicted as fanatics and fundamentalists using every pretext to stage ethno-religious war against all non-Muslim inhabitants of these areas. It is true that the Orthodox patriarchs and clergy from Athens to Moscow are political tools of their respective governments, but it is also true that the religious, moral and political commitments of the believers of these official churches are rather weak; and compared to some Islamic societies in the Middle East, the Balkan and Caucasian brands of Islam belong to the liberal variety and are often highly secularized. This is so for the Muslims of Bosnia and, even more so, of Albania. Explanations like 'history,' 'ethno-radicalism' and 'religious fundamentalism' also ignore the fact that it is often tiny political élites which, from time to time, succeed in using ethnicity and religion to mobilize, polarize and radicalize larger target groups who only then give up their generally multi-ethnic, multilingual and multireligious outlook.

What really complicates things in Eastern Europe is not its long historical record of conflict, nor a predilection for ethnic radicalism and religious fanaticism, let alone a genetic inclination towards violence. Rather, it is the fact that the new nationalist principle, introduced here in the second half of the nineteenth century (i. e. the trinity of 'history,' 'land' and 'people'), is even more impracticable in this subregion of Europe than in the western part of the continent. The large number of ethnic groups and their high degree of mixture leads to the presence of many more nationalisms in a much smaller area than to the west of Leitha and Oder. In addition, the borders of the Eastern European nation-states are in general not older than 50, and at most 100 years, and these borders have been changed over and over again during and after the wars of the twentieth century. The political situation here is therefore much more volatile than in Western Europe, where the nation-states have solved their mutual problems in a long series of protracted religious and ethnic wars from the seventeenth to the mid-twentieth century.

My argument is that, in analyzing ethnic conflict in Eastern Europe, one should first and above all turn to empirical evidence and fresh data, treat historical analogies with great caution and beware of the many and often hidden biases, prejudices and stereotypes concerning this new part of the Old World. I shall discuss the six most common scenarios of internal and external threat to the Republic of Macedonia in the light of factual and circumstantial evidence and suggest alternative interpretations. I shall not describe either the difficult and contradictory process out of which the East Southslav speaking Orthodox population of Macedonia emerged as a Macedonian nation (cf. Bernath 1971; de Jong 1984; Kofos 1986; 1989; Matzureff 1978; Palmer 1971; Troebst 1992; 1993a), or the equally complicated road from a Yugoslav republic to an independent state (cf. Libal 1993; Perry 1992a:44-6; 1992b:16; 1992c:12-9; 1993:31-7; 1994:118-21; Poulton 1993:22-30; Reuter 1993a; 1993b; Weithmann 1993) which was fraught with international complications (cf. Axt 1993; Danforth 1993; Magnusson 1993; Pettifer 1992; Rondholz 1993; Valinakis 1992).[9]

The most common forecasts concerning Macedonia involve Serbian aggression, the spillover to Macedonia of an inter-ethnic civil war in Kosovo, the partition of Macedonia by some or all of its neighbours, a re-absorption of the Macedonian nation by Bulgaria, a violent conflict between the Macedonian authorities and the local Albanian minority and an economic, social and political breakdown followed by the voluntary return of Macedonia to rump Yugoslavia. Although some of these scenarios are not at first sight connected with ethnic conflict they would, if they materialized, result in ethnic conflict.

Serbian aggression

International organizations, national foreign ministries and the media regard Serbian military aggression, aiming at the reincorporation of Macedonia into rump Yugoslavia, as possibly the most likely and certainly the most dangerous scenario of all. The best proof of the seriousness with which the world regards this prospect has been the stationing of UN and US troops on Macedonia's border with Kosovo and Serbia proper. It is assumed that, as the end of the war in Bosnia approaches, Greater Serbian nationalists will turn their attention to 'Southern Serbia,' as they call Vardar Macedonia, that is today's Republic of Macedonia.

---

9 There is a huge literature on the historical background. For two short introductions see Wilson 1987 and Völkl 1993.

In sharp contrast to Greater Serbian expansionist propaganda directed towards Croatia and Bosnia, however, only in a very few instances have Serbian government officials, or ultra-nationalists, made historical, ethnic and territorial claims on Macedonia. Paramilitary radicals like Vojislav Seselj and Zeljko 'Arkan' Raznatovic do indeed consider, for historical reasons, that the Vardar Valley is an integral part of Serbia and that the Slav-speaking, Eastern Orthodox majority population there that is, the Macedonians, are 'South Serbs' or 'Mountain Serbs.' Also, Seselj's followers have tried to whip up nationalist feeling among the small Serbian minority community in Macedonia in order to turn them into a 'fifth column' in the service of a Greater Serbia. The results, however, have been more than disappointing and, apart from the distribution of leaflets and the waving of the Yugoslav (not even Serbian) flag, nothing materialized (Weilguni 1993). The same applies to official Serbia and its president Milosevic. It is true that, in late 1992, he caused the Serbian Orthodox Church to issue a declaration according to which the Republic of Macedonia and its own Orthodox Church should be treated as part of the Serbian bishopric of Nis, but that was all (Krizan 1993). There is no strong evidence for a Serbian plan to invade its southern neighbour nor are there Serbian threats to do so.[10] Bearing in mind Serbia's overall strategy, such aggression would make little sense. The Serbian-dominated Yugoslav National Army (YNA) had strong forces stationed throughout Macedonia but these were withdrawn in April 1992. It seems unlikely that the Serbian leadership would have given up such a favourable position only to return later by force, particularly after the international presence on the Serbian-Macedonian border was reinforced by some 1,100 UN peace-keepers and dozens of CSCE, EU, SAM and other international monitors.

There are two more serious indicators pointing away from the possibility of Serbian aggression. Firstly the ethnic and political orientation of almost the whole population of Macedonia and especially of its three main political camps—former communists, new nationalists, and Albanian parties (Perry 1992c)—are, if not thoroughly anti-Serbian, at least not pro-Serbian. The former communists are still frustrated by the dominance exercised by their Serbian colleagues in the former League of Communists of Yugoslavia and by the latters' patronizing attitude towards what they regarded as a former Serbian colony; the new nationalists and their strongest political party, the VMRO-DPMNE (Internal Macedonian Revolutionary Organization-Democratic Party for Macedonian National Unity), are fiercely anti-Yugoslav and thus staunchly anti-Serbian; and the Albanian and other Muslim minorities in Macedonia naturally abhor Serbia's treatment of its

---

[10] Brigadier General Finn Særmark Thomsen, commander-in-chief of UNPROFOR Macedonia Command until the end of 1993, indicated in the summer of 1993 that he did not consider the Serbs a threat to Macedonia (Krsteski 1993:7-9).

own Albanians and Muslims in the Kosovo and the Sandzhak. There is thus no major political group in Macedonia which sympathizes with Milosevic. Secondly the Serbian minority in Macedonia is incapable of playing a role analogous to that of the Serbian population in Croatia and Bosnia. For one thing, the 46,000 Macedonian Serbs are numerically weak, accounting for only 2.2 per cent of the population (Republika Makedonija [Census] 1992: 17, 59-70; cf. Bubevski 1985; Pekevski 1974; Preinerstorfer 1962); in addition, they are geographically dispersed and socially divided. Only a small part of the Serbian minority is composed of autochthonous villagers living in border areas adjacent to Serbia and Kosovo. Another portion consists of descendents of Serbian military colonists who were settled predominantly in the mountainous areas of eastern and southern Macedonia during the interwar period; by now this group has become acculturated (Apostolov 1992). But most of the Serbian minority are members of the former party *nomenklatura* and technical intelligentsia who moved to Macedonian towns after 1944. The 'Serbianness' of these three different groups varies considerably, and their capacity to work together politically appears to be minimal.[11]

With no strong Serbian minority in Macedonia and therefore no strong ethnic base, and with no political sympathies there, let alone a pro-Serb movement, Macedonia seems, from Belgrade's point of view, an indigestible item on the Greater Serbian expansionist menu. As in the interwar period, any Serbian regime of occupation in Macedonia would also tie down a disproportionate share of Serbia's already overstretched military and security forces that might be more urgently needed elsewhere.

To sum up, there are few signs that the 'Serbian scenario' could become a reality in Macedonia. In military, political, and ethnic terms, the conditions for a Serbian conquest are much less favourable here than in eastern Slavonia, Krajina, or most of Bosnia. Indeed, it appears that the costs of a Serbian occupation of Macedonia would be much higher than Belgrade could afford to pay.

Spillover of inter-ethnic war in Kosovo

The scenario of Macedonian involvement in an inter-ethnic war in Kosovo comes in two variants. The first assumes that Macedonia, and especially the western and northern parts of the country, could become a theatre of military operations either by the Albanian Army or by paramilitary formations of

[11] There are at least three different Serbian political organizations in Macedonia: (1) a small group of Seselj-followers in the Kumanovo area; (2) the 'Domestic Party of the Serbs in Macedonia,' which recently sacked its Bitola-based leader Boro Ristic; and (3) an 'Association of Serbs and Montenegrins in Macedonia' led by Bosko Despotovic from Skopje (*Puls* 1993; Damoski 1993).

Macedonian Albanians (or both) supporting Albanian insurgents in Kosovo, which could result in armed incursion by Serbian troops. The second variant predicts that a wave of up to one million refugees from Kosovo could flood into Macedonia and destabilize the country socio-economically and ethno-politically.

Both variants of the 'Kosovo scenario' are plausible, but only on one condition: that an outbreak of violent conflict in Kosovo is likely in the near future. Available analyses of current political conditions in this formerly autonomous part of Serbia indicate, however, that, while ethnic tension is indeed very high, a reasonably stable balance prevails between the Serbian security forces and the Albanian majority population. Thus, an eruption of mass violence in Kosovo does not seem likely in the short and medium term (Neier 1994; Schmidt 1993a; 1993b). According to intelligence collected by the Macedonian general staff in early 1993, the 1.8 million ethnic Albanians in the Kosovo—including some 500,000 men between fourteen and sixty years of age—face a well-armed Serbian security force of 100,000 men. Some 30,000 members of this force belong to the regular security formations, which include two tank brigades, three mechanized infantry brigades (each including a tank battalion), three artillery regiments, and some 10,000 policemen. In addition, the local authorities can call upon three volunteer brigades of heavily armed Seselj and Arkan followers, each numbering up to 1,200 men, and some 65,000 well-equipped Serbian reservists living in Kosovo, who can be mobilized within several hours. The deterrent effects that the presence of this massive force exercises on the Albanian population has been obvious in the frequent cases of maltreatment of ethnic Albanians by the Serbian authorities. Even public killings have generally not provoked the Albanian majority into violent acts of protest or revenge. The Kosovo Albanians and their political leadership, namely the shadow government of Ibrahim Rugova, which the Serbs tolerate even as they claim it is illegal, know perfectly well that a violent response to Serbian state terrorism would result in a military catastrophe and a large-scale exodus of refugees (Schmidt 1993a). But the Serbian leadership also seems to be aware that it has virtually nothing to gain from provoking an Albanian insurrection in Kosovo. First of all, since Kosovo *is* already a part of Serbia—something international diplomacy and the media seem to forget—there is no need for Serbia to underscore its claim by an invasion or conquest of the region. Second, the ethnic balance between Albanians and Serbs in the Kosovo is so tilted to the disadvantage of the latter—outnumbered by at least 8:1—that even massive ethnic cleansing and/or ethnocide would not profoundly change this ratio in favour of the Serbs. It would, however, definitely cause severe damage to Serbia's already isolated international position and possibly even lead to direct Western military intervention. The symbolic stationing of 310 US soldiers on the Macedonian border with Kosovo and southern Serbia can be interpreted as confirmation of this assumption.

Finally, there is another strong reason why both sides, the Serbian authorities and the Kosovo Albanians, should not provoke mutual bloodshed on a large scale. The solution of the Kosovo problem will very likely be at the core of any future general settlement between Serbia and the international community and thus one of the decisive objects of negotiation. It is quite possible that the West will 'buy back' autonomy for Kosovo either by helping to reconstruct Serbia's ruined economy or even by letting Belgrade keep some Croatian territory. The Kosovo Albanians, for their part, know that autonomy under Belgrade's auspices is probably the best they can expect for quite some time, since backward Albania is struggling with interlocking crises of transformation and modernization.

There is, of course, a decisive *caveat* to be added to the alternative scenario outlined here: the condition that the present legal situation of the Kosovo Albanians, unsatisfactory as it may be from a human-rights point of view, is not further worsened by radical new measures of repression on the part of the Serbian authorities. This includes a possible crackdown on the free movement of Albanians from Kosovo via Macedonia to the centers of labor emigration in Western Europe through the introduction of new Serbian passport regulations or even Macedonian visas. Only the lifeline provided by Macedonia's airports in Skopje and Ohrid has guaranteed that the steady outflow of emigrants from Kosovo is matched by an influx of large amounts of Western currency, which has done much to stabilize the economic and social position of the Albanian community in war-weary Serbia. If this lifeline is cut off, then social tension in the Kosovo pressure cooker will soon build up to the point that all political attempts to head off an explosion will fail. All three governments involved —the Serbian, the Macedonian and the provisional Kosovo Albanian—are perfectly aware of this fact and, thus far, common sense has induced them to behave accordingly.

Partition by neighbouring countries

The spectre of a partition of Macedonia, already somewhat outdated after a brief vogue in 1991 and early 1992, was revived in November 1993 after a demonstrative closing of ranks between Milosevic and the new Greek government of Prime Minister Andreas Papandreou. Due to problems involving military weakness, economic transformation and political disruption, neither Albania nor Bulgaria is currently in a position to translate its historical and ethnic aspiration for Macedonian territory into concrete political and military action. For its part, however, Greece would be a highly unlikely partner in any partition of its northern neighbour, notwithstanding all the rhetorical hysteria over Macedonia's name and flag and the economic obstructions that have issued from Athens over the past two years. Such a step would jeopardize Greek membership in Western security organizations such as NATO and the West European Union (WEU) and would endanger Greece's even more vital economic ties with the EU. Also, the pan-Hellenic vision, espoused by nationalist extremists, of a multilateral exchange of territories (Albania ceding northern Epirus to Greece in exchange for western Macedonia) is nothing more than a pipe dream. The only remaining candidate for a partition of Macedonia is thus Serbia, which brings us back to the first scenario.

'Re-Bulgarization'

At first glance, this scenario does not imply violence, but a 'peaceful' and 'voluntary' return of the Slavic-speaking Orthodox Macedonians to 'mother Bulgaria.' On a closer look, however, it does imply violence, because the large and densely settled Albanian minority in Western Macedonia definitely would not agree to any 'reunification' scheme and would turn instead to secession, with unforseeable political and territorial consequences. There is no need to go more deeply into this scenario. There is an idea that the majority of today's Macedonians see their ethnic identity as forced upon them by the 'rabid' regime of Josif Broz Tito and that they would willingly 'return' to the Bulgarian identity most Slavic-speaking Orthodox Macedonians adopted during the years of Serbian assimilationist policy from 1912 to 1915 and from 1918 to 1941. This is mere nostalgia and wishful thinking, however, cultivated exclusively in Sofia.

Two periods of Bulgarian wartime occupation (the first from 1916 to 1918 and the second and decisive one from 1941 to 1944) left a very unfavourable impression in Macedonia, and the steady stream of anti-Macedonian propaganda that issued from Sofia in the postwar years did little to improve matters (Troebst 1983). In fact, the process of nation-building that unfolded in Macedonia after 1944 was not nearly as artificial or volatile as the Bulgarians still believe. In the (quite reliable) Yugoslav census of 1991, only 1,370 citizens of Macedonia declared their 'national affiliation' as Bulgarian, and only 1,161 named Bulgarian as their mother tongue (*Popis na naselenieto* 1992:59, 71). There are no indications that these figures have changed significantly since then. A Gallup poll published in Bulgaria in the summer of 1993, for example, revealed that 78 per cent of the Macedonian citizens interviewed were of the opinion that "the Macedonians have always been a separate nationality," while only 4 per cent thought that "Macedonians are Bulgarians." Although pro-Bulgarian activist are present in some Macedonian towns (notably Strumica and Bitola), their influence is marginal, even at the local level.

There are several reasons for this. One is that, particularly in eastern Macedonia where many families have relatives on the other side of the border, people have been appalled by Bulgaria's opportunistic policy of exploiting the economic and transport problems Macedonia has encountered as a result of the international embargo against Serbia and the Greek blockade. Secondly the numerous statements by Bulgarian officials that their country's recognition of the Macedonian *state* (15 January 1992) by no means implies a recognition of the Macedonian *nation* have also proved unacceptable, even to Macedonian political groups that look to Sofia for political support. Thus, even the most powerful pro-Bulgarian party, the VMRO-DPNME of Ljupco Georgievski, deeply resents the Bulgarian view that the Macedonians are not an independent nation but merely the western outposts of the Bulgarian people. Sofia has thus squandered a huge amount of the political sympathy it had won by its early recognition of Macedonia. Attempts to raise political support among Macedonians by Bulgarian parties and movements (notably the oppositionist Union of Democratic Forces and its front organizations for Macedonian matters, the Bulgarian nationalist Internal Macedonian Revolutionary Organization-Union of Macedonian Congregations (VMRO-SMD))[12] have been unsuccessful.

A third reason for Bulgaria's diminishing influence in Macedonia is Sofia's uncompromising attitude towards its own ethnic Macedonians in the southwestern part of Bulgaria. While the repressive nationality policies of the Bulgarian communist regime of Todor Zhivkov since 1989 have been mitigated in relation to the Bulgarian Turks, the Bulgarian Muslims and, to some extent, even the Roma (Gypsies), those Bulgarians who still dare to define themselves ethnically as Macedonians (6,000 in the 1992 census compared with 188,000 in 1956) continue to face severe discrimination (Troebst 1994d). Thus, the Bulgarian model does not appear to be attractive, even to the Slav part of the population of Macedonia who do not show the slightest sympathy for 're-Bulgarization.'

Macedonian-Albanian conflict

Ethnic tension between the large Albanian minority—442,000 people or 21.7 per cent of Macedonia's total population, according to the 1991 census[13]—and the Macedonian state or ethnic Macedonians has existed for decades. It was particularly strong in the 1980s when, in the wake of the

---

[12] When nationalists and 'Greater Bulgarian' organizations call themselves 'Macedonian,' they use the term in a geographical sense, since they do not consider themselves to be 'ethnically' Macedonian.

[13] In 13 out of the 35 Macedonian municipalities this census was boycotted by part of the Albanian population. The quoted census results are figures extrapolated by the Macedonian authorities. Although the figures seem reliable, the Albanian political élite in Macedonia claims that the real percentage of their co-nationals is 30-35 per cent, while some even mention as many as 48 per cent. Serious assessments, however, indicate 24 per cent as the highest percentage for the Albanians in Macedonia. I estimate that they add up

Kosovo riots of 1981, federal and republican authorities embarked on open repression of Macedonian Albanians. In the decisive winter months of 1991 and 1992, when Macedonian independence came about, Albanian radicals in Western Macedonia organized a referendum on a separate republic ('Ilirida'), while the two more moderate Albanian parties—the larger Party of Democratic Prosperity (PDP) and the much smaller National Democratic Party (NDP)—also seemed to be in favour of secession. The horrifying effects of the war in Bosnia, however, which was perceived in Macedonia as a conflict between Christians and Muslims, brought about a change.

In the summer of 1992, both Albanian parties joined a coalition government with the former Macedonian Communists and some Macedonian centrist parties. Today, five out of twenty-two cabinet posts are held by Albanians, and there are twenty-five Albanians among the 120 deputies in Macedonia's Sobranie, the national parliament. In almost all other spheres of public life, however, Albanians are clearly under-represented, and the rebuilding of Albanian cultural and educational institutions that had existed up to the early 1980s is proceeding very slowly. There is also a deep ethnic, religious, and above all cultural cleavage between the Macedonian titular nation and the Albanian minority. The overwhelming majority of Albanians in Macedonia form a highly traditional community isolated from almost all other sections of society. There are thus very few lines of communication between Albanians and Macedonians in the country (Austin 1993; Mickey & Albion n.d.; Moore 1992; Perry 1992c; Poulton 1993; Reuter 1987).

It is therefore hardly surprising that political observers have seen the interethnic tension between Albanians and Macedonians that has appeared since 1991 as an indication of a coming clash between the two groups. In particular, two events have been interpreted as clear evidence that a violent conflict is in the offing. One was the riot at the open market of Skopje (*Bit pazar*) on 6 November 1992 in which three Albanian men and a Macedonian woman were killed by the police (*Puls* 1992); the other was the Macedonian authorities' discovery in early November 1993 that a secret paramilitary organization which called itself the All-Albanian Army was operating within the Army of the Republic of Macedonia and was evidently in contact with government officials in Tirana (Jovanovski & Velinovska 1993; Mihajlovski

---

only to about 20 per cent; this estimate is strengthened by the fact that in 1991 non-Albanian ethnic groups, such as the Albanized Roma and Slavic-speaking Muslims, called Torbesh, declared themselves Albanians under pressure from members of the Albanian Muslim clergy. These uncertainties led the Council of Europe to take into consideration a 1992 proposal by Erik Siesby, Chairman of the Danish Helsinki Committee, to hold an extraordinary census in Macedonia, 70 per cent of the costs of which were to be borne by the European Community. The proposal was accepted by both the Macedonian government and the Albanian parties but, due to financial, organizational and other problems the census has not yet taken place (Statistical Office 1992; Siesby 1993).

1993). Despite their ethno-political backgrounds, however, a closer look at both events reveals that the first was a criminal affair while the second was most likely a case of espionage.

The culprit in the *Bit pazar* riot was the local Albanian mafia, which controls the illegal trade in cigarettes, Western currency, drugs, and arms in the Macedonian capital. Alarmed by tighter police controls over the open market, the mafia succeeded in mobilizing residents from central Skopje's Albanian quarters to protest against the measure. After the demonstration had been dispersed by the police, some mafia leaders tried to provoke a showdown by resorting to firearms. This provided the pretext for special police forces to storm the Albanian neighbourhood of Serava. It is significant that the clash produced no serious political echo, either from the Albanians of western Macedonia or from the leadership of the PDP and NDP. The All-Albanian Army affair, according to the evidence that has come to light, involved a group of ten persons, including two high-ranking members of the PDP occupying posts in the present coalition government. The group is said to have collected the personal data of 21,630 ethnic Albanian recruits from army registers and to have accumulated larger stocks of light weapons (Geroski 1993a).

In addition to these two incidents, there have been several outbreaks of ethnic tension between Albanians and Macedonians at the local level. For example, in the village of Dlapkindol, near Kicevo, Albanian parents set up a private gymnasium without the approval of the state school authorities, and similar developments have taken place near Struga. In predominantly Albanian Tetovo, ethnic Macedonian deputies on the city council have refused to cooperate with the Albanian majority.

While such examples of inter-ethnic tensions are important and revealing, it should be remembered that they are not unusual in ethnically mixed societies and not atypical at times of economic crisis and international instability. It is difficult to judge, therefore, whether these Albanian-Macedonian tensions represent the tip of an iceberg or are merely isolated phenomena. Reaching a conclusion is all the more complicated because no such thing as a single Albanian community in Macedonia exists; instead, one is faced with a bewildering array of social strata, interest groups, and political parties and factions, each favouring divergent strategies and options. Even the leading Albanian party, the PDP, has been unable to follow a single policy owing to a protracted power struggle that has largely occurred behind closed doors. Recently, a radical autonomist wing under Menduh Thaçi forced the party leadership (which was, to a certain extent loyal to the new Macedonian state) to resign along with the entire party presidium. At present, both the new 'loyalist' leadership around Xheladin Murati and the Thaçi group use the name PDP for their organizations, but in fact the party has already split into two parts. While on the one hand, this split may have negative results for the present coalition government formed by Albanians and former communists it may, on the other, contribute to the inner-Albanian process of clarifying the political aims of the different interest groups.

In general, it seems that a clear majority of the Albanians living in Macedonia, after carefully assessing the advantages and disadvantages of being a citizen of the new state, wish to remain under Skopje, despite instances of serious ethnic discrimination and an informal 'pariah' status. In the last analysis, Albanians in Macedonia are far better off in political, economic, social, legal, cultural, and educational terms, than their fellow nationals in Kosovo and even in Albania, while the number of minority rights enjoyed by them is increasing because of their parliamentary strength and activism. The Albanian language will become sooner or later the second official language of Macedonia, an Albanian faculty will be opened at Skopje University, and even some form of territorial autonomy in northern and western Macedonia is not out of the question.

So much for the factors binding Albanians to the new Macedonian state. Among the forces pushing them towards this allegiance, the most important of course is the fear of Serbian expansionism, which is felt even more acutely by Muslim Albanians than by Orthodox Macedonians. The leaders of the Macedonian Albanians are also aware that secession from Macedonia would open up the dangerous issue of frontiers in the southern Balkans—something that no one, particularly not the Albanians of Macedonia, would profit from. In addition, the economically and socially backward Albanian 'motherland' exerts little attraction for the relatively more advanced Albanian communities of Macedonia. Indeed, Macedonia's Albanians exhibit a certain degree of suspicion towards their more secular brethren beyond the Albanian border. Among certain currents in the Albanian leadership in Macedonia, this attitude has culminated in the idea of Western Macedonia as a kind of Albanian Piedmont—the modern, prosperous, and pious center of an otherwise poor, immobile, and pitiable Albanian periphery in Kosovo and Albania proper.

Thus, from the point of view of the moderate majority of Macedonia's Albanians, the political, economic, and other advantages of belonging to the new Macedonian state clearly outweigh the numerous disadvantages and, in particular, the uncalculable risks of trying to change the territorial *status quo*. One of several indications of the growing acceptance of Macedonian statehood by the Albanian minority is the increasing number of ethnic Albanian conscripts in the Macedonian Army. While in 1992 only 7.5 per cent of all serving conscripts belonged to this largest minority (which meant, in effect, that three out of every four Albanian draftees had avoided military service), by July 1993 some 26.5 per cent of the new conscripts were Albanians, a figure that roughly corresponds to the size of this minority in the total population (Geroski 1993a).[14]

---

[14] In the wake of the All-Albanian Army affair of November 1993, some Macedonian

If the Macedonian Albanians themselves show no inclination for ethnic warfare, what about the anti-Albanian sentiment of the Macedonian nationalist opposition and other ethnic Macedonians? After all, the nationalist VMRO-DPMNE, with its 35 deputies, is the largest faction in the Macedonian parliament. Apart, however, from some rude and threatening statements, its members have engaged in only a few instances of harrassment. Moreover, it seems likely that, should the possibility of forming a new coalition government arise before the elections scheduled for November 1994, the VMRO-DPNME would prefer the Albanian parties as political partners to the former Macedonian communists. The reason for this is the deep mutual suspicion and long-standing political feuds which exist between the leading cadres of both Macedonian camps. And while a solid majority of ethnic Macedonians harbour anti-Albanian sentiments, they also know that reasonably good inter-ethnic relations in the Republic are an indispensable precondition for the continued existence of this multi-ethnic state. Recent Macedonian opinion polls, furthermore, show a considerable weakening of public support for VMRO-DPNME and other nationalist groups (down from 30 per cent to some 10 per cent). Something similar to the Bulgarian situation could, therefore, take place also in Macedonia. In Bulgaria, the only numerically stable political parties are those of the minorities (due to the 'conservative' electoral behaviour of the minority population), while the parties of the dominant ethnic group are either locked in a stalemate or get drastically changing results from one election to the next. In either case, the minority parties form the only element of continuity in an otherwise fluctuating political environment and/or tip the scales for simple mathematical reasons. While the coming election will most probably not change the current number (25) of the Albanian Sobranie seats, the average number of seats of the approximately six to nine old and new Macedonian parties will drop to an average of around ten. And since the political divides between these different Macedonian parties is much deeper than the ethnic divides between them and the Albanian parties, that political camp will form the government which succeeds in winning the Albanians over.

By the beginning of 1994 it appeared that a break-up of Macedonia along ethnic lines was less likely than it had been at the beginning of the decisive year 1992. The political experience of the following two years resulted in an ethno-political arrangement that was less vulnerable to disruption by local inter-ethnic tensions or by the activities of radicals on either side.

journalists interpreted the increase of Albanian conscripts as a deliberate strategy to infiltrate the regular army (Geroski 1993a:14-5).

Voluntary return to rump Yugoslavia

The scenario envisaging a voluntary return of Macedonia to rump Yugoslavia is based on two assumptions which, while correct in themselves, have become distorted through exaggeration. The first is that the Macedonians are fundamentally pro-Yugoslav. It is noted, in support of this, that the Macedonian leadership, like the Bosnian, tried to preserve a Yugoslav federation well into 1991, long after the political élites of Slovenia and Croatia had determined to secede. The second assumption stems from the commonplace observation that the Macedonian economy is dependent on the former Yugoslav (and especially Serbian) economy, and this in a particularly one-sided way, namely by trading raw materials for finished products. According to this scenario, the Macedonian leaders are being pulled toward Belgrade, not only by their ideological stance but also by economic necessity.

Three factors, however, make such a conclusion highly improbable. The first has already been touched upon. Since rump Yugoslavia is dominated by Serbian nationalists, a Macedonian rapprochement with Belgrade would mean incorporation into Greater Serbia. That would amount not only to a complete U-turn for Macedonian policymakers who, since 1991, have opposed Serbian military activism, but also to a momentous ethno-political change: a capitulation of Macedonian ethnic identity to the former Serbian occupier. As has been shown above, none of the three political camps in Macedonia—the former communists, the nationalist opposition and the Albanian parties—is in favour of such a policy. Furthermore, no Macedonian government would survive such a move.

Secondly, it is true that many of Macedonia's current economic problems have been caused by the UN embargo against Serbia and Montenegro, which cuts off Macedonia from the important Serbian market. But it is not true that these problems would be solved by Macedonia rejoining rump Yugoslavia. Indeed, it makes little sense for Macedonia to throw in its lot with a state which is not only in even deeper economic trouble than itself but which is also under an embargo. The average monthly wage in rump Yugoslavia is now (1994) DM 20, as opposed to the Macedonian average of DM 220; inflation in Serbia is skyrocketing, while in Macedonia it is currently some 20 per cent per month; Serbian unemployment is well over 60 per cent, as opposed to 30 per cent in Macedonia (Wyzan 1992; 1993a; 1993b). If Macedonia's economic problems were indeed to become so overwhelming as to force its government to look for a neighbouring state to join, the least logical candidate would be Serbia.

Moreover—and this is the third factor—it is by no means certain that the country's economic situation is as desperate as Macedonian politicians have led the delegation from the International Monetary Fund and the World Bank to believe. According to Wyzan a leading Western economist specializing in specializing in Macedonia, despite the negative effects of the UN embargo against rump Yugoslavia and the partial blockade of Macedonia by Greece, Macedonian economic performance has been satisfactory if not good. In response to the question, whether Macedonia is "an economically viable nation," he has given a carefully balanced affirmative verdict:

> A stable new currency has been introduced, the economy has performed better than that of any other former republic besides Slovenia's, minorities have been brought into the government, liberal economic legislation has been passed, interest-group pressure for give-aways in the privatization process has been resisted, new trading opportunities and partners have been found, and successful application for membership in international organizations has been made. Serious problems remain, of course, especially with respect to gaining sovereignty over all economic activity on its territory and restructuring a very poor and distorted economy. Everything considered, however, the Macedonian experience suggests that a poor part of a larger country can indeed make its own way (Wyzan 1993b: 20).

In short, the scenario of an economically enforced return to Milosevic's rump Yugoslavia is built on premises which do not correspond to the actual situation.

Conclusion

By questioning the six most common scenarios of external and internal threat to the integrity of Macedonia, it has not been my aim to diminish the grave ethnic, economic, diplomatic, and security problems the country is facing. But the Macedonian experience shows that, through skilful diplomacy and a balanced domestic policy, even a volatile state without the backing of a great power or security guarantees from a friendly military alliance can be steered through the troubled waters of post-Tito Yugoslavia and post-communist southeastern Europe. Despite Macedonia's manifold problems, no military threat is imminent from any of its four neighbours, no militant irredentist or separatist movements are operating on either side of the border, no fifth columns under the control of foreign powers are undermining the integrity of the country, and no violent majority nationalism is threatening its minorities.[15] A combination of international factors, security interests, military equilibria, domestic checks and balances and, probably, even a healthy dose of political realism caused by the

[15] This is definitely not a traditional trait of the Macedonian 'national character' as Peter Hill has claimed: "Macedonians have a long tradition of non-violence" (Hill 1989). On the contrary, the Macedonian national movement in the nineteenth and twentieth centuries was notorious for its outstanding brutality and for having popularized modern forms of terrorism such as kidnapping, taking hostages, or placing bombs in public places (Perry 1988; Troebst 1987). In Bulgaria, for example, the ethnic stereotype of a Macedonian includes cruelty and martial behaviour, and the expression *makedonska rabota*, 'a Macedonian job,' means something violent and bloody.

'Bosnian shock' has prevented Macedonia from being turned into another Balkan theatre of war. It even seems probable that the country has a good chance of avoiding such involvement in the medium and long term future.

It can also be argued that the Macedonian example is not just a happy exception and thus an isolated case, but that it represents one of two general types of ethnic conflict in Eastern Europe, which I would term the 'non-kin-state type' and the 'kin-state type.' In the 'non-kin-state type' no neighbouring country, regional or global great power, nor a military alliance system actively and persistently supports one or several of the opposing parties. The Albanians, Serbs, Turks and Bulgarians of Macedonia do, of course, have their respective 'kin-states'—Albania, rump Yugoslavia, Turkey and Bulgaria—but none of these has tried to instigate ethnic conflict. Another 'non-kin-state' example is provided by the Czechs and Slovaks, who do not have kin-states outside the former federation. It is no coincidence that it was the authors of the 'silk revolution' who managed also to stage a 'silk divorce.'

A typical 'kin-state type' is Bosnia with its record of ethnic war. The Bosnian Serbs broke away from the Republic of Bosnia-Hercegovina with the backing of rump Yugoslavia and the active support of the Yugoslav National Army. The Bosnian and Hercegovinian Croats then made sure that they would get the political, financial, material, and finally military support of the Republic of Croatia. Only the so-called 'Bosnian Muslims' or 'Muslims as a Nation' were unable to counter these combined secessionist and annexationist moves by securing support from a kin-state of their own (Calic 1993a, 1994; Gow 1993; Hayden 1993; Moore 1993). No Near Eastern and Middle Eastern state nor the Islamic Conference volunteered to act as such, let alone the EU, NATO or the USA (Calic 1993b; Schlotter *et al.* 1993). A similar situation is to be found in the Caucasian conflicts between Azerbaijan and Armenia, the latter acting as the kin-state of the Arzakh Armenians in Nagornyj Karabakh, and between Georgia and its Ossetian and Abkhaz minorities. These are supported by the North Caucasian Autonomous Republics of the Russian Federation, by the central government in Moscow and by the CIS. A more complicated case then is Moldova, where both types of ethnic opposition are to be found. The Transnistrian crisis zone with its Russian population and the 14th Russian Army belongs to the 'kin-state type,' whereas the situation in the other parts of the country resembles the 'non-kin-state type,' since neither the Gagauz nor the Bulgarian minorities are looking to Ankara or Sofia for support.

The dividing line between violent and non-violent ethnic conflict is not exactly parallel to the division between the 'kin-state' and 'non-kin-state types' of ethnic tensions. In 'non-kin-state types' the threshold of open violence is crossed only occasionally; this is most often the case when clashes occur between members of a dominant nationality and/or government authorities on the one side, and Roma-Gypsy minorities, a 'non-kin-state' ethnic group par excellence, on the other. In 'kin-state types' of tension, violence is far from being a necessary ingredient. Thus, the deep ethnic cleavages in the Baltic countries between the governments formed by the dominant nationalities and the Russian minorities, has not led to open conflict despite the presence of Russian troops. Nor has the high ethnic tension between Bulgarians and the Turkish minority in Eastern Bulgaria. The reason, in both cases, is the significant difference in power between the kin-state and the country where the minority lives—Russia vs. Estonia, Latvia and Lithuania, and Turkey vs. Bulgaria. Where, however, a political and military equilibrium prevails within the 'kin-state pattern', as between Armenia and Azerbaijan or between the Serbs on the one hand and the combined military forces of the Bosnian Croats and the Bosnians on the other, extended violence is most likely.

In and around Macedonia this danger is not acute so far. It could become so, however, in the wake of a significant deterioration of inter-ethnic relations between the Albanian minority and the dominant nationality in the country. Thus, the key to the internal stability and external security of the new republic is in the hands of the political representatives of the Macedonian Albanians and the two large Macedonian political camps of former Communists and new nationalists. Despite some recent signs of increasing ethnic radicalism, particularly on the part of the Albanians, it does not seem over-optimistic to hope that the danger of ethnic, civil and inter-state war in Macedonia will be warded off for the foreseeable future.

References

[Abbreviation: RFE/RL RR = Radio Free Europe/Radio Liberty Research Report]

Apostolov, A.
1992 *Kolonizacijata na Makedonija vo stara Jugoslavija.* [The Colonization of Macedonia in Old Yugoslavia]. Skopje: Kultura.

Austin, R.
1993 Albanian-Macedonian relations: confrontation or cooperation? *RFE/RLRR,* vol. 2, no. 42, 22 October 1993, pp. 21-25.

Axt, H.-J.
1993 Mazedonien: ein Streit um Namen oder ein Konflikt vor dem Ausbruch? *Europa Archiv* 48: 65-75.

Bernath, M.
1971 Das mazedonische Problem in der Sicht der komparativen Nationalismusforschung. *Südost-Forschungen* 29: 237-248.

Beyme, K. von
1992 Demokratisierung in der Sowjetunion. In *Die Chancen der Freiheit. Grundprobleme der Demokratie.* H. Münkler (ed.), pp. 169-188. München-Zürich: Piper.

Boden, M.
1993 *Nationalitäten, Minderheiten und ethnische Konflikte in Europa. Ursprünge, Entwicklungen, Krisenherde. Ein Handbuch.* München: Olzog Verlag.

Bubevski, D.
1985 Nekoi aspekti na nacionalniot sostav na naselenieto vo SRM Makedonija. [Some aspects of the national composition of the population of the Socialist Republic of Macedonia]. In *Problemi na demografskiot razvoj vo SR Makedonija.* K. Bogoev (ed.), pp. 537-550. Skopje: Makedonska akademija na naukite i umetnostite.

Bugajski, J.
1994 *Ethnic Politics in Eastern Europe. A Guide to Nationality Policies, Organizations, and Parties.* Armonk, NY: M. E. Sharpe.

Calic, M.-J.
1993a Der Krieg in Bosnien-Hercegovina. Ursachen, Verlaufsformen und Lösungsmöglichkeiten. Ebenhausen: Internes Papier der Stiftung Wissenschaft und Politik.

1993b Jugoslavienpolitik am Wendepunkt. *Aus Politik und Zeitgeschichte* no. B 37/92, 10 September 1993, pp. 11-20.

1994 Düstere Ausichten für Bosnien-Herzegovina. *Europa-Archiv* 49 (3): 71-79.

Cohen, B., & G. Stamkoski
1992 Macedonia ready for recognition? *Euromoney Supplement* London: Euromoney.

Connor, W.
1978 A nation is a nation, is a state, is an ethnic group, is a.... *Ethnic and Racial Studies* 1: 377-400.

Damoski, A.
1993 Baranja na partijata na srbite vo Makedonija: Faktite ubivaat. [The demands of the Party of the Serbs of Macedonia: convincing facts]. *Nova Makedonija,* no. 16 524, 23 January 1993, p. 13.

Danforth, L. M.
1993 Claims to Macedonian identity: The Macedonian question and the breakup of Yugoslavia. *Anthropology Today* 9 (4): 3-10.

The Economist
1993 Minorities: That other Europe. *The Economist* 25 December 1993: 17-20.

Elwert, G.
1989 Nationalismus und Ethnizität. Über die Bildung von Wir-Gruppen. *Kölner Zeitschrift für Soziologie und Sozialpsychologie* 41: 440-464.

1991 Fassaden, Gerüchte, Gewalt. Über Nationalismus. Merkur 45: 318-332.

Enzensberger, H. M.
1992 *Die Grosse Wanderung. Dreiunddreissig Markierungen. Mit einer Fussnote "Über einige Besonderheiten der Menschenjagd."* Frankfurt/M: Suhrkamp.

1993 *Aussichten auf den Bürgerkrieg.* Frankfurt/M: Suhrkamp.

Furkes, J., & K.-H. Schlarp (eds.)
1991 *Ein Staat zerfällt. Der Balkan - Europas Pulverfass.* Reinbek: Rowohlt Taschenbuch Verlag.

Ganzer, B.

1990 Zur Bestimmung des Begriffs der ethnischen Gruppe. *Sociologus* 40: 3-18.

Geroski, B.

1993a Albancite vo ARM - dilemi i nedoumci. Koga kvota ke nè smota.... [The Albanians in the Army of the Republic of Macedonia - dilemmas and suspicions]. *Vecer-Europe*, no. 5, 8 November 1993, pp. 14-15.

1993b Pres-konferencija na Ministerot za vnatresni raboti dr Ljubomir Frckovski: Krugot e zatvoren! [Press conference of Minister of the Interior Dr. Ljubomir Frckovski: The circle is closed!]. In *Vecer-Europe*, no. 6, 15 November 1993, p. 13.

Glotz, P.

1990 *Der Irrweg des Nationalstaats. Europäische Reden an ein deutsches Publikum.* Stuttgart: Deutsche Verlagsanstalt.

Götz, R., & U. Halbach

1992 *Politisches Lexikon GUS.* München: C. H. Beck.

Gow, J.

1993 One year of war in Bosnia and Herzegovina. *RFE/RL RR,* vol. 2, no. 23, 4 June 1993, pp. 1-13.

Gow, J., & J. Pettifer

1993 Macedonia—Handle with Care. *Jane's Intelligence Review* September 1993: 387-388.

Hayden, R. M.

1993 The partition of Bosnia and Herzegovina, 1990-1993.*RFE/RL RR,* vol. 2, no. 22, 28 May 1993, pp. 1-14.

Heckmann, F.

1992 *Ethnische Minderheiten, Volk und Nation. Soziologie inter-ethnischer Beziehungen.* Stuttgart: Ferdinand Enke Verlag.

Hill, P.

1989 *The Macedonians in Australia.* Carlisle, Western Australia: Hesperian Press.

Höpken, W.

1993 Geschichte und Gewalt. Geschichtsbewusstsein im jugoslawischen Konflikt. *Internationale Schulbuchforschung* 15: 55-73.

Jong, J. de

1984 Die makedonische Nationswerdung - eigenständige Integration oder künstliche Synthese? In *Jugoslawien. Integrations-probleme in Geschichte und Gegenwart. Beiträge des Südosteuropa-Arbeitkreises der Deutschen Forschungs-gemeinschaft zum V. Internationalen Südosteuropa-Kongress der Association Internationale d'Études Sud-Est Européen.* Belgrad 11.-17. September 1984. K.-D. Grothusen (ed.), pp. 164-177. Göttingen: Vandenhoeck & Ruprecht.

Jovanovski, V., & M. Velinovska

1993 Policijata apsi "vojnici". [Police arrest "Soldiers"]. *Puls*, no. 147, 12 November 1993, pp. 10-12.

Kofos, E.

1986 The Macedonian question: The politics of Mutation. *Balkan Studies* 27: 157-172.

1989 National heritage and national identity in nineteenth- and twentieth century Macedonia. *European History Quarterly* 19: 229-267.

Krsteski, E.
1993 "Sinite" ostanuvaat vo Makedonija. Intervju: Fin Tomsen. [The "Blue Ones" Remain in Macedonia. Interview with Finn Thomsen]. *Puls* [Skopje], no. 137, 3 September 1993, pp. 7-9.

Krizan, M.
1993a Wirtschaftsprobleme Makedoniens. *Osteuropa* 43: A 462-A 465.
1993b Die makedonische orthodoxe Kirche und die makedonische Nation. *Osteuropa* 43: A 646- A 652.

Lador-Lederer, J.
1986 Im Irrgarten der Ethnoterminologie. *Europa Ethnica* 43 (2): 64-67.

Libal, W.
1993 *Mazedonien zwischen den Fronten. Junger Staat mit alten Konflikten.* Wien-Zürich: Europaverlag.

Macdonald, Captain D. S. M.
1944 Report on Mission Brasenose. 18 November 1944. In *Military Missions*, vol. 209: Reports from the field: Macedonia Sept.-Nov. 1944. War Office 202; War of 1939-1945; Military Headquarters Papers. London: Public Record Office.

Magnusson, K.
1993 Den makedonska frågan. *Internationella studier* 1: 7-12.

Mark, R. A.
1993 *Die Völker der ehemaligen Sowjetunion. Ein Lexikon.* Opladen: Westdeutscher Verlag.

Matzureff, G. D.
1978 The Concept of a "Macedonian Nation" as a New Dimension in Balkan Politics. Ph. D. Thesis, University of Washington, DC.

Mickey, R. W., & A. S. Albion
n.d. (In press) A miracle in the Balkans? Albanian-Macedonian relations. In *Minority Rights and Responsibilities: Challenges in a New Europe.* New York: East-West Studies.

Mihajlovski, G.
1993 Tajmerot po evropsko vreme. [The timer set to European time]. *Vecer-Europe*, no. 6, 15 November, 1993, p. 11.

Moore, P.
1992 The "Albanian question" in the former Yugoslavia. *RFE/RL RR,* vol. 1, no. 14, 3 April 1992, pp. 7-15.
1993 Endgame in Bosnia and Herzegovina. *RFE/RL RR,* vol. 2, no. 32, 13 August 1993, pp. 17-23.

Neier, A.
1994 Kosovo survives! *The New York Review of Books* 41 (3), February 3, 1994, pp. 26-28.

Oswald, I.
1993 *Nationalitätenkonflikte im östlichen Teil Europas.* Berlin: Landeszentrale für politische Bildungsarbeit.

Palmer, S. E., & R. R. King
1971 *Yugoslav Communism and the Macedonian Question.* Hamden, CT: The Shoe String Press.

Pekevski, B.
1974 Demographic situation and ethnic characteristics of the population of SR Macedonia. In *The Socialist Republic of Macedonia.* M. Apostolski & H. Polenakovic (eds.), pp. 175-187. Skopje: Macedonian Review.

Perry, D. M.
1988 The Politics of Terror. *The Macedonian Revolutionary Movements,* 1893-1903. Durham, NC: Duke University Press.

1992a [The media:] Republic of Macedonia. *RFE/RL RR*, vol. 1, no.39, 2 October 1992, pp. 44-46.

1992b The Military in the Republic of Macedonia. *RFE/RL RR,* vol. 1, no. 46, 20 November 1992, p. 16.

1992c The Republic of Macedonia and the odds for survival.*RFE/RL RR*, vol. 1, no. 46, 20 November 1992, pp. 12-19.

1993 Politics in the Republic of Macedonia: Issues and parties.*RFE/RL RR,* vol. 2, no. 23, 4 June 1993, pp. 31-37.

1994 Macedonia: From independence to recognition. *RFE/RL RR*, vol. 3, no.1, 7 January 1994, pp. 118-121.

Petkovski, M., G. Petreski & T. Slaveski
1993 Stabilization efforts in the Republic of Macedonia. *RFE/RL RR*, vol. 2, no. 3, 15 January 1993, pp. 34-37.

Pettifer, J.
1992 The New Macedonian question. *International Affairs* 68: 475-485.

Popis na naselenieto
1992 *Popis na naselenieto, domakinstvata, stanovite i zemjodelskite stopanstva vo 1991 godina. Osnovni podatoci za naselenieto po opstini. Definitivni podatoci.* [Census of the Population, Households, Apartments, and Agricultural Enterprises in 1991. General Data on Population by Municipalities. Final Results]. Skopje: Republicki zavod za statistika.

Poulton, H.
1993 The Republic of Macedonia after UN recognition. *RFE/RL RR,* vol. 2, no. 23, 4 June 1993, pp. 22-30.

Preinerstorfer, R.
1962 Die Volksgruppen der VR Mazedonien. *Österreichische Osthefte* 4: 386-393.

Puls
1993a So dialog do sozivot. [Through dialog to co-existence]. *Puls*, no. 105, 21 January 1993, pp. 12-13.

1993b Albancite ja sakaat ARM. [The Albanians like the Army of the Republic of Macedonia]. *Puls*, no. 142, 8 October 1993, p. 5.

Rathfelder, E. (ed.)
1992 *Krieg auf dem Balkan. Die europäische Verantwortung*. Reinbek: Rowohlt Taschenbuch Verlag.

Reiterer, A. F.
1992 Die politische Konstitution von Ethnizität. In *Minderheitenfragen in Südosteuropa. Untersuchungen zur Gegenwartskunde Südosteuropas*, 27. G. Seewann (ed.), pp. 37-52. München: R. Oldenbourg Verlag.

Reuter, J.
1987 Die albanische Minderheit in Mazedonien. *Südosteuropa* 36: 587-597.
1993a Makedonien - der jüngste Staat auf der europäischen Landkarte. *Aus Politik und Zeitgeschichte* no. B 37/93, 10 September 1993, pp. 21-29.
1993b Politik und Wirtschaft in Makedonien. *Südosteuropa* 42: 83-99.

Riedel, S.
1993 Bulgarien und Makedonien als Betroffene des UN-Handelsembargos gegen Jugoslawien. *Südosteuropa* 42: 318-325.

Rondholz, E.
1993 Zankapfel Mazedonien. Historische Hintergründe des Streits zwischen Athen und Skopje. *Blätter für deutsche und internationale Politik* 38: 871-881.

Rupnik, J.
1990 Eisschrank oder Fegefeuer. Das Ende des Kommunismus und das Wiederwachen der Nationalismen. In *Osteuropa - Übergänge zur Demokratie?* K. Michalski (ed.), pp. 132-141. Frankfurt/M.: Verlag Neue Kritik.

Schlotter, P., P. Billing, G. Krell, H.-J. Schmidt & B. Schoch
1993 *Der Krieg in Bosnien und das hilflose Europa. Plädoyer für eine militärische UN-Intervention.* Frankfurt/M: Hessische Stiftung für Friedens- und Konfliktforschung.

Schmidt, F.
1993a Kosovo: The time bomb that has not gone off. *RFE/RL RR*, vol. 2, no. 39, 1 October 1993, pp. 21-29.
1993b Has the Kosovo crisis been internationalized? *RFE/RL RR,* vol. 2, no. 44, 5 November 1993, pp. 35-39.

Siesby, E.
1993 An extra-ordinary census in the Republic of Macedonia. In *Bulletin of the Office for Democratic Institutions and Human Rights of the Conference on Security and Cooperation in Europe* 1 (1): 6-8.

Sperling, R. A. C.
1928 *Foreign Office* [report]. Sofia, 22 March 1928. F. O. 371, vol. 12 856, no. C2670/42/7. London: Public Record Office.

Stark, J.
1988 Völker, Ethnien, Minderheiten. Bemerkungen zur Erkenntnistheorie und Terminologie der Minderheitenforschung. *Jarhbuch für ostdeutsche Volkskunde* 31: 1-53.

Statistical Office of the Rep. of Macedonia
1992 *Conditions and activities that should be ensured for the realization of an extraordinary census of the population in the Republic of Macedonia.* Skopje, 10 July 1992.

Sundhaussen, H.
1993 *Experiment Jugoslawien. Von der Staatsgründung bis zum Staatszerfall.* Mannheim: B. I. Taschenbuchverlag (Meyers Forum, 10).

Troebst, S.
1983 *Die bulgarisch-jugoslawische Kontroverse um Makedonien 1967-1982.* Untersuchungen zur Gegenwartskunde Südosteuropas, 23. München: R. Oldenbourg Verlag.

1987 *Mussolini, Makedonien und die Mächte. Die "Innere Makedonische Revolutionäre Organisation" in der Südosteuropapolitik des faschistischen Italien.* Köln-Wien: Böhlau Verlag.

1990a Nationale Minderheiten. In *Südosteuropa-Handbuch.* Bd. VI: *Bulgarien.* K.-D. Grothusen (ed.), pp. 474-489. Göttingen: Vandenhoeck & Ruprecht.

1990b "Macedonia heroica". Zum Makedonier-Bild der Weimarer Republik. *Südostforschungen* 49: 293-364.

1992 Makedonische Antworten auf die "Makedonische Frage" 1944-1992: Nationalismus, Republiksgründung, nation-building. *Südosteuropa* 41: 423-442.

1993a Aufgaben und Ziele vergleichender historischer Forschung zur ethnischen Struktur und zu den Nationalisten Osteuropas. Drei Vorüberl'egungen. *Südosteuropa-Mitteilungen* 33: 146-156.

1993b Demokratie oder Ethnokratie? Nationalitätenpolitik im Nach-"Wende"-Bulgarien. In *Südosteuropa zu Beginn der Neunziger Jahre, Reformen, Krisen und Konflikte in den vormals sozialistischen Ländern.* H. Sundhaussen (ed.), pp. 35-72. Berlin-Wiesbaden: O. Harassowitz.

1994a Macedonia: Powder Keg Defused? *RFE/RL RR*, vol. 3, no. 4, 28 January 1994, pp. 33-41.

1994b Macedonia in a Hostile International and Ethnopolitical Environment (Six Scenarios). *Balkan Forum* [Skopje] 2 (1): 25-44.

1994c Präventive Friedenssicherung durch internationale Beobachtermissionen? Das Beispiel der KSZE-Spillover-Monitormission in Makedonien 1992-1993. In *Sicherheitspolitisches Symposium Balkankonflikt. Instrumente des internationalen Krisenmanagements.* Vom 25. bis 27. Juni 1993 an der Universität Bayreuth. W. Puehs, T. Weggel & C. Richter (eds.), pp. 125-154. (Schriftenreihe des Verbandes der Reservisten der Deutschen Bundeswehr: Wehrdienst und Gesellschaft, 3). Baden-Baden: Nomos Verlagsgesellschaft.

1994d Ethnopolitics in Bulgaria: The Turkish, Pomak, Macedonian and Gypsy Minorities. *Helsinki Monitor* 5 (1): 32-42.

Valinakis, Y.
1992 *Greece's Balkan policy and the "Macedonian issue".* Ebenhausen: Internes Papier der Stiftung Wissenschaft und Politik.

Verdery, K.
1991 *National Ideology Under Socialism. Identity and Cultural Politics in Ceausescu's Roumania.* Berkeley, CA: California University Press.

Völkl, K.
1993 Makedonien/Mazedonien. In *Der ruhelose Balkan. Die Konfliktregionen Südosteuropa.* M. W. Weithmann (ed.), pp. 218-252. München: Deutscher Taschenbuchverlag.

Weilguni, W.
1993 Die serbische Minderheit in Makedonien. *Osteuropa* 43: A 520-A 525.

Weiner, M.
1971 The Macedonian syndrome. An historical model of international relations and political development. *World Politics* 23: 665-683.

Weithmann, M. W.
1993 Makedonien - "Land zwischen vier Feuern". *Aussenpolitik* 44: 261-270.

Wilson, M.
1987 The Macedonian question. In *Border and Territorial Disputes.* A. J. Day (ed.), pp. 79-85. A Keesing's Reference Publication. London: Keesing.

Wolkow, W. K.
1991 Ethnokratie - ein verhängnisvolles Erbe in der postkommunistischen Welt. *Aus Politik und Zeitgeschichte* 20 December 1991, no. B 52-53/91: pp. 34-43.

World Bank
1992 *The Challenge of Economic Recovery and Social Harmony in the Former Yugoslav Republic of Macedonia.* Report prepared by the Section Europe and Central Asia Region in the Central Europe Department of the World Bank.

Wyzan, M. L.
1992 *First Steps to Economic Independence in Macedonia: The Struggle for Survival in a Hostile Environment.* Working Papers, 59. Stockholm: Institute of Economics.

1993a Monetary independence and macroeconomic stabilisation in Macedonia: an initial assessment. *Communist Economies & Economic Transformation* 5: 351-368.

1993b An economically viable nation? Paper delivered at "First steps toward economic independence: new states of the post-communist world", a conference organized by the Stockholm School of Economics on 23-24 August 1993.

OROMO NATIONAL LIBERATION, ETHNICITY AND POLITICAL MYTHOMOTEURS IN THE HORN OF AFRICA

THOMAS ZITELMANN

Freie Universität Berlin, Institut für Ethnologie, Drosselweg 1-3, D-14195 Berlin

A pressing problem in the analysis of ethnic conflicts in the Horn of Africa concerns the relation between material factors, notably competition between groups for scarce resources, and the "material dimension" of the "cultural" and "symbolic" elements employed in the conflicts (Markakis 1994:217-37). I argue here for the relative autonomy of the cultural field, which may include levels of conflict formation not directly linked to the issue of material scarcity and resource competition. I shall discuss two topics. One takes up the view that ethnicity is about classification and cognition (involving both the observer and the observed) and about creating new boundaries of cultural difference or redefining old ones (O'Brien & Roseberry 1991:1-18; Tonkin *et al.* 1989:1-18). I shall add to this a hierarchical perspective. Every policy to overcome a low collective status in this hierarchical field implies what Fukuyama calls a "struggle for recognition" (1992:135). Secondly, I shall focus on the function of myth as a mobilizing and legitimating factor for political actions which seek a change of status. This takes up Sorelian ideas and gets support from the notion of a "mythomoteur" as employed by Armstrong (1982:9).

Discussing the ethnic prehistory of European nationalism, Armstrong introduces the idea of "mythomoteurs," that is, basic legitimating myths for collective political action which consist of continuously disseminated sets of complex symbols. One very strong and persistent mythomoteur in European history was, according to Armstrong, the "antemurales myth," that is, the confrontation between imperial structures and nomadic peoples and, later, the Islamic empire in Eastern and Western Europe. The Horn of Africa has its own set of such myths. Their continuous dissemination is a material fact in its own right, which does not necessarily have an immediate link to material scarcity. Collective changes of status due to a successful struggle for recognition at one level can easily lead to the revival of such myths at another level. Conflict involving the Oromo-speaking population in the Horn of Africa will be my case in point.

The Ethiopian setting

Conflicts in the Horn of Africa are like Russian dolls. The larger dolls always contain smaller ones. Conflict solutions are part of the same structure. The disappearance of conflict at one level brings it to the surface at another. The Ethiopian situation is an example of this. After the ousting of Mengistu Haile Mariam and his government in the Summer of 1991, the victorious Tigray People's Liberation Front (TPLF) opted for the decentralization of Ethiopia along ethno-linguistic lines. Having first created an umbrella organization called the Ethiopian Peoples' Revolutionary Democratic Front (EPRDF) to govern the central state, the TPLF leadership inundated the country with so-called 'People's Democratic Organizations' (PDO), allied to the EPRDF, and covering each sizable ethno-linguistic unit. The intention was to maintain the continuity of the Ethiopian borders as they had been shaped under Menelik II (1889-1913) and to introduce a degree of regional and local autonomy while preserving the hegemony of the TPLF and its control over the central state. In some cases the creation of these PDOs was fiercely resisted by organizations with earlier claims on the national representation of ethno-linguistic units and which had a history of resistance to the former regime. This was in particular the case among the Oromo, but also among the Afar, the Somali and other populations in southern Ethiopia like the Gurage, Walamo, Hadya and Kambata. The case of the Oromo became the most pressing because Oromo-speakers make up roughly half of Ethiopia's total population of 50 million people and live in a part of the country which has the richest natural resources (Asafa Jalata 1993; Zitelmann 1994).

In the Oromo case, an administrative unit called 'Oromiya' came into existence under the control of the Oromo People's Democratic Organization (OPDO) which was, in March 1990, one of the first organizations created by the TPLF according to the PDO pattern. The intention was to outflank four already existing political groups, all of which demanded independence rather than autonomy for Oromiya. These groups had their roots in the political milieu of the 1960s and the early 1970s: the Oromo Liberation Front (OLF), the Islamic Front for the Liberation of Oromiya (IFLO), the Oromo-Abbo-Liberation Front (OALF), and the United Oromo People's Leadership, for (Jihad and) Liberation (UOPLL). Apart from a common commitment to Oromiya as a political unit, there was little else that the five organizations agreed about in the Summer 1991. One additional agreement was that the administrative language within Oromiya should be Oromo (*afaan oromoo*) and that it should be written using Roman characters, not the Ethiopian script.

In the Summer of 1991, the OPDO and OLF joined the transitional government and all five organizations joined the representative council, or parliament. The acceptence of 'Oromo' as a political cause was far from complete during the 1960s. This was partly due to political pressure from the imperial government under Emperor Haile Selassie and, partly, to obstacles within the Oromo-speaking communities themselves. But the term 'Galla,' used at that time to identify the ethno-linguistic unit as a whole, became thoroughly disliked because of its derogatory implications. Sometimes, regional terms were used to identify political pressure groups like the Macha-Tulama-Association (1963-1967). But one can see continuity, both in ideology and action, between the Macha-Tulama-Association and the foundation of the OLF in 1974. The IFLO broke away from the OLF in 1978 and adopted an Islamic agenda in 1986, but the political career of its leading member, Sheikh Jaaraa Abba Gada (Abdulkarim Muhammad Ibrahim), had already begun in the late 1960s.

The OALF and the UOPLL are off-spring of the 'Somali-Abbo Liberation Front.' Although bearing an artificial name which had been imposed on Oromo-speakers by the Somali government during the second half of the 1970s, the Somali-Abbo Liberation Front derives from the Bale uprising (1963-1971) among the Arsi and other Oromo-speakers. Core networks of political activists had remained stable since then. The OALF is linked to the Dadhi-Tarre family, which has a strong base among mixed Oromo and Somali speakers in Bale and Sidamo, and the UOPLL is linked to Waqo Guto Usu, the foremost political and military leader of the Bale uprising. What distinguished these networks of activists, in the eyes of observers, from simple extensions of 'clan' or 'tribe' was, initially, their organizational efficiency (Gebru Tareke 1991:152).

The notion of 'Oromo culture' (*aada oromo*) as a symbol of social and political mobilization is now increasingly accepted (Baxter 1994). For more than a decade it was mainly the secular and modernist OLF-leadership which fostered the current symbols of national Oromo culture. This was particularly true for the age and generation system (*gada*), which became for the OLF a mythomoteur and symbol of secular Oromo nationalism. Gada was not cherished in the same way by other organizations. What all five organizations were engaged in, with different degrees of success and using different means, was the "symbolic construction of community" (Cohen 1985) or "we-group construction" (Elwert 1989), using blue-prints drawn from contested traditions.

Oromo culture became a rallying cry in this process of construction, but its proper definition is still not agreed upon (Zitelmann 1993). The debate is carried on within a context which is controlled by the EPRDF/TPLF and by its extension, the OPDO. Although not independent and although living under far from democratic conditions, the Oromo today have a degree of cultural autonomy unknown since their inclusion in the Ethiopian Empire. The political rallying cry of 'being Oromo' has advanced beyond the limited field of organized nationalist activists. The language issue, including the problem of which alphabet should be used, has become a broad issue concerning all Oromo-speakers, because it now touches on such questions as administration and schooling. These reforms, however, are also likely to contribute to the redefinition and even reinforcement of older cultural boundaries.

The discourse of ethnicity

The very fact that the insurgents of the Bale uprising had an efficient organization had already, during the 1960s, provoked the charge that communism was involved (Gebru Tareke 1991). With the disappearance of the socialist block, rationalizations like 'building up socialism' or 'national liberation' or even the more recent 'democratization,' have lost their power to legitimate power struggles. Instead of communism, a vision of four 'apocalyptic riders' now haunts the imagination of a conflict-bound world: nationalism, ethnicity, culture and religion. Such foci of traditional values became identified as possible obstacles to global 'democratization' and the universality of the 'civic' (Fukuyama 1992:215). Defining 'ethnicity' or 'culture' as obstacles to something else is, in the Ethiopian case, not so new. It is no coincidence that, during the regime of Mengistu Haile Mariam, applied ethnography was the "study of harmful cultures"[1]—harmful to socialism of course! It is difficult to imagine sustainable civic political institutions being established in Ethiopia which did not recognize the cultural particularities of the populations involved. There are problems here, however, which have to be faced.

In the 1980s, there were two conventional ways of analyzing conflicts in the Horn of Africa. One was to identify intra-élite tensions (civil/intellectual/military) which the cold war powers or their regional stooges exploited to fuel nationalistic, ethnic and religious feelings (Halliday & Molyneux 1981; Lefort 1981; Ottaway 1983). The other form of analysis stressed internal frictions and deprivations and brought culture and ethnicity into the picture (Bereket Hapte Sellassie 1980; Braukämper 1983; Lewis 1983; Tamene Bitima *et al.* 1983), sometimes in a spirit of romantic Herderianism, but often also to reconcile, at least theoretically, the divergent Utopias of class and nation (Gebru Tareke 1991). In the case of the Ethiopian Empire, ethnicity became a 'wild-card,' used whenever one had to explain why peasants and agro-pastoralists did not follow the organizational principle of class; and, where class was seen as a true organizational principle, it often represented a secular argument for the territorial continuity of the empire.

Another approach to ethnic conflict in the Horn of Africa has recently been offered by Fukui and Markakis (1994:1-11). The distinction between three spheres of conflict—at the centre, at the margin and in-between—allows for a formal structural differentiation of the groups involved and of causes and responses. It further provides a theoretical perspective relating the different spheres to each other, without losing sight of regional and local particularities. According to this view, conflict at the centre is marked by

---

[1] The official Amharic terminology was *ya-goji bahil tinat.* I owe this information to Getachew Chemeda Nadhabasaa.

competition for state power. Conflict at the margin is still characterized by feuds and raids, as in the classical anthropological writings on 'stateless' societies, but it is bolstered now by new military technology. The supply of light weapons—especially the AK 47—links conflicts at the margins with conflicts at the centre. Conflict in-between brings populations into confrontation with the state, either involuntarily or in pursuit of objectives at the regional or local level (Fukui & Markakis 1994:3). In general, the contributors to Fukui and Markakis avoid narrow definitions of ethnicity and rely instead on a situational approach. Some problems, however, remain.

Most of the populations engaged in conflicts at the margin are numerically too small to have any immediate interest in competition for state power. In the Oromo case, however, conflict at the centre and at the margin takes place within one ethno-linguistic unit. The OLF's use of Gada symbolism for community construction draws largely on the working Gada system among Borana pastoralists in the Ethio-Kenyan borderlands who are engaged in raids and feuds at the margins. According to the social anthropological ('structural-functionalist') analysis of such warfare, raids and feuds are part of a larger social order and contribute to the reproduction of that order. The introduction of new arms technologies certainly disturbs this equilibrium but what happens when activists at the centre use symbols drawn from the margin to symbolize the boundaries of their 'we-group' in the competition for state power? One can distinguish between a customary 'culture of violence' and the modern 'cult of violence' (Scheffler 1991:3). While a 'culture of violence' is part and parcel of a given social order, a 'cult of violence' is part of a modern propaganda effort to transcend a given social order. Authors like Sorel, Pareto, Sartre and Fanon represent the latter, while classical social anthropology in the Horn of Africa offers many examples of the former. There is an important linkage between a supposed culture and a cult of violence. Once political organizations consciously develop, and use, a symbolic system to mobilize adherents *as if* the bygone 'warrior tradition' (Ali Mazrui 1977) and the related social order could be re-established, it means operating with myth in the Sorelian sense. From the perspective of core activists, it blurs the distinction between competition for state power and the other two spheres of conflicts, although they have no means of intervening in these spheres.

The attempt of Markakis to identify "objective factors" which give ethnicity the potential for political conflict poses further problems. One factor he identifies is "competition for resources in conditions of great scarcity" (Markakis 1994:217), which includes natural resources and uneven regional development. This factor seems to link ethnic conflict at the centre and at the margin. Scarcity makes mobility necessary for many people in the Horn and this leads to conflict. Conflict at the centre derives from scarcity, in so far as the state is the sole institution controlling natural resources and development. One can hardly deny the impact that droughts, erosion and desertification, together with international uneven development and the decline of producers' prices, have had on politics in the Horn of Africa in recent decades. But to see the political history of the Horn solely from the perspective of scarcity is a very recent fashion which may well be confined in future to a museum collection of "images of Africa." A stress on "scarcity" obviously supports a "materialist" perspective on ethnicity and conflict, and makes it difficult to accommodate "cultural elements" and their "material dimension" (Markakis 1994:226).

Though it seems useful, for the Ethiopian case, to recognize the political nature of "ethnicity" (Markakis 1994:236), I find it difficult to distinguish between universal markers of group identity, such as nationalism, socialism and religion on the one hand, and a parochial 'ethnicity' on the other (Markakis 1994:236). In the Ethiopian case 'ethnicity' has become a means by which academics and activists close to the centre argue about the parochial people at the margins.

Ethnicity in the regional context

In a recent discussion of twentieth century's peasant wars in Ethiopia, Gebru Tareke describes northern Ethiopia (Abyssinia) as sharing "a common mode of production, a common polity, the same Christian tradition, and an 'etiological charter composed of a script, art and literature'" (1991:198). While 'mode of production' stands here for the core lands of the Ethiopian Empire, 'ethnicity' stands for kinship, locality and parochialism. This classification appears to be part and parcel of the very process the author attempts to clarify. Theoretical abstractions are in this case code words for a much deeper classification which sets the Christian tradition of the imperial core—elevated to the position of a Marxist 'mode of production'—apart from local 'ethnic' traditions at its periphery.

Imperial and Christian Abyssinia (the northern parts of present-day Ethiopia) had its own 'antemurales myth,' in the sense used by Armstrong, seeing itself surrounded by a "sea of Muslims and heathens." The Shoan expansion which led to the present territorial borders of Ethiopia during the time of Menelik II (1889-1913), made much use of this myth. Among the Amhara and Tigray, the imperial legacy was marked by the Semitic language, the Christian religion and the existence of a Holy Scripture and a written language. This led to a number of structural oppositions: Ethiopian/Semitic versus African/Negro; Christian versus Muslim/pagan; state versus non-state; sedentary versus nomadic; and literate versus non-literate (Mohamed Hassen 1990:3). There were also hierarchic ethnic labels, like 'Galla,' a class of 'uncivilized' pagans speaking Cushitic languages and, even further down, the enslavable 'Shankalla,' speakers of Omotic and Nilotic languages (Donham 1986:13).

There were changes in the use of such labels during the late eighteenth and early nineteenth centuries. Crummey, arguing against the relevance of 'ethnicity' for the imperial polity during the eighteenth century, nevertheless recognizes changes in the use of the term Galla in the imperial chronicles. He identified a "disapprobation which frequently arose from grounds far removed from the ethnic," the latter still being narrowly defined as "objective descent and a degree of non-semitic blood" (Crummey 1975:278). In this case, any study of ethnicity would imply first an ethnography of disapprobation, a study of what is to be disapproved by whom. The Ethiopian situation concerning mythomoteurs is even more complex. There is, in addition, an Islamic perspective with a complementary classificatory hierarchy, including the legacy of an empire. The historical empire reached its height during the first half of the sixteenth century, under the Imam Ahmed Granj. It subsequently split into sub-units, leaving part of its former territorial space for the Somali clan polities, the petty Sultanates of the Afar and the Gada polities of some Oromo. Classificatory hierarchies linked to this Islamic perspective emphasize the central position of law (the Islamic *shari'a*) *vis-à-vis* local custom and tradition (Ali Moussa Iye n.d.; Zitelmann 1993b:17-8).

Some people fall between such hierarchical classifications and this has an impact on their choice of mythomoteur for collective political action. In particular, among the Oromo, we find very complex articulations of ethnicity within a linguistically homogeneous population.

Gada as a mythomoteur for political activism

During my fieldwork among Oromo refugees in the Sudan and in Somalia (intermittently between 1984 and 1989), I was impressed by the way people developed the idea of a reified, essentialist 'Oromo culture' (*aadaa oromoo*) (Zitelmann 1994). It was a weapon in the struggle but it became also, in the classical anthropological sense, part of their *persona*, a mask perhaps, but an essential one. 'Oromo culture' became instrumental in the struggle, but it was also a mask which was put on to face the host societies. In the Sudan, marginal Oromo refugees, long despised as 'Hàbasha,' had become, in 1989, respected 'Urumu,' a term which hardly any Sudanese knew in 1984. In practical terms it meant simply that the 'Urumu' distanced themselves from the Sudanese stereotype of the 'Hàbasha' as someone given to drinking, gambling, and prostitution (Zitelmann 1994:126 ff.). It was truly a 'struggle for recognition.'

This newly gained respected status was partly due to the cultural and social engineering of a liberation front which the Sudanese authorities had, since 1977/78, allowed to use the Sudan as a retreat area for its inroads into the Oromo areas in southwestern Ethiopia. Sudanese state security helped to make this possible, as did the UNHCR and international NGOs. The process of developing a reified idea of Oromo culture, however, took place within the OLF and through interaction within the international Oromo diaspora. Each diaspora had its own problems with its particular host society and, far from seeing 'culture' as a repository of traditional values, I experienced it as a reaction to external demands, whether in Berlin, Khartoum or Toronto. Being somebody, a *persona*, meant having a culture.

In its struggle for a nation-state, the OLF stressed 'conscientization' and the creation of 'new personalities,' invoking the theories of Paolo Freire. The restoration of dignity and self-respect was to be achieved through *aadaa oromoo* and literacy and education became the backbone of this process. During the 1980s the OLF drew on the classical age and generation grading system (Gada) in the military, politically and administrative fields (Zitelmann 1991a:266 ff.). This increased, if anything, when the OLF joined the Ethiopian transitory government in 1991.[2]

Gada appears to be an example of a classical mythomoteur for collective action in the political sphere. Up to 1991, however, only the OLF made it the core of its programme. The smaller Islamic Front for the Liberation of Oromiya (IFLO) attempted to combine Islam with Gada, but stressed its legal aspects rather than the warrior tradition. Furthermore, any traditional elements which were reminiscent of a non-Islamic past were avoided in IFLO's propaganda. Where the OLF spoke about the *aada oromoo,* the IFLO described the *aadaa* as something 'local' (*mahali*), thus elevating the Islamic legacy above non-Islamic traditions (Zitelmann 1994). In the case of the OALF, recourse to Gada was not appropriate because the people concerned had a low status in the former Gada-polities dominated by the Borana. Islam was for them a symbol of emancipation (Schlee & Shongolo 1993).

The OPDO took no stand on tradition but its emergence reveals something about the struggle for recognition. The militarization of Ethiopia under the former regime offers wide scope for research into the process of gaining political awareness. Forced conscription into the militias in 1976 and the general conscription of high school graduates in 1984 influenced individuals to take refuge in neighbouring countries and provided an incentive to join opposition movements. During the last years of the former government, many young men in the rural areas were forcibly drawn into

2 An American election observer, who was later expelled from Ethiopia, took part in a mass meeting at the OLF headquarters. He reported having taken part in the initiation ritual of a new class of fighters for the organization. According to the observer, the ritual was in line with the centuries old Gada practice. It was presented as a rediscovery of their identity (*The Indian Ocean Newsletter,* No. 534, 4th July, 1992, p. 1). Reading this, I remembered that, in 1984, refugees in the Sudan, belonging to the mass organizations of the OLF, had meetings about Gada and that the OLF leadership was in need of more academic ethnographic material about it.

the army, but some also went to gain status. The peasant associations had a quota of young men to be sent but we know little about the criteria used for selection. Processes like these are usually linked, in a very complex way, to local social structures and may include marking out the village 'undesirables.' This is also a field where the status issue, linked to basic categories like honour and shame, may easily play a part. Although no studies have been done on this subject, one may assume that an organization like the OPDO is able to exploit this contradiction.[3] The struggle for recognition has thus an external as well as an internal dimension.

Strangers and devils

There is much to be said about the regional and social differentiation within the Oromo organizations, including the linkages between landholding classes, intellectuals, bureaucrats and the 'people' (Zitelmann 1993). While violence and the support of the EPRDF/TPLF allowed the OPDO to gain the upper hand in the control of Oromiya, many of the cultural demands which had hitherto fuelled the conflict at the centre were satisfied. But there are other levels of potential strife which are not immediately linked to narrowly definable groups and interests. In what follows I shall illustrate with two short case studies how mythomoteurs like the 'stranger' and the 'devil' make possible additional levels of conflict. Remarkably, it was not until 1991 that all organizations finally identified themselves as 'Oromo,' a process which took nearly three decades. This was particularly the case for the groups which emerged from the Somali-Abbo movement, the leaders of which had, for a long time, cooperated with the Somali government, mostly in open antagonism to the OLF. The shift towards Oromo identity had already emerged during the second half of the 1980s, and was perhaps linked to rising tensions within Somali society. Locating the 'stranger' became one expression of this tension (Zitelmann 1991b:120).

In two of the refugee-camps in the Hiraan region (Southern Somalia) where I did fieldwork in 1988, lived Arsi-Oromo from the Ethiopian region of Bale (Zitelmann 1994:162 ff.). Some used to have linkages with the Somali-Abbo movement and others with the OLF but, in 1988, all identified themselves as Oromo. The OLF's educational material was present in the camps and historical texts gave a uniform picture of a golden Oromo past, when democracy was flourishing under the Gada system, and Ethiopian

3 Immediately after the EPRDF/TPLF took power in Addis Ababa in the Summer of 1991, so-called 'peace-and stability-committees' were formed at the level of local neighbourhoods. There was a strange tendency in Addis Ababa to denounce the members of such commitees as 'outsiders,' as 'people without honor,' as not having a status as *ilma nama* (sons of persons).

colonialism had not yet disturbed the peace of the green pastures. Although Somali officials did not interfere with the change from Somali-Abbo to Oromo, they had a tragic impact on school education in the camps. Since their language was no longer considered to be a Somali (-Abbo) dialect, the primary school teachers were no longer permitted to use the Oromo language. Teaching had to be in Somali. Because teachers in the private Koranic schools continued to teach in the Oromo language, attendance at these schools increased, while attendance at the primary schools decreased. Islam, which once had provided the pivotal link between the Arsi and their Somali neighbours, suddenly became a boundary.

Other elements of distinctiveness were connected with ideals of lineage solidarity and of neighbourhood. In the case of the Ogaden Somali, the fiction of lineage was used to delineate the realms of solidarity and antagonism. The Arsi Oromo expressed the same ideas in terms of 'good' and 'bad' neighbourhood. In both cases, solidarity combined mutual assistance and the exchange of spouses. Apart from their relevance at the local level, both models included wider social and political dimensions. In the Somali case, the fiction of lineage provided a strategy for the negotiation of alliances at the national level while, in the Oromo case, the ideal type of 'good neighbourhood' stood for a lost way of life even as it expressed a hope for the future. People had left Ethiopia because of 'bad neighbourhood' (with the Amhara) and they still longed for the re-establishment of 'good neighbourhood.' The dilemma for the Arsi was that they saw no way of escaping from 'bad neighbourhood': "The Amhara call us 'Galla' and the Somali call us 'gaal' (stranger). Where shall we go? We live between two people."

The case for membership of the Somali-Abbo, from which the Arsi in the Hiraan camps had distanced themselves in 1988, gives us a clue to the hierarchical order of ethnicity, seen from a perspective which combines Islam with pan-Somalism.[4] The basic argument runs as follows (Ibrahim Abdallah Muhammad 'Mah' 1982:92-111). Galla is not a race, nor is it synonymous with the Arabic 'muhajir' (emigrant), as has often been speculated. The word means, in ancient Somali, 'camel' and the *gaala* were nomadic herders of long-distance camels. Beginning as a label for people who followed a certain livelihood, *gaal* came to include any non-Islamic population (and hence strangers), whether white or black. As early as the

4 The role of Islam in creating social cohesion and political alliances in the Oromo-Somali border areas in southern Ethiopia has been far from exhaustively discussed. Abbas Hajji has recently described how the Muslim Arsi for a long time identified their being Arsi with the concept of the Islamic "Umma" (1992:266); I. M. Lewis saw mutual veneration of Islamic saints and their tombs, like the famous Sheikh Hussein, as one basis for the Somali-Oromo interaction during the 1970s (1980:409-15); Oromo refugees in the Hiiraan camps stressed in 1988 the point that the Somali had promised them education (!) and arms for the alliance as Somali-Abbo (Zitelmann 1988:19).

time of Sultan Saad-ed-Din (1387-1414), Abbo/Galla, Afar and Somali joined the armies of the Islamic empire, fighting against the Christian empire. During the time of Ahmed Granj, the Abbo, Afar and Somali formed the nucleus of Granj's armies. The subsequent war between the Muslims of Harar and the Galla, wrongly called the 'Galla migrations' by European researchers, was a civil war. On one side were the 'civilized' Muslims (Galla and Somali) and on the other the pagan nomads (Galla and Somali), who kept to their tradition (Arabic: *ada*). The 'Galla migrations' into the Christian highlands were organized Islamic raids under Galla leadership. On the other hand, those Galla who, in 1567 besieged the town of Harar, were 'heathen' Borana, who had no political aims and were only interested in acquiring cattle, horses and arms.

Turning to the term 'Oromo,' Ibrahim tells us that 'Uruma' is a new political name, introduced by certain intellectuals, following the lead of Yilma Deressa, a minister close to Emperor Haile Selassie. Since it is a term linked to Addis Ababa and Christian culture, and not directed against Amhara colonialism, the aim of introducing it was to prevent a separation from the Amhara. Ibrahim agrees that 'Uruma' was the name of a man who lived in ancient times, outside the Horn of Africa, and that his offspring can be found among the Galla and the Somali. For the 'Somalian Oromo peoples,' however, it is one of many tribal names which "does not carry in its meaning any necessary message for change and liberation" (Ibrahim Abdallah Muhammad 'Mah' 1982:96). This is taken as evidence that 'Uruma' was never a name for all the Galla, but rather for the "few heathens in the country." The message is clear. 'Oromo' represents the continuity of 'unbelievers' and 'strangers.' Gada and the *aadaa oromoo,* so central for the OLF style of thought, is 'heathen,' 'uncivilized' and pre-political.

One central issue which all Oromo organizations had agreed on in the Summer of 1991 was that the Oromo language, using the Roman script, should be the administrative language for the future territory of Oromiya. Following the regional elections in the Summer of 1992, the TPLF-sponsored OPDO took power in Oromiya.[5] The newly established parliament, in a 'gadaizing' idiom known as *chaffee* decided, in its first session, to implement the language issue immediately. Schoolbooks were soon available, thanks to the research undertaken in the first year of the new government and the suddenly flourishing printing business. Administrators were obliged to take courses in the Oromo language and people flocked to new literacy classes to learn the Roman alphabet known as *qubee.* Soon afterwards, voices were raised against the use of *qubee* from the Ethiopian-Orthodox Church, from northern settler communities in Oromiya. Amhara intellectuals started a campaign against the use of *qubee*, calling it

---

[5] For this part of the chapter I owe much to information supplied by Tamene Bitima who did research in Ethiopia in the Autumn of 1992.

a 'devil's script.' "We have two big enemies, Qubee which is taken from the land of the Franji (Whites) and the Sheetan" (Toleeraa Tasaammaa 1993:18). This campaign is still going on and is beginning to embrace other features of what is considered to be Oromo culture.

Up to the Summer of 1991, the *qubee* script was used idiosyncratically by the Oromo refugees and exile communities. The rationale for its use was that it made it easier to express the shifts in vocalization (single and duplicating) which are so characteristic of the Oromo language and which are difficult to express in the Ethiopian syllabic script known as *fidal.* Inside Ethiopia, the use of *qubee* was prohibited. It was not simply a technical matter, then, but was also strongly connected to a political boundary mechanism which the government of Mengistu Haile Mariam intended to control. In addition, the government defended the 'civilizing' role of the Christian empire, to which the Ethiopian script is essentially bound.

Although all Oromo organizations supported the use of the Roman script, it was only the OLF and the international Oromo diaspora linked to it which had used it continuously since the late 1970s. Within the OLF network, the *qubee* script was used for administrative, technical, educational, artistic and propaganda reasons. It was here too that the 'gadaizing' idiom and the use of archaic words was developed (Tamene Bitima 1990:647). Literacy was one of the symbolic hallmarks of the OLF's attempts to give a corporate identity to its followers. The IFLO (which, in its most recent programme, is quite clear that the Koran should be studied in the Roman script) put little emphasis on literacy up to 1991/1992. For propaganda, it used mainly audio or video tapes. Although the Somali-Abbo movement among refugees in Somalia was influenced by the Somali use of the Roman script, it did not develop much material. When the OPDO was formed in the Spring of 1990, it started to publish pamphlets in the Ethiopian script, but shifted after some months to the Roman script. The EPRDF/TPLF leadership, which had been engaged since the Summer of 1991 in a world-wide search for Oromo intellectuals who were equally opposed to the government and to the OLF, seems to have accepted that writing the Oromo language in the Roman script does not necessarily mean the break-up of Ethiopia. For more than a decade, the OLF was the backbone of the campaign to adopt the Roman script. With the changes in Ethiopia and growing literacy in the Oromo language, the language issue has become a public matter and the OLF has become redundant as an agency for cultural nationalism.

As long as *qubee* was used only by Oromo refugee and diaspora communities, the cultural specialists of the Abyssinian core did not care much about it. When it had to be taken seriously, the reaction was to have recourse to the Abyssinian imperial mission as a fight between light and darkness, good and evil, with God on the imperial side and with its enemies guided by the Sheetan (Markakis 1974:32). In the late nineteenth century, the French-trained Shoan court historian Asma Giorgis argued forcefully against such an approach to the Oromo and their language. But, for some clerics, it was still a language taught by the devil to make people forget their Christian tongue (Bairu Tafla 1987:91).

Blaming the Sheetan for political activities among the Oromo is part and parcel of the Abyssinian antemurales myth. Its re-emergence in the context of administrative reforms in Ethiopia sheds a disturbing light on possible expressions of communal hatred and violence. As long as the issue of *qubee* was confined to the narrow realm of formally organized nationalism, certain organizations could be blamed as culprits. With *qubee* as a free-floating symbol, the hierarchical classifications may again ultimately concern 'a people.'

Conclusion

Internationally observable changes in the pattern of violent conflict have provoked a number of new academic hypotheses. Global power shifts and disturbances of the international equilibrium even came to be regarded as conducive to local attempts to change power relations by any means, including violence (Toffler 1990). Are skinheads in the local neighbourhood and warlords in savanna and jungle perhaps expressions of related phenomena? Combining the global with the local, the older theory of 'structural violence' comes to mind (Galtung 1976). When does violence become a means to achieve power and when is it a means of survival in the context of a violent social reality (Nordstrom *et al.* 1992:4)? As with 'structural violence' the stress here is more on interactive relationships within a larger 'culture of violence' than on essentialist notions of violence-prone values. Structural violence always implies an interactive relationship between those in power and an opposing agency. This view of politics owes much to Hannah Arendt's distinction between "violence" as an instrumental means and "power" as the "human ability to act in concert" (1969:106). Groupings in the political arena are never a simple reflection of material scarcity and resource competition, as Markakis implies for the Ethiopian case, but a necessary part of the emergence of any plural or heterogenous political system.

There can be many mythomoteurs for collective political action; some may vanish or become unimportant, new ones may be added. As Sorel has shown for the "general strike" (1941), they are certainly not confined to an 'ethnic' sphere. Mythomoteurs can be inclusive, like our modern 'multi-culturalism,' or exclusive like 'racism.' They can be overtly civic and 'polis-minded,' as apparently in Sarajevo; or clannish and anti-urban, as in Mogadishu; and there can be changes over a generation. Addis Ababa was burned and looted by its population when Emperor Haile Selassie fled in 1936, escaping from the Italian invasion. In 1991, when the troops of the

Tigray Peoples' Liberation Front (TPLF) and of other armed fronts chased out the government of Mengistu Haile Mariam, the multi-ethnic population of Addis Ababa showed a remarkable sense of civic urbanism in keeping the war away from the town. Violence, however, does not need parochial ethnicity: it can also flourish with universal socialism, as it did in Ethiopia during the period of the so-called 'white' and 'red' terrors (1977/1978).

Mythomoteurs and classificatory hierarchies which include 'the stranger' and 'the devil' form part of the regional expression of structural violence in the Horn of Africa. There may be immediate material reasons for the intensity of this expression in political discourse, but once a mythomoteur is set in motion, its side effects are beyond control. In the Oromo case, the disapprobation enshrined in the two classificatory hierarchies (Abyssinian and Islamic) focus on the same Galla/Oromo subject, for different reasons, but with similar consequences for the same set of people. It is difficult to imagine that a political solution will be found without recognition of the curious cultural mask the Oromo persona wears in modern civil society. In his discussion of ethnicity among the Kenyan Kikuyu, John Lonsdale argues that "Deep debates are supressed by high faction" (1992:468). This would describe also the Oromo situation. Lonsdale proposes, as an alternative, a "debated ethnicity" which could provide a public space for the discussion of differences. The Ethiopian situation demands a similar approach.

Acknowledgements—This chapter is based on research supported, between 1987 and 1992, by the German Foundation for Research.

References

Abbas Hajji
1992 L'Ethiopie va-télle éclater? Conflits politiques, économie et société en pays arssi (1900-1935). *Cahiers d'Études africaines* 126 (XXXI-2): 239-283.

Ali Moussa Iye
n.d. Le Verdict de l'Arbre - Le Xeer Issa - Étude d'une 'Democratie Pastorale.' Dubai.

Arendt, H.
1969 *On Violence*. New York: Harcourt, Brace & World.

Armstrong, J. A.
1982 *Nations Before Nationalism*. Chapell Hill: University of North Carolina Press.

Asafa Jalata
1993 *Oromia and Ethiopia - State Formation and Ethnonational Conflict, 1868-1992*. Boulder/London: Lynne Rienner Publishers.

Bairu Tafla (ed.)
1987 *Asma Giorgis and His Work, 'History of the Galla and the Kingdom of Sawa.'* Stuttgart: Franz Steiner.

Baxter, P. T. W.
1994 The Creation and Constitution of Oromo Nationality. In *Ethnicity and Conflict in the Horn of Africa.* K. Fukui & M. Markakis (eds.), pp. 167-186. London: James Currey.

Bereket Hapte Selassie
1980 *Conflict and intervention in the Horn of Africa.* New York: Monthly Review Press.

Braukämper, U.
1983 Ethnische Probleme in Aethiopien. In *From 'Scramble for Africa' to 'East-West-Conflict.'* Friedrich-Ebert-Stiftung (ed.), pp. 111-128. Bonn: Friedrich-Ebert-Stiftung.

Cohen, A. P.
1985 *The Symbolic Construction of Community.* Chichester/London/ New York: Ellis Horwood Ltd. & Tavistock Publications.

Crummey, D.
1975 Society and Ethnicity in the Politics of Christian Ethiopia during the Zamana Masafent. *The International Journal of African Historical Studies* 8 (2): 266-278.

Donham, D.
1986 Old Abyssinia and the New Ethiopian Empire: Themes in Social History. In *The Southern Marches of Imperial Ethiopia - Essays in History and Social Anthropology.* W. James & D. Donham (eds.), pp. 3-48. Cambridge: Cambridge University Press.

Elwert, G.
1989 Nationalismus, Ethnizität und Nativismus - Über die Bildung von Wir-Gruppen. In *Ethnizität im Wandel.* G. Elwert & P. Waldmann (eds.), pp. 21-50. Saarbrücken: Breitenbach Verlag.

Fukui, K., & J. Markakis
1994 Introduction. In *Ethnicity and Conflict in the Horn of Africa.* K. Fukui & J. Markakis (eds.), pp. 1-11. London: James Currey.

Fukuyama, F.
1992 *The End of History and the Last Man.* London: Penguin.

Galtung, J.
1976 *Eine strukturelle Theorie des Imperialismus.* In *Imperialismus und strukturelle Gewalt - Analysen über abhängige Reproduktion.* D. Senghaas (ed.), pp. 29-104. Frankfurt: Suhrkamp.

Gebru Tareke
1991 *Ethiopia: Power and Protest. Peasant Revolts in the Twentieth Century.* Cambridge: Cambridge University Press.

Halliday, F., & M. Molyneux
1981 *The Ethiopian Revolution.* London: Verso.

Ibrahim Abdalla Muhammad 'Mah'
1982 *Al-hazima at-thalatha* (The Third Defeat). Cairo: Maktaba an-Nahdha al-Masriyya.

Lefort, F.
1981 *Ethiopie - La Revolution hérétique.* Paris: Maspero.

Lewis, I. M.
1980 The Western Somali Liberation Front (WSLF) and the Legacy of Sheikh Hussein of Bale. In *Modern Ethiopia*. J. Tubiana (ed.), pp. 409-415. Rotterdam: Balhema.

1983 *Nationalism and Self Determination in the Horn of Africa*. I. M. Lewis (ed.). London: Ithaca Press.

Lonsdale, J.
1992 The Moral Economy of Mau Mau: Wealth, Poverty and Civic Virtue in Kikuyu Political Thought. In *Unhappy Valley. Conflict in Kenya and Africa, Book 2: Violence and Ethnicity*. B. Berman & J. Lonsdale (eds.), pp. 315-504. London: James Currey.

Markakis, J.
1974 *Ethiopia: Anatomy of a Traditional Polity*. Oxford: Oxford University Press.

1987 *National and Class Conflict in the Horn of Africa*. Cambridge: Cambridge University Press.

1994 Ethnic Conflict and the State in the Horn of Africa. In *Ethnicity and Conflict in the Horn of Africa*. K. Fukui & J. Markakis (eds.), pp. 217-237. London: James Currey.

Mazrui, A. (ed.)
1977 *The Warrior Tradition in Africa*. Leiden: Brill.

Mohamed Hassen
1990 *The Oromo of Ethiopia: A History 1570 to 1860*. Cambridge: Cambridge University Press.

Nordstrom, C., & J. Martin
1992 The Culture of Conflict: Field Reality and Theory. In *The Paths to Domination, Resistance, and Terror*. C. Nordstrom & J. Martin (eds.), pp. 3-17. Berkeley/Los Angeles/Oxford: California University Press.

O'Brien, J., & W. Roseberry
1991 Golden Ages, Dark Ages. In *Imagining the Past in Anthropology and History*. J. O'Brien & W. Roseberry (eds.), pp. 1-18. Berkeley/Los Angeles/Oxford: California University Press.

Ottaway, M.
1983 Revolution and 'Social Question.' In *From 'Scramble for Africa' to 'East-West-Conflict'*. Friedrich Ebert-Stiftung (ed.), pp. 35-47. Bonn: Friedrich-Ebert-Stiftung.

Scheffler, T.
1991 Einleitung: Ethnizität und Gewalt im Vorderen und Mittleren Orient. In *Ethnizität und Gewalt*. T. Scheffler (ed.), pp. 9-32. Hamburg, Deutsches Orient Institut.

Schlee, G., & Abdullahi A. Shongollo
1993 Oromo and Somali Ethnicity and the Concept of Nationhood. Paper presented for the seminar within the framework of the 19th Congress of the Union of Oromo Students in Europe, Berlin, 16th July 1993.

Sorel, G.
1941 *Reflections on Violence*. New York: Smith.

Tamene Bitima
1990 Oromo Technical Terms. *Africa* (Roma) 45 (4): 639-658.

Tamene Bitima & J. Steuber
1983 *Die ungelöste nationale Frage in Aethiopien: Studie zu den Befreiungsbewegungen der Oromo und Eritreas.* Frankfurt/Bern: Peter Lang.

Toffler, A.
1990 *Power Shift: Knowledge, Wealth and Violence at the Edge of the 21st Century.* New York: Bantam.

Toleeraa Tasammaa
1993 Sheexanaa fi Qubee (The Devil and Qubee). *Madda Walaabuu* (Addis Abeba/Finfine) 1: 17-19.

Tonkin, E., M. McDonald & M. Chapman
1989 Introduction: History and Social Anthropology. In *History and Ethnicity.* E. Tonkin, M. McDonald & M. Chapman (eds.), pp. 1-21. London/New York: Routledge.

Zitelmann, T.
1988 'We have Nobody in the Agencies': Somali and Oromo Responses to Relief Aid in Refugee Camps (Hiraan Region/Somali Democratic Republic). *Sozialanthropologische Arbeitspapiere* Nr. 17. Berlin: Das Arabische Buch.

1991a Politisches Gemeinschaftshandeln, bewaffnete Gewalt, soziale Mythen: Die Oromo Liberation Front (OLF) in Aethiopien. In *Ethnizität und Gewalt.* T. Scheffler (ed.), pp. 251-272. Hamburg: Deutsches Orient Institut.

1991b Refugee Aid, Moral Communities and Resource Sharing: A Prelude to Civil War in Somalia. *Sociologus* 41: 119-138.

1993a Violence, pouvoir symbolique et mode de representation des Oromo. *Politique Africaine* 50: 45-58.

1993b Oromo and Islam. The Integration of Two Religious Pasts in a Pan-Movement. Paper submitted to the conference, The Anthropology of Ethnicity, Amsterdam, 15th - 19th December 1993.

1994 *Nation der Oromo: Kollektive Identitäten, nationale Konflikte, Wir-Gruppenbildungen.* Berlin: Das Arabische Buch.

WAR IN THE POST-WORLD WAR II WORLD: SOME EMPIRICAL TRENDS AND A THEORETICAL APPROACH

KLAUS JÜRGEN GANTZEL

Institut für Politische Wissenschaft, Universität Hamburg, Allende-Platz 1, D-20146 Hamburg

During the East-West conflict the term 'war by proxy' was frequently used to explain the roots of 'local wars,' particularly those in or between Third World states. The term was misleading, or even an example of propaganda. It implied that governments and their opponents, such as liberation movements and guerilla groups, were only puppets of major powers. Since the end of the East-West conflict, it has become fashionable to use another term in order to categorize violent conflicts which *prima facie* are not conflicts between states, social classes, interest groups or political parties, namely 'ethnic war.' In order to find out whether the term makes explanatory sense one has to do more than focus on the phenomena themselves. Comparative time-series data and an encompassing conceptual approach are necessary. For this purpose I shall present some empirical findings and a theoretical interpretation as a background for the discussion of the connection between ethnicity and war.[1]

A typology

Any comparative description of reality requires an operationalization of the phenomena. According to our former Hungarian colleague Istvàn Kende (1971:6; 1978:227) we at the *Arbeitsgemeinschaft Kriegsursachenforschung* (AKUF) (Study Group on the Causes of War[2]), define war as any armed

[1] I shall not discuss my own doubts about the usefulness of 'ethnicity' and 'ethnic war' as concepts in social sciences, and in political language. Max Weber suspected that, after precise research on "ethnically conditioned common acting (...) the collective 'ethnic' certainly would be thrown overboard" (1964:313, trans.). Kathrin Eikenberg (1987:69) drew attention to the fact that it was not until the late sixties that social scientists began to apply the term 'ethnic conflict' to unrest in large US cities; to the appearance of militant ethnic minorities and regional movements in Europe struggling for separation from the central state or for greater autonomy; and to the many political crises and violent conflicts in the Third World which came about at the end of decolonization. Because of its origin, I suspect the concept has an ideological background and, in part, a colouring of arrogance or even racism.

[2] The AKUF, located in the Unit for Research on Wars, Armament and Development of the Institute of Political Science, Hamburg University, was founded by the author in 1978 but greatly expanded and intensified its studies after the Carl-von-Ossietzky Guest-

conflict in which all of the following criteria obtain:

- the engagement of regular armed forces of the government (military, police forces, supporting paramilitary forces, etc.) at least on one side;
- a certain degree of organization and organized fighting on both sides, even if this extends to organized defence only; and
- a certain continuity between armed clashes, however sporadic. It is irrelevant whether the fighting takes place on the territory of only one society or one state, or whether it extends to two or more territories.

Like any empirical definition of societal phenomena, our definition creates some difficulties which I cannot discuss here (cf. Gantzel *et al.* 1986:3-11; Gantzel *et al.* 1995:24-48). It is enough to say that we try to avoid too broad a spectrum of collective violence and to preserve the original meaning of 'war.' At least on one side, therefore, the government or the state must directly and actively participate with armed forces, and both sides must be organized and must fight in a planned, organized manner. We do not distinguish, *a priori* between international and domestic war, and we do not use quantitative criteria like number of troops or of casualties. We distinguish between several types of war, as follows.

Type A: Anti-regime wars. These are domestic wars fought against the government in power with the aim of changing the political, or even the whole societal, system (revolution, fundamental reforms, counter-revolution), or to replace a 'bad' government with a 'better' one, or simply to open up access to state benefits for other élite groups.

Type B: Other domestic wars. In most cases these are struggles of a national or regional minority for secession or more autonomy.[3]

Type C: Inter-state wars. These are wars between sovereign states.

Type D: Decolonization wars. These are wars of liberation, fought against colonial powers.

In many wars, two or sometimes three types are combined, or the type changes during the war. We call these cases *mixed types*. In a very few cases (3 out of 184) more than two types are combined simultanously or successively, for instance ABC or ABD; we call these *complex wars.* We recognize that this typology is crude and that it is not always easy to decide

---

Professorship of Istvàn Kende (Budapest, 1917-1988) in 1982, continuing thereafter the work of data collection and trend analysis of war. Presently the AKUF has about 40 members chosen among advanced students who have completed their second academic year, in addition to a few salaried part-time project assistants. Two long-term projects are the most important: (1) the build-up and permanent up-dating of a computerized data-bank on wars and their characteristics; (2) the construction and stepwise typological differentiation of a comparative theory on the causes of war.

3 We are unhappy with the definition of type B wars which we 'inherited' from Kende. It encompasses too many heterogeneous cases to be grouped together in a residual category of 'others.' We have, however, postponed improvement until our theoretical work is more advanced.

into which category a war should be placed. In future we shall try to improve the typology, although any refinement will create new problems.

For each type there are two subtypes: wars *with intervention* (symbolized by '-1') and *without intervention* (symbolized by '-2'), that is, with or without the participation of one or more third parties (other groups of the same or another country; other states). For intervention, only cases in which the third party actively and directly participates in fighting are counted. Other forms of intervention, such as armament sales or gifts, financial aid and support by military advisers are excluded as typological criteria, since otherwise we should hardly find a single war without intervention.

The history of the term 'Third World' reflects changes in global development after World War II. Since the end of the East-West conflict the term has lost much of its original meaning. We continue to use the term because, after the peak of the 'Cold War,' it became a broadly used label for the totality of developing societies. Consequently, the expressions 'First World' and 'Second World' now refer to industrialized societies of the capitalist (or liberal, or Western) type, or of the former socialist (or Eastern) type. The People's Republic of China belongs to the Third World.

Empirical insights[4]

In the period of 48 years from 1945 to 1992, 184 wars occurred. The data collected show (see fig. 5.1) that the annual frequency of war outbreaks oscillates in an irregular way. This irregularity does not differ from previous periods (cf. Small *et al.* 1982). However, the graph which shows the annual number of active wars is significant and, more important, after some ups and downs until the end of the fifties, a constant and considerably increasing trend began. This means that each year since 1960 at the latest, more wars began than ended, and that the new wars lasted longer.[5] The longest of these wars is the war or, more precisely, the complex of interrelated wars, in Burma which started in 1948. At the end of 1992 the trend resulted in a peak of 51 ongoing wars. Table 5.1 presents the situation at the end of 1993, when 42 wars were in progress, with a cumulative total of about 4 million military and civilian deaths. I assume that this disastrous trend will continue, with small oscillations.

Whereas, after World War II and again after the Rejkjavik meeting between Presidents Reagan and Gorbachov, there was great hope of more peace in the world, the contrary has been true. Thus the graph in fig. 1

4 For additional, and more detailed, information, tables and figures cf. Gantzel *et al.* (1995).

5 During the period 1945-1992, in any year there was, on average, nearly one more war than the year before. The linear trend equation is $y = 4.1 + 0.95x$.

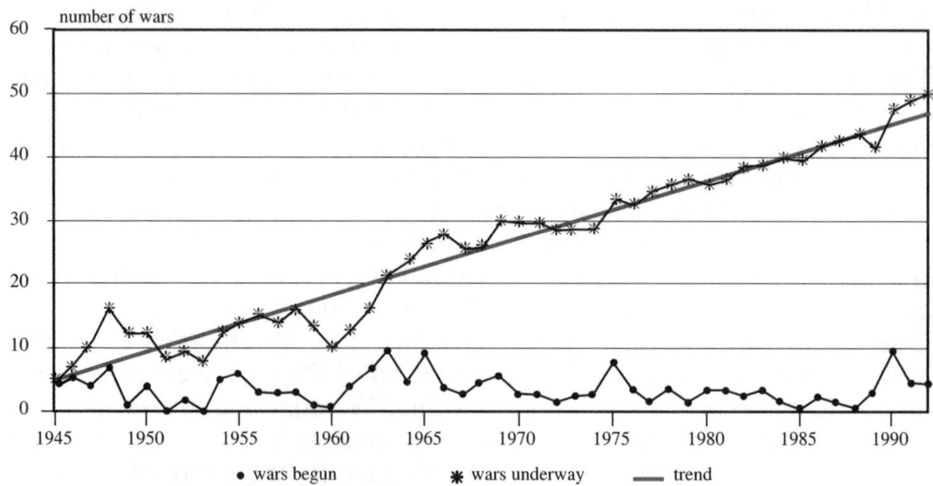

Fig. 5 - 1 - Annual frequency of wars, 1945-1992

allows us to draw two conclusions: (a) war is becoming a 'normal' feature of global development; and (b) the East-West conflict did not have a significant influence on the occurrence of war. One has to look, therefore, for more deeply rooted and longer-term world developments in which the East-West conflict was nothing more than a historical episode.

A more precise indicator shows the yearly total of months the war-affected nations were at war (fig. 5.2). In fact, some wars ended after one or a few months, or broke out later in the year, while others continued throughout the year. This graph shows almost the same trend as the number of ongoing wars in a given year. For the purpose of this chapter we can therefore neglect this more precise indicator.[6]

Figure 5.3 highlights another very important phenomenon: the overwhelming majority of domestic (internal or intra-national) wars. It underscores an essential historical leap. Beginning in the nineteenth century, the proportion of domestic wars began to increase, gradually but constantly. The percentage of inter-state wars, however, remained higher until World War II.[7] Since then the relationship became inverted, as domestic wars became the majority—and an increasing one. All true internal wars since

6 A valid and more precise indicator for the occurrence of war would consist in the number of military and civilian deaths due to war as a measure of the intensity of a war. Even though such data are extremely unreliable, or simply lacking, we are working on this problem to try to improve our data-bank.

7 This relationship is calculated from the database of Small *et al.* (1982) although they operated with another, much more restrictive and partly ideologically biased, definition of international and civil wars. With this reservation in mind, the frequency of international wars relative to internal wars developed as follows: 1816-1899, 1:0.6; 1900-1943, 1:0.9; 1944-1980, 1:1.5 (cf. Gantzel 1987:58).

Table 5.1

*List of ongoing wars in 1993 (as of December 31st, 1993)**

Region and country	Beginning of war		Type of war	Number of deaths
Europe				
Northern Ireland		1969	B-2	3,000
Croatia/Serbia	July	1991	BC-2	>10,000
Bosnia-Herzegovina	March	1992	B-1	>100,000
Africa				
Algeria		1992	A-2	>3,000
Angola	Febr.	1961	ABC-1/A-2	750,000
Ethiopia (Oromos)		1976	AB-2	<10,000
Djibuti	Oct.	1991	AB-2	<1,000
Liberia	Dec.	1989	A-1	>20,000
Mali & Niger (Tuaregs)	May	1990	B-2	1,000
Mozambique		1975	AC-2/A-1	>1,000,000
South Africa	June	1976	AB-2	14,500
Rwanda	Oct.	1990	A-1	5,000
Senegal (Casamance)	April	1990	B-2	200
Somalia	May	1988	AB-1	300,000
Sudan (Southern area)	Sept.	1983	BA-2	260,000
Chad	June	1966	ABC-1	>20,000
Near and Middle East				
Afghanistan	Oct.	1978	A-1/A-2	1,000,000
Armenia/Azerbaijan	Jan.	1990	B-2	16,000
Georgia (Gamsachurdia)	Sept.	1991	A-2	n.k
Georgia (Abkasia)	Aug.	1992	B-2	2,000
Iraq (Curds)	May	1976	BA-1	7,000
Iraq (Shiites)	March	1991	A-2	12,000
Lebanon	April	1975	ABC-1	150,000
Israel (Palestine)		1968	B-2	12,300
Russia (Northern Ossetia)		1992	B-2	340
Tadzhikistan	Aug.	1992	A-1	15,000
Turkey (Curds)	Aug.	1984	B-2	10,000
Asia				
Bangladesh (Chittagong Hills)		1973	B-2	>2,000
Burma, or Myanmar	Jan.	1948	AB-2	>15,000
India (Kashmir)	Jan.	1990	B-2	>7,000
India (Punjab)	July	1982	B-2	20,000
Indonesia (East Timor)	Aug.	1975	B-2	70,000
Cambodia	Dec.	1975	C-2/A-1	>26,000
Papua New Guinea (Bougainville Island)	Febr.	1989	B-2	6,000
Philippines (Mindanao Island)		1970	B-2	>21,000
Philippines (New Peoples Army)		1970	A-2	>25,000
Sri Lanka (Tamils)	July	1983	B-2/AB-1/B-1	>25,000
Latin America				
Guatemala		1980	A-2	100,000
Colombia (FARC)	May	1964	A-2	15,000
Colombia (ELN)	Jan.	1965	A-2	n.k.
Peru (Sendero Luminoso)	May	1980	A-2	30,000
Peru (MRTA)	Nov.	1987		n.k.
Totals		42 wars		approx. >4,978,000

* Armed conflicts which do not fit all definitional criteria of war were not included.

Symbols and abbreviations:

A = anti-régime war; B = other domestic war; C = interstate war;
-1 = with outside intervention; -2 = without outside intervention.
> = more than; < = less than; n.k. = not known.

Source: Arbeitsgemeinschaft Kriegsursachenforschung
c/o Research Unit War, Armament and Development,
Institute of Political Science, Hamburg University,
Allende-Platz 1, D-20146 Hamburg.

For more detailed information on above wars see: Siegelberg (1991); Gantzel *et al.* (1992). and Gantzel *et al.* (1994).

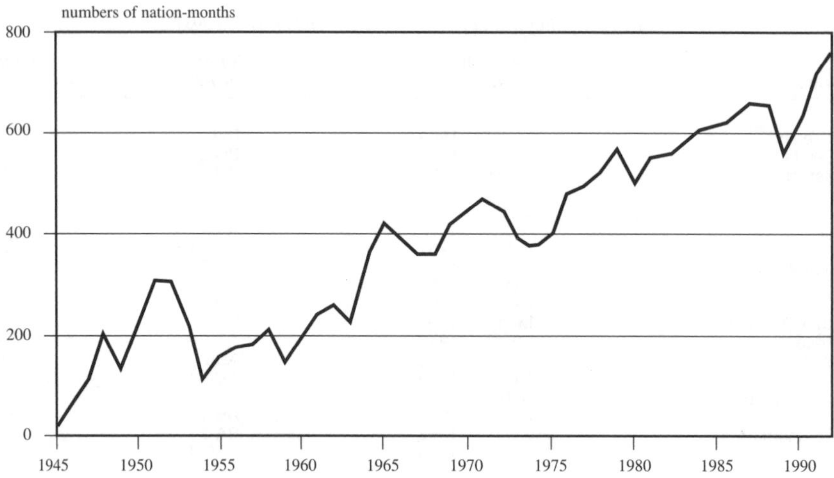

Fig. 5.2 - Annual nation-months of ongoing wars, 1945-1992

1945 taken together, including mixed AB-types, amount to two thirds (66 per cent) of all wars, while international wars, including wars of decolonization, count for less than a quarter (23 per cent); a further 11 per cent are intra- and international mixed or complex wars.

Figure 5.4 shows the same phenomenon in a time series graph. It is very clear that the increase in the yearly occurrence of wars is essentially caused by the growth and duration of domestic wars. On the other hand, the proportion of ongoing international wars decreases slowly after the mid-seventies.[8] It is not surprising, therefore, that the proportion of domestic-international mixed type wars is increasing too, but more slowly than pure domestic wars. It is possible that in the near future the number of inter-state wars, particularly in the south-Caucasian region and in south-eastern Europe, will increase because of the recent dissolution of the Soviet empire and of socialist systems. It is likely, however, that most formal inter-state disputes, about borders for example, will be solved fairly soon, while internal conflicts concerning political power and social integration will continue. Mainly since World War II, the international community has developed many regulations, procedures, mechanisms and organizations which, although as yet insufficient, make the settling of inter-state quarrels easier. The international community of states and organizations is, however, mostly helpless when dealing with domestic wars. The structure of the UN, of international law, and of international military 'police' forces, composed more or less accidentally from case to case, are hardly appropriate for the

8 One has to keep in mind also that the 12 decolonization wars are counted as 'international wars.' The period of formal political decolonization has been a specific historical phenomenon. It ended after the mid-sixties.

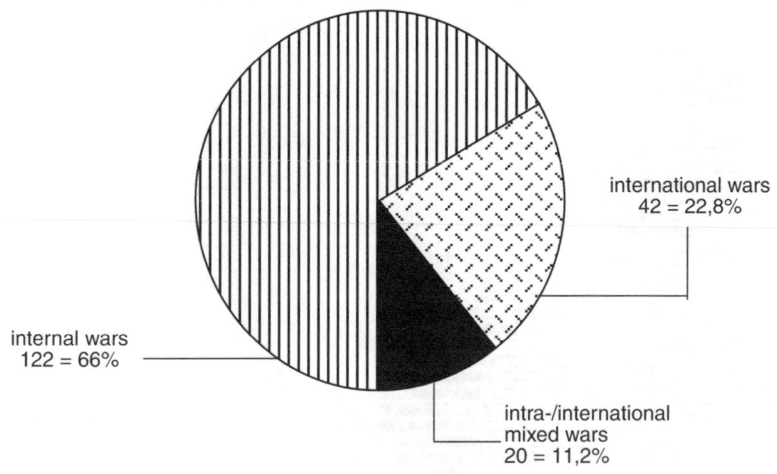

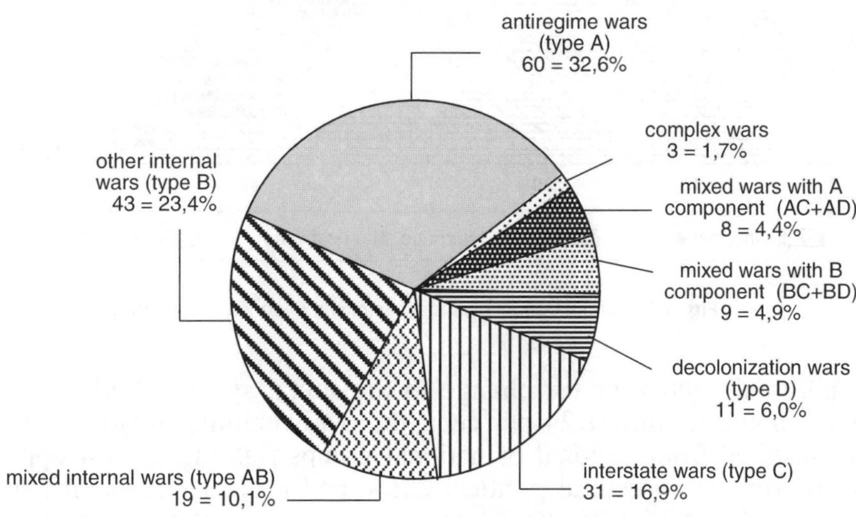

Fig. 5.3 - Frequencies of types of war, 1945 -1992

solution of internal disputes, although improvements may be expected.[9]

Returning to domestic wars (see fig. 5.3), one can see that most of the internal clashes consist in anti-regime wars (32 per cent), that is, struggles

9 Developments in the field of Human Rights and their growing relevance for political legitimacy are important indications of this.

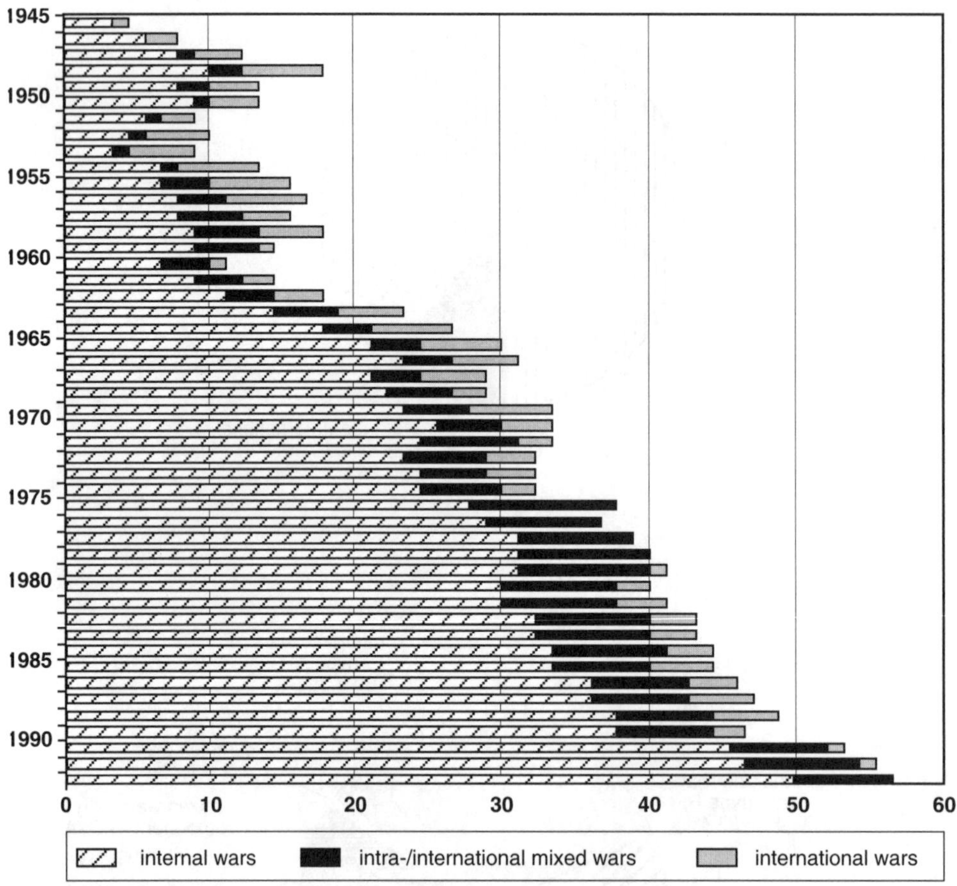

Fig. 5.4 - Annual frequencies of types of war underway, 1945-1992

for political control or for change in the social system. 'Other domestic wars' amount to almost 24 per cent, the overwhelming majority of which have resulted from regional or national groups fighting against oppressive and discriminatory central political élites, or for greater autonomy or even secession. In addition to the 10 per cent of wars in the AB category, one should also take into account the 11 per cent of intra- and international mixed wars which have an A or B component. Bearing in mind that about 93 per cent of all wars since 1945 were, or are still being, fought in the Third World, we suggest that these statistics are the expression of a general historical process of state-consolidation, nation-building and modernization. As the histories of the highly developed societies of Western Europe and North America illustrate, this process is always conflictual and violent.

Figure 5.5 presents wars with or without interventions. First of all, it is obvious that the great majority of wars are free from direct intervention. In spite of our restrictive definition of intervention, this empirical finding contradicts the popular impression. It parallels the suggestion just made about the general background of the majority of internal wars. The diagram of percentages, on the other hand, underscores the global importance of state-formation processes in the Third World: anti-regime wars, in addition to all mixed types with an A component, are relatively more liable to intervention than other types of war.

Table 5.2 shows that Third-World wars, that is, wars without any direct intervention by states of the 'First' or 'Second' World, amount to three quarters (76 per cent) of all wars. Table 5.3 is even more interesting, since it shows that the frequency of interventions by industrial powers in Third-World wars is decreasing significantly. The developing world is more and more 'at war with itself.'

Table 5.4 shows that Asia is the leading region with respect to the number of wars since 1945.[10] This relates mainly to South and South-East Asia, whereas the Far East has been almost free of war since the end of the fifties. Africa and the Middle East are ranked in second and third place. These three regions suffer most from the consequences of colonialism and from problems of socioeconomic development. Latin America, including the Caribbean, follows at some distance. This is the region where decolonization, with few exceptions, dates back about 170 years and where, on the whole, the process of state-building and state-consolidation is considerably more advanced than in several parts of Asia and Africa.[11] In Europe only twelve wars occurred, although this region has been the germ-cell of two world wars in our century,[12] and all the Post-World-War-II wars

---

[10] It is quite complicated to draw reasonable boundaries between regions or to subdivide the continents into regions. It is not a question of geography but of political, economic, social and cultural aspects. The considerable difficulties cannot be discussed here. From the beginning of our project we always made a clear distinction between North America (the USA and Canada), Central America (including Mexico and the Carribean) and South America. After criticisms of our previous publications, we have subdivided Africa into five regions. We now have the problem of how to subdivide Europe (into two or three regions?), South-/South-East Asia (into three regions, including Oceania?) and the Near and Middle East (i.e. the region from Egypt to Afghanistan, including Eastern parts of Turkey) where it is hardly possible to make any reasonable subdivision because of interconnected systems and conflicts. We have just started a project in order to make theoretically valid subdivisions. Our region-related statistics in Table 5.4 should, therefore, be read with caution. The detailed statistics on Africa should be understood more as an indication of methodological problems than as an important insight.

[11] The case of Haiti should not be taken as a counter-argument.

[12] In my opinion, these world wars, viewed from the standpoint of the epochal structuring of world-history, belong more to the 19th than to the 20th century. The first real 'world wars' took place in the 16th and 17th century between England and Spain, and between England and the Netherlands.

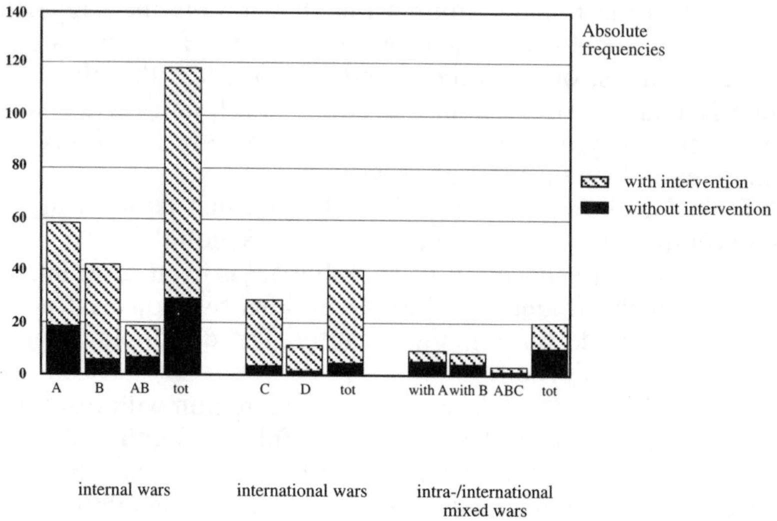

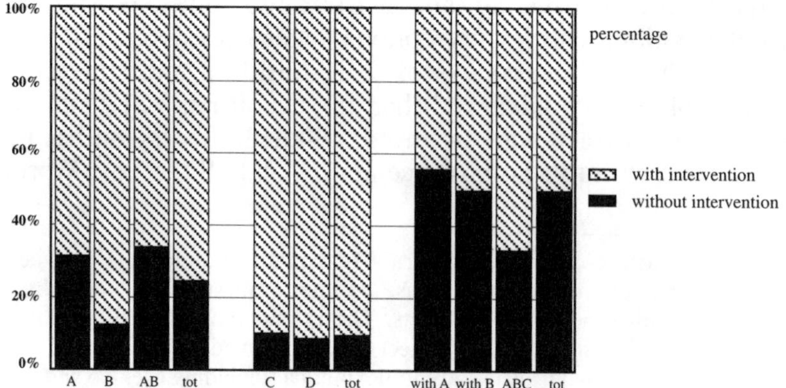

Fig. 5.5 - Frequencies of war types with or without intervention, 1945-1992

in Europe occurred on its peripheries (Greece [2 wars], Spain [2 wars], Cyprus [3 wars], Hungary, Northern Ireland, Rumania, Moldavia, ex-Yugoslavia).[13] Like the highly industrialized countries of Europe, Canada and the United States were immune from war within their territories. We should not forget, however, that even East Asia has experienced no wars[14]

13 The war between Turkey and the Kurds belongs to the Near East.

14 The Chinese invasion of India in 1962 and the Chinese war against Vietnam (to aid Cambodia against the Vietnamese invasion) are counted among South/South-East Asian wars.

Table 5.2

Frequency of wars in the Third World, 1945-1992

Third World wars	Intranational wars	International wars*	Intra-/Internat. mixed wars	Totals n	%
Without outside intervention	84	20	4	108	63
With interventions of Third World countries only	16	1	6	23	13
Total endogenous Third World wars	**100**	**21**	**10**	**131**	**76**
Third World wars with interventions of 'First' or 'Second' world countries	12	22	7	41	24
Total Third World wars	**112**	**43**	**17**	**172**	**100**

* Inter-state and decolonization wars.

Table 5.3

Percentage development of Third World wars by decades, 1945-92

Third World wars	1945-54 %	1955-64 %	1965-74 %	1975-84 %	1985-92 %
Without outside intervention	38	45	74	59	82
With interventions of Third World countries only	3	10	13	27	11
Third World wars with interventions by 'First' or 'Second' World countries	59	45	13	14	7
Totals	**100**	**100**	**100**	**100**	**100**

Table 5.4

Regional distribution of wars, 1945-92

Region		Frequency of wars n	%
North America	-	-	
Europe		12	6.5
Central America incl. Mexico and the Caribbean		15	8.2
South America		14	7.6
Near and Middle East		41	22.3
South and South-East Asia		47	25.5
Hither India	20		
Farther India	13		
Other SE Asia and Oceania	14		
East Asia		7	3.8
Africa		48	26.1
Northern Africa	9		
West Africa	8		
Central Africa	10		
East Africa	13		
Southern Africa	8		
Totals		**184**	**100.0**

since the early sixties. This has been due mainly to the provisional territorial and structural consolidation of the People's Republic of China, the internal reforms of Taiwan, the US-protected freeze in the conflict between South and North Korea and the strength of the Japanese peace economy.

Shifting from war as the unit of analysis to the countries affected by war, Table 5.5 shows that the United Kingdom, the United States and France belong to the group with highest frequencies of war involvement since 1945.[15] This seems to contradict what has just been said, but all the wars in question took place outside the core territories of these states (except for the war in Northern Ireland).[16] Whenever the UK and France waged war, as was the case for Belgium, the Netherlands or Portugal, they did so in their colonies, to defend their colonial influence, or they intervened in the internal struggles of their ex-colonies, in some cases even on behalf of the UN. The colonial maps are still implanted in governmental brains. The frequent war involvement of the USA can be explained by two factors. In the first place, the US on several occasions behaved like a colonial power towards Latin America and the Caribbean, or at least claimed to control the Western Hemisphere. In the second place, since 1945 the US has been the leading Western hegemonic power, its global commitment being the consequence of its role of securing and safeguarding the 'free' world, that is, the capitalist world system.[17]

The list in Table 5.5 shows another interesting fact: the seven members of the highest ranked group account for nearly a quarter of all national war involvements since 1945. If we add only nineteen further countries, with seven or five involvements apiece, we can account for 52 per cent of all war participations. The remaining 48 per cent are accounted for by 93 other countries.[18] While we can see a fairly strong concentration of war involvement among a few countries, we cannot categorize these countries according to any recognizable pattern. They include major and minor powers; large and small countries; highly and less developed societies;

---

15 'War involvement' includes participation as one of the two conflicting parties and direct intervention, whether as part of UN forces or not.

16 As to the 1982 war in the Falklands or Malvinas between Argentina and the UK, international lawyers may object that these distant islands are part of the UK, not a colony, even though many more sheep live there than British subjects. In the context of our world-historical view, the lawyers' argument is irrelevant.

17 It is not important whether the US fulfilled this function well or not, and whether it also pursued national interests within that role. On the other hand there is the historical irony of any hegemonic system: the leading role of the US finally damaged its own economy, whereas the protected smaller capitalist societies saved a lot of costs.

18 At the end of 1992 there existed 191 generally acknowledged states, not all of them UN members, and many tiny states with less than 500,000 inhabitants. Based on this number, two thirds of all countries in the world have experienced war since 1945.

Table 5.5

Frequencies of war involvements by country, 1945-92

Rank	Country	Frequency of war involvement** n	%
1.	United Kingdom	18	4.8
2.	India	14	4.2
3.	Iraq	12	3.2
	United States of America	12	3.2
4.	France	11	2.9
5.	China, or PR of China	10	2.7
6.	Syria	8	2.1
Total (7 countries)		**87**	**23.3**
7.	Ethiopia	7	1.9
	Zaire	7	1.9
	Indonesia	7	1.9
	Israel	7	1.9
	Pakistan	7	1.9
	South Africa	7	1.8*
	Egypt (United Arab Rep.)	7	1.8*
Cumulated totals (14 countries)		**136**	**36.4**
8.	Democratic PR of Yemen	5	1.4*
	Yemen (Arab Rep., incl. of Yemen Rep.)	5	1.4*
	Colombia	5	1.4*
	Greece	5	1.4*
	Iran	5	1.3
	Laos	5	1.3
	Nigeria	5	1.3
	Philippines	5	1.3
	Thailand	5	1.3
	Turkey	5	1.3
	USSR or Russian Federation	5	1.3
	Vietnam (united)	5	1.3
Cumulated totals (26 countries)		**196**	**52.4**
9.	Belgium	4	1.1
	Costa Rica	4	1.1
	Honduras	4	1.1
	Jordan	4	1.1
	Cuba	4	1.1
	Morocco	4	1.1
	Nicaragua	4	1.1
	Vietnam (united)	4	1.0*
	Peru	4	1.0*
	Spain	4	1.0*
Cumulated totals (36 countries)		**236**	**63.1**
10.	Algeria	3	0.8
	Australia	3	0.8
	El Salvador	3	0.8
	Georgia	3	0.8
	Guatemala	3	0.8
	Lebanon	3	0.8
	Libya	3	0.8
	New Zealand	3	0.8
	Netherlands	3	0.8
	Portugal	3	0.8
	Saudi Arabia	3	0.8
	Somalia	3	0.8
	Sudan	3	0.8
	South Vietnam	3	0.8
	Taiwan	3	0.8
	Tanzania	3	0.8
	Uganda	3	0.8
	Zimbabwe (formerly Rhodesia)	3	0.8
Cumulated totals (54 countries)		**290**	**77.5**
11.	19 countries with two involvements each	38	10.2
12.	46 countries with one involvement each	46	12.3
Cumulated totals (119 countries)		**374**	**100.0**

* Percentages indicated by an asterisk have been increased or decreased by 0.1 to make the sums conform to the partial totals while avoiding an excess of fractional figures. However, it is understood that they are no different from the other percentages in the same section.

** Actions on behalf of the UN are included since they actually led to participation in direct combat as, for instance, in the Korean War, in the Second Gulf War against Iraq, and in Somalia.

democracies, and authoritarian regimes and even dictatorships; ethnically homogeneous and heterogeneous societies; and states with and without regional, imperial or hegemonic aspirations. We therefore need to delve deeper to find an encompassing theoretical approach.

We have not yet categorized the causes of war. This is the most difficult task and it presupposes a further development of the theory we are working with. Table 5.6 presents a preliminary taxonomy of the conflicts which have been at the root of wars since 1945. Since nearly all wars were caused by several types of conflicts, the number of conflicts shown in Table 5.6 (294) is higher than the number of wars (184). The largest number of conflicts concerned territorial questions,[19] and the majority of these were about autonomy, or secession from the central state. The second largest group comprises heterogeneous cases which have in common only the fact that they are single-issue conflicts. These issues are: change in the governing party, distraction from other problems or crises, specific resource conflicts, ethnic confrontations,[20] and disputes about military-strategic positions. The latter include fighting between China and Taiwan for islands of military importance, the Chinese offensive against Vietnam (1979-1988) to support the Khmer Rouge in Cambodia against the Vietnamese and the war of attrition between Egypt and Israel in the Western part of occupied Sinai (1969-1970). In the third group, the actors are fighting for revolution, reform or restoration of the system. The fourth and smallest group contains conflicts which are directly involved with colonialism and with situations where one side is struggling for hegemony or for greater influence over another country or a whole region.

The regional distribution of kinds of conflict seems to be symptomatic. System conflicts are most frequent in Latin America and partly in the southern and south-eastern regions of Asia. In Europe, revolutionary or reformist ambitions and 'national' questions (Cyprus, Northern Ireland, the Basques) prevailed. In Africa, conflict was mostly concerned with

---

[19] Disputes over territory (space) are often only the concrete 'material' expression of temporarily uneven phases of socioeconomic development.

[20] We have found ethnic confrontations to be an original cause of war in three cases only, the conflict between Hutu and Tutsi in Burundi and Rwanda being the most outstanding example. But even here, the very long quasi-feudal history of conflict between immigrating nomads (Tutsi) and autochthonous peasants (Hutu), the misuse of these tensions by colonial powers and recent economic, political, social and foreign (Uganda) conditions have been very important in triggering these wars. The low number of 'tribal' confrontations does not mean that ethnic factors are irrelevant to the outbreak of war; on the contrary, they play a role in many wars. We have to remember, however, our definition of war, which presupposes a state apparatus as an actor at least on one side. Secondly, rivals for power often make use of ethnic differences as a political resource, but the differences themselves are not responsible for war. Thus specific mobilization strategies are a cause of war, not ethnic cleavages *per se* (cf. Tetzlaff *et al.* 1992).

Table 5.6

Types of conflict at the root of wars, 1945-92

Type of conflict	Regions* 1	2	3	4	5	6	7	Totals n	%
Total change of system (revolution)	2	5	3	3	4	13	3	33	11.2
Basic reforms	7	5	3	1	5	4	-	25	8.5
System restoration (counter-revolution)	4	-	-	-	3	3	-	10	3.4
Totals of system conflicts	**13**	**10**	**6**	**4**	**12**	**20**	**3**	**68**	**23.1**
Replacement of government without change of system	4	3	-	21	7	1	-	36	12.2
Outlet for other domestic problems	1	1	-	1	2	1	-	6	2.0
Conflict on special particular interests	-	3	-	11	2	4	-	20	6.8
True ethnic conflict	-	-	-	2	1	-	-	3	1.0
Military strategic motives	-	-	-	1	8	3	3	15	5.1
Totals of single issue conflicts	**5**	**7**	**-**	**35**	**20**	**9**	**3**	**79**	**27.0**
Territorial expansion	-	-	-	1	5	4	4	14	4.8
Restoration of previous borders	-	-	1	-	10	3	1	15	5.1
Revision of existing borders	-	-	2	2	6	6	5	- 21	7.1
Secession or more autonomy	1	1	6	14	13	19	1	55	18.7
Totals of territorial conflicts	**1**	**3**	**9**	**21**	**34**	**31**	**6**	**105**	**35.7**
Colonial rule or decolonization	-	-	1	13	1	4	-	19	6.5
Regional influence or hegemony	4	-	1	-	10	7	-	22	7.5
Totals of conflicts on foreign dominance	**4**	**-**	**2**	**13**	**11**	**11**	**-**	**41**	**13.9**
Grand Totals	**23**	**20**	**17**	**74**	**77**	**71**	**12**	**294**	**100.0**

*

1 = Central America incl. Mexico and the Caribbean
2 = South America
3 = Europe
4 = Africa
5 = Near and Middle East
6 = South- and South-East Asia
7 = Far East

decolonization and, later, with political power, competition between special interests, and ambitions for secession or autonomy. The Middle East is affected mainly by territorial disputes and regional hegemonic aspirations, but many of the other kinds of conflict also play a role here. The main reasons for conflict in South and South-East Asia were again problems of national minorities and of revolutionary attempts, mainly until the end of the Vietnam War and the Vietnamese military retreat from Cambodia. As for the Far East, territorial disputes, revolutionary ambitions and calculations of military strategy were most frequent.

To complete the picture, Table 5.7 provides a glance at the ways wars ended. No clear trend appears. On the whole, two modes prevail: mediation by third parties, mostly the UN or regional governmental organizations, such as the OAU, the OAS or the Arab League; or a military victory of the side which was originally attacked. Only 24, or 18 per cent, of the 130 wars which ended were concluded by the military victory of the aggressor. It seems that military aggression no longer pays, and that there is a broad interest on the part of third parties all over the world to end wars. Let us hope that this fact may be clearly remembered by actors who wage war and that it may have some peacemaking effect. In spite of these hopeful

Table 5.7

How wars ended

Type of end of war	1945-54		1955-64		1965-74		1975-84		1985-92		Totals	
	n	%	n	%	n	%	n	%	n	%	n	%
Military victory of the attacking or war initiating side	8	33	2	6	2	6	5	25	7	33	24	18
Military victory of the defending side	7	29	13	39	10	31	7	35	2	10	39	30
Breaking off the fighting	1	4	5	15	1	3	1	5	2	10	10	8
Agreement without mediation from a third party	1	4	3	9	6	19	2	10	3	14	15	12
Mediation by a third party	7	29	10	30	13	41	4	20	7	33	41	32
Unknown	-	-	-	-	-	-	1	5	-	-	1	1
Totals	**24**	**100**	**33**	**100**	**32**	**100**	**20**	**100**	**21**	**100**	**130**	**100**

tendencies, data which are not presented here lead me to inject a drop of pessimism. Mediation is most successful in ending inter-state wars, that is, wars which represent a relatively small and decreasing proportion of all wars, which are relatively short and which cause relatively fewer casualties. Domestic wars, on the other hand, are mostly the result of world-historical developments and change in basic structures, which can hardly be influenced by the goodwill of mediators.

Theoretical approach

Comparative research on the causes of war has achieved virtually no cumulative results since the 1920s, when systematic empirical investigations began. The results are 'atomistic' and often contradictory because of different empirical indicators, even for the same aspects, and because of the different time periods and regions under investigation.[21] The reasons include ideological biases, different methodological premises and theoretical approaches, badly integrated levels of analysis and incompatible definitions and frames of reference. I cannot go into details about all this here, but would like to stress one important point.

Since wars have taken place throughout human history, they seem to be a universal phenomenon, an anthropological 'constant,' as some ethologists would have us believe. That, of course, is a very superficial conclusion. Nobody will deny that war is a social phenomenon, and all must acknowledge that societies are changing and therefore possess an historical

[21] It is significant that a greater effort appears to have been made (through, for example, the publication of overviews and compilations of abstracts) to sum up the 'state of the art' in this field, with its tiny group of researchers from the international community, than in almost any other field of social science research.

nature. It follows that war has a historical nature too. There is no doubt that the structures of societies, the interests and aims of war-waging actors, the norms and means of warfare and the circumstances and consequences of war have changed significantly since the beginning of human history. Nevertheless, in comparative research on the causes of war, the *historicity* of war has been widely neglected. This is not the same methodological point made in traditional historiography, namely that any event is a unique one and that no event can be compared with another. The very opposite is implied, namely a social theory, or at least a frame of reference based on systematic general categories, in which the historical-developmental aspect is reconstructed with respect to different epochs and which takes into account the structural dynamics which condition the emergence and behaviour of actors.[22]

Since World War II, the highly industrialized countries have been almost immune from war in their own territories and have experienced only a few, and mostly low-intensity, wars on their peripheries. All these societies are of the capitalist type and may be described by the following attributes: a highly differentiated system of work specialization, based on the private ownership of the means of production and labour; exchange is coordinated and regulated mainly through markets; the use of violence is monopolized by the state and legitimated and limited by law; democratic participation by the public; a well functioning and controlled bureaucratic apparatus; stable social integration as a consequence of complex interdependencies and of welfare policy; conflict regulation based on a consensus about certain basic principles; strong self-discipline; and loyalty to the law by both governed and governing. Let us call them 'civil societies.'[23]

For about 50 years they have enjoyed sustained peace domestically and they no longer wage war among themselves. This is the end-result of a development which lasted almost a millennium, having started in the early Middle Ages. This historical process was analyzed by Karl Marx with respect to economic dynamics; by Norbert Elias with respect to the monopolization of violence by the state and the parallel process of individual self-control of emotional impulses and by Max Weber through his precise definitions and conceptualizations.[24] Until about the middle of this

---

22 In the following paragraphs our theoretical approach is only sketchily outlined. For more details and reasons, cf. Gantzel *et al.* 1991; Jung 1995; Siegelberg 1994.

23 This characterization does not imply that the most developed capitalist part of the world is like paradise. Indeed, it has many deficiencies. Even present capitalist development in North America, Western Europe or Japan has not reached its peak. The notion of 'Late Capitalism,' frequently used by the 'Left' in the late sixties and during the seventies, was borrowed from Leninist wishful thinking and did not have any substance.

24 It is impossible to describe these theories and the corresponding historical processes here (cf. Elias 1980; Marx 1857/58, 1867, 1894; Siegelberg 1994; Weber 1964).

century, the process was very violent and bloody. Capitalism, in the end, brings peace, but its realization in its European cradle and its penetration of traditional societies all over the world has been quite violent. The process of creating the conditions for capitalism is always accompanied by war and other forms of violence, but capitalism itself tends to non-violent forms of conflict because violence is counter-productive to its economic, political and social interests.

Moreover, as I suggested some time ago (Gantzel 1972:117 ff.), the socialist counter-model in the Soviet Union and other East European states may be considered a special form of the so-called North-South conflict. It has been obvious since 1989/1990 that the socialist experiment has failed; it was nothing more than an episode in history. There is no alternative to the model of capitalist, bourgeois society, or civil society, in the foreseeable future.[25] As already mentioned, that formation of society has already penetrated, or at least deeply affected, all the world populations. 'Civil society' must serve as the theoretical yardstick, a kind of *tertium comparationis*. All developments in the Third World and all observed triggering factors and causes of wars must be compared and interpreted by that yardstick.[26] For historical reasons, this yardstick must take into account the uneven speeds and the specific conditions and strategies of development in different countries and regions. From this point of view, the wars in the Third World today resemble wars in the feudal and early bourgeois periods in Europe. Some initial conditions for the Third World are different, of course, and I shall return to them.

---

[25] Even if formulated in an extreme form, a well known passage in the analytical part of the *Communist Manifesto* clearly highlights the irresistible drive of the capitalist economic system. The passage begins with the following sentence: "The need of a constantly expanding market for its products chases the bourgeoisie over the whole surface of the globe," and it ends with these words: "Independent, or but loosely connected provinces, with separate interests, laws, governments and systems of taxation, became lumped together into one nation, with one government, one code of laws, one national class-interest, one frontier and one customs-tariff" (Marx/Engels, 1848:38-40).

[26] Because of this point of departure, we are often accused of being 'eurocentric.' Indeed, we are. We do not have any other choice (apart from the psychological and intellectual limits of cultural empathy). Beginning with the Portuguese during the reign of Henry the Navigator (1394-1460) followed by Columbus and others, Europeans have conquered the world and, gradually, they have impressed their laws of reproduction and development on all the people of the world. The implosion of the Soviet Union and the Eastern bloc is the most recent evidence of the above trend, and even the 'old men' of the People's Republic of China or of North Korea must envisage their own twilight. On the other hand, US hegemony also seems to be on the wane, and the exercise of hegemonic power has tended to become a difficult collective effort between North America, Western Europe, and Japan. After a few decades, some East-European countries and some 'Newly Industrializing Countries' in Latin America, Asia and Africa may be added to the list.

I should like to sum up our general theoretical approach with the following quotation from a previous publication (cf. Gantzel *et al.* 1991:22-3).[27]

> According to the view set out above, the bloody process of global expansion and development of capitalist socialization (*Vergesellschaftung*), which has led to peaceable forms of social intercourse in Europe since the 15th century...is still in full swing in peripheral societies. Since the end of the process of decolonization, however, the capitalist transformation of pre-bourgeois living conditions has no longer been taking place in the form of a process coercively imposed from outside by colonialism and imperialism. With the independence of peripheral societies as formally sovereign states, the more developed forms of global socialization created the conditions by which the—always conflicting—forging ahead of capitalist living conditions became mainly an internal matter of these states. The subsequent consolidation of superimposed statehood has become the task of the heterogeneous social forces inside these states. Thus the social conflicts bound up with the horizontal and vertical penetration by capitalism have become the 'Third World's' own 'endogenous' problem. The form of the dissemination of capitalist socialization within these societies does not differ fundamentally from the forms known to us from European history—since the horizontal and vertical form of this dissemination is the only societal form by which the contradiction develops between use-value and exchange-value within the commodity as a product of labour....
>
> However, one should not ignore the elementary differences in the conditions determining the European process of development in the past and the present process of transformation. It makes a difference whether this process develops from inside or is imposed from outside, whether it develops gradually or rapidly, whether it creates the world market or results from it, whether the form of government is organic or has been implanted, etc.; it makes a difference when and in what form capitalist penetration begins, whether capital has already developed or is still in the process of developing, and so on; and above all it makes a difference against which existing forms of social life the revolutionizing forces of capital are running. In all these aspects the original European process of the development of capitalism differs from the present forms of its global advancement. And it is precisely the quite different pre-capitalist living conditions which leave their mark not only on cultural differences in these societies but also on their different ways of settling social conflict.
>
> From the point of view of historical epochs, three structural lines of conflict are thus discernible as causes of war in the 'Third World': (1) lines of conflict carried over from traditional and partly pre-colonial relationships; (2) lines of conflict resulting from the contradiction between capitalist and traditional socialization; (3) lines of conflict resulting from the inherent contradictions of capitalist socialization itself.... The main causes of most of the hostile conflicts in the 'Third World' can be reconstructed from a combination of these structural elements....

As to the differences between European history and the process of transformation in our time, I would like to add that, even in Europe and North America, the origins, forms, cultural conditions, strategies, and speed

---

[27] I did not translate this article, which was originally published in German. I have changed a few sentences and phrases in the passage quoted.

of capitalist modernization were different and uneven; but in the end these societies became very similar, and the process is continuing.[28] Nobody planned this history. Once set in motion, the dynamics of capitalism dissolve all traditional forms of societal structure and reproduction. The societies of the Third (and 'Second') World started out on the long road to capitalist socialization with preconditions which differ from the previous European ones. The following conditions are particularly important and can explain why most wars since 1945 have been domestic wars.

(a) Whereas in Europe the modern state was able to grow slowly out of feudal struggles, absolutism and then democratization, most Third World countries have inherited from the colonial era a state apparatus and, particularly, modern armed forces without an adequate social basis and rules of behaviour. The state here is nothing more than a shell: it is not a rationally working apparatus. A modern rational, legal, stable and legitimate system of government cannot be created on the spur of the moment.

(b) A bourgeois class which, as in Europe, could accumulate private capital by economic activities, often under the protection of kings or princes interested in taxes and credits, is generally lacking. The colonial powers were not interested in creating indigenous middle classes which would limit their own profit and future investments. Very often, therefore, state power and force are used for private enrichment. And because those groups which are excluded from the state fleshpots have almost no chance of coming to power by democratic procedures, they try to do so by violent ones. It will be very interesting to see whether a bourgeois class emerges from the enriched state class.

(c) While Europeans conquered the rest of the world, destroyed traditional economies and social relations, substituted for them a dependent colonial economy and created the world market, the Third World with its weak and deformed economies is confronted with an already existing world market, dominated by industrialized nations and transnational corporations.

(d) Although the colonial or semi-colonial economies mobilized large parts of the population, they hardly contributed to the continuous increase of functional differentiation and the division of labour, both of which are preconditions for social interdependence, integration and self-discipline (cf. Elias 1980). On the contrary, large portions of the population are uprooted but cannot be absorbed by modern sectors of the economy. Old integrating social values have been destroyed or have lost their original social functions, but modern values cannot work without adequate material living conditions. For this reason it is almost impossible to build up mass political parties based on rational common interests, a secular ideology and loyalty to state and law. Political leaders, or those who want to achieve power, therefore,

---

[28] For example, the banishing of words of Anglo-Saxon origin by the French Minister for Cultural Affairs two years ago is nothing more than a joke of history.

often make use of ethnic, religious, or other cultural attributes in order to attract followers. This is fatal for the development of a pluralist party system because, while it is possible to change interests, programmes and ideology, it is not possible to change ethnic characteristics quickly. The unavoidable, disintegrating effects of relatively rapid but incomplete capitalist modernization produce 'political ethnicity' and 'ethnic war,' as well as religious fundamentalism and separatist nationalism.

Acknowledgements—I am very grateful to Torsten Schwinghammer and Wilhelm Nolte who prepared the tables and figures from the AKUF data bank on wars, to my collaborator Klaus Schlichte for suggestions about the concept of ethnicity, to my collaborator Jens Siegelberg for his contributions to the general theoretical outline and to all the students and project collaborators of AKUF for collecting the data and their efforts to create a theory of the causes of war, one of the scourges of mankind.

References

Eikenberg, K.
1987 Ethnische Konflikte in der Dritten Welt. In *Jahrbuch Dritte Welt 1987*. Deutsches Uebersee-Institut Hamburg (ed.), pp. 69-83. Munich: Beck.

Elias, N.
1980 *Ueber den Prozess der Zivilisation. Soziogenetische und psychogenetische Untersuchungen*. 1st vol.: Wandlungen des Verhaltens in den weltlichen Oberschichten des Abendlandes. 2nd vol.: Wandlungen der Gesellschaft, Entwurf zu einer Theorie der Zivilisation. Frankfurt am Main: Suhrkamp.

Gantzel, K. J.
1972 Zu herrschaftssoziologischen Problembereichen von Abhaengigkeitsbeziehungen in der gegenwärtigen Weltgesellschaft. In *Imperialismus und strukturelle Gewalt - Analysen ueber abhaengige Reproduktion*. D. Senghaas (ed.), pp. 105-120. Frankfurt am Main: Suhrkamp.

1987 Tolstoi statt Clausewitz!? Überlegungen zum Verhältnis von Staat und Krieg seit 1816 mittels statistischer Beobachtungen. In *Kriegsursachen*. R. Steinweg (ed.), pp. 25-97. Frankfurt am Main: Suhrkamp.

Gantzel, K. J., & J. Meyer-Stamer (eds.)
1986 *Die Kriege nach dem Zweiten Weltkrieg bis 1984. Daten und erste Analysen*. Munich: Weltforum Verlag.

Gantzel, K. J., & J. Siegelberg
1991 War and Development. Theorizing about the Causes of War, with Particular Reference to the Post-1945 Period. *Law and State: A Biannual Collection of Recent German Contributions to These Fields*. No. 44: 7-29.

Gantzel, K. J., T. Schwinghammer & J. Siegelberg
1992 *Kriege der Welt. Ein systematisches Register der kriegerischen Konflikte 1985 bis 1992*. Bonn: Stiftung Entwicklung & Frieden.

Gantzel, K. J., & K. Schlichte
1994 *Das Kriegsgeschehen 1993. Daten und Tendenzen der Kriege und bewaffneten Konflikte im Jahr 1993.* Bonn: Stiftung Entwicklung und Frieden.

Gantzel, K. J., & T. Schwinghammer
1995 *Die Kriege nach dem Zweiten Weltkrieg bis 1992. Daten und Tendenzen.* Muenster, Hamburg: Lit-Verlag.

Jung, D.
1995 *Tradition - Moderne - Krieg. Grundlegung einer Methode zur Erforschung kriegsursächlicher Prozesse im Kontext globaler Vergesellschaftung.* Münster, Hamburg: Lit-Verlag.

Kende, I.
1971 Twenty-five Years of Local Wars. *Journal of Peace Research* 8 (1): 5-22.
1978 Wars of Ten Years (1967-1976). *Journal of Peace Research* 15 (3): 227-241.

Marx, K.
1857/58 *Grundrisse der Kritik der Politischen Oekonomie.* Berlin/GDR (1974): Dietz.
1867 Das Kapital - Kritik der Politischen Oekonomie, 1st vol., *Marx-Engels-Werke, no.23.* Berlin/GDR (1972): Dietz.
1894 Das Kapital - Kritik der Politischen Oekonomie, 3rd vol., *Marx-Engels-Werke, no.25.* Berlin/GDR (1973): Dietz.

Marx, K., & F. Engels
1848 Manifest der Kommunistischen Partei. *Marx-Engels-Werke, no.4*, pp. 459-493. Berlin/GDR (1983): Dietz. (Here quoted from the English edition: Manifesto of the Communist Party. *Selected Works of Marx and Engels.* London: Lawrence & Wishart Ltd., 1968, pp. 35-63.)

Schlichte, K.
1994 Is Ethnicity a Cause of War? *Peace Review* 6 (1): 59-65.

Siegelberg, J.
1991 *Die Kriege 1985 bis 1990. Analyse ihrer Ursachen.* Münster, Hamburg: Lit-Verlag.
1994 *Kapitalismus und Krieg. Eine Theorie des Krieges in der Weltgesellschaft.* Münster, Hamburg: Lit-Verlag.

Small, M., & J. D. Singer
1982 *Resort to Arms. International and Civil Wars, 1816-1980.* Beverly Hills: Sage Publishing Co.

Tetzlaff, R., C. Peters & R. Wegemund
1992 Politicized Ethnicity: An Underestimated Reality in Post- colonial Africa. Law and State. *A Biannual Collection of Recent German Contributions to These Fields.* No. 46, pp. 24-53.

Weber, M.
1964 *Wirtschaft und Gesellschaft. Grundriß der verstehenden Soziologie.* J. Winckelmann (ed.). Köln, Berlin: Kiepenheuer & Witsch.

NATIONALISM AND ETHNICITY: ETHNIC NATIONALISM AND THE REGULATION OF ETHNIC CONFLICT

JAKOB RÖSEL

Arnold Bergstraesser-Institut für Kulturwissenschaftliche Forschung, Windausstrasse 16, D-79110 Freiburg

In this chapter I concentrate on two closely related but not identical ideological phenomena—nationalism and ethnicity. Far from losing their importance during the process of political and cultural modernization, both phenomena constitute a major threat, whether to the maintenance of the prevailing system of states or to the integration of single states. In the first part of the chapter I compare the different theoretical foundations—or nationalisms—of the liberal and ethnic nation-state. As I will show, it is the doctrine of ethnic exclusiveness and ethnic nationalism which creates the image of a closed and primordial group and which provokes the emergence of secondary and competing ethnic movements and self-perpetuating conflicts. In the second part of the chapter I concentrate on the dangerous escalation of these ethnic conflicts and the difficulty of finding solutions to them. I cannot do justice to the complexity of both phenomena but focus, firstly, on a rather abstract, theoretical distinction and, secondly, on possible political solutions. My perspective is that of a political scientist and I approach the phenomena of nationalism and ethnicity from a normative and pragmatic viewpoint. As this viewpoint might seem naïve to some observers, it calls for an explanation.

To many observers, the attempt to distinguish between a liberal and an ethnic nation-state will seem futile. This is because they view most variants of nationalism as a kind of politicized ethnicity writ large, an ethnicity operating on the level of intra- and inter-state political competition. Although conceding that there might, in theory, exist some difference between a liberal and an ethnic nation-state, they emphasize that in political practice, in nationalist rhetoric and in propaganda, the different concepts can no longer be distinguished. Against this reductionist or sceptical viewpoint, I insist on the need to distinguish, ideologically and historically, between the theoretical and ethical foundations of each concept of nation. Not to do so would mean that we could no longer distinguish between the different kinds of loyalty these two concepts of state can legitimately demand from their subjects— citizens or members of a tribe. It would mean that we would be tempted to see any attachment to a democratic polity as tainted with ethnic chauvinism. Simultaneously, we would be tempted to adopt a short-sighted realism which postulated that any state—indeed any social group—is entitled to some kind of primordial, ethnocentric attachment. Failure to distinguish, therefore, would exact a political and moral price. We would no longer be able to distinguish between the legitimate and illegitimate bases of the cultural and moral cohesion of a democratic polity; democratic societies would be put on a par with non-democratic ones; and we would not be able to define the uniqueness of their new patterns of identity, nor judge their legitimacy and performance. The fact that liberal nation-states have often failed fully to evolve these new patterns of identity and that they are continuously tempted to embrace some variant of ethnic nationalism makes this attempt to distinguish between a liberal and an ethnic nation-state all the more indispensable.

The growth and cultivation of ethnic loyalties in one group, in one nation, facilitates the emergence and proliferation of mutually hostile ethnic identities and nationalisms among other ethnic groups. Nevertheless, there still exist more ethnic groups than ethnic conflicts and most of these conflicts have not become politicized and radicalized to the extent that they have turned into civil war. Yet, it is these self-sustaining conflicts which threaten the legitimacy and integrity of multi-ethnic states and the prevailing system of states. It is therefore on this comparatively small number of escalating and self-sustaining ethnic conflicts that I focus in the second part of this chapter. Again, this attempt to address an empirical problem with solutions that have largely failed in practice might be seen as futile. And yet to dispense with the optimistic assumption that these conflicts are, in the last analysis, political conflicts and therefore amenable to political solutions would replace a practical predicament with a moral one: it would make the political scientist a hapless bystander.

Nationalism: the liberal and the ethnic nation state

Nationalism, like liberalism and socialism, is one of the most important doctrines, 'world views' and historical forces to have emerged during the nineteenth century in Europe. Like its two predecessors, it arose from new theoretical insights and seemingly self-evident truths. It reflected and strengthened new political, social and cultural institutions and, to the degree that it created new modes of thought and organizations, it spread both vertically and horizontally. It not only influenced the course of European history, through the consolidation of old states and the emergence of new ones, it was also transmitted, through the rise of nineteenth century colonialism and imperialism, to the 'Third World.' As it was adapted to ever more varying local situations and political circumstances, the doctrine diversified. Simultaneously, it began to interact and compete with the antagonistic as well as complementary doctrines of liberalism and socialism (Kedourie 1971:22-77).

Put in the simplest of terms, nationalism proclaims a new political ideal, the nation, and a new political structure, the nation-state. It thus postulates a new and necessary relationship between a newly proclaimed ideal, the Nation, and a long, and by now well-established structure, the State. It postulates that a nation is in need of its own state and that a state is in need of a nation. It shifts the emphasis to a new political ideal: to be legitimate and to be able to function, the state from now on needs its nation. From a morally selfsufficient and historically incidental structure, from an end in itself, the state is transformed into a legitimate entitlement and a practical tool of nationhood. The demand to provide the nation with its as yet non-existent state, and the ambition to provide the state with its as yet non-existent nation becomes a powerful force to strengthen and to weaken, to make or to unmake new and old states (Gellner 1991:8-17). Yet while the various existing states of Europe, as well as the structure of a modern state, could be clearly described and defined, this was—and is—not possible for nations. At least in Europe, there existed a bewildering variety of nations. Nations with and without states; self-proclaimed new and self-confident old nations; and nations which had constituted themselves and nations which had been defined by others now stood besides or against each other. Often these nations overlapped and sometimes they denied each others' very existence.

This confusion had two causes which were well recognized by contemporary observers. Firstly, two mutually incompatible concepts of the nation were, by now, well entrenched in politics and ideological debate. Secondly, although both concepts could deal, each in its own way, with the generalized question 'What is the nation,' they gave inconclusive or contradictory answers when they were confronted with the specific and always politically biased question 'Is *this* a nation?' (Renan 1882/1993: 290-310). These two, mutually exclusive, concepts of the nation are, on the one hand, the ideal of an open and democratic nation and, on the other, the ideal of a closed and ethnic nation. Although both concepts are normally found in the same modernizing societies and although they are sometimes difficult to disentangle in political practice and ideological debate, they have to be clearly differentiated if we want to understand the nature, form and consequences of nationalism in modernizing societies —not only in Europe, but in the Third World.

The two concepts of nation

The concept of an open and democratic nation, or as Hans Kohn has put it, the ideal of the voluntaristic and subjective nation, arose first (Kohn 1962:309-14, 550-3). It was influenced by liberalism and it was necessarily linked to the basic concepts of a liberal or 'civil' society: the rule of law and democratic government. The open and democratic nation consists of all those individuals who have lived together under a common system of law and who, as a result of political reform and revolutions, have acquired the right of democratic self-determination. It is the memory of having lived under a common rule of law, the existence of a democratic constitution and the constant practice of self-government which impart to these diverse individuals a common, a national identity. This nation is not only democratic, it is also open: since its members are not defined by any common biological or social substance, but through a common political relationship, any other individual is in principle (but dependent upon democratically determined economic and social conditions) allowed to enter into this same relationship. He or she thus becomes a member of the nation (Lepsius 1993:209-12). Democratic states have thus evolved into nation-states but they do not have a general theory of the nation. Instead, their concept of nation describes, in general and abstract terms, the boundaries and the cohesion of their respective civil societies.

The contrasting concept is that of the closed and ethnic nation, or as Hans Kohn has put it, the deterministic and objective nation (Kohn 1962: 309-14, 550-3). This nation is not defined through a political (legal and democratic) relationship between its many and vastly different members but through a common biological or social bond, which overrides the various differences among its members. This bond is derived from common descent, religion, culture, language or history and it creates an ethnic identity and ethnic nation, as the commonalities of descent, religion, culture, language and history are no longer seen as separate, incidental elements or functions of society. Instead, they are perceived as the external manifestations of an ageless, unique and primordial community. This community is therefore unified through a common substance and fate, not through ephemeral and individual interests. The ethnic nation is a closed nation. As it is defined by a common substance, by common descent or by social traits which signify or substitute for common descent, outsiders are either excluded in principle or they have to be completely assimilated. Over various periods of time they might acquire the unique physical or social substance which defines and demarcates the ethnic nation (Lepsius 1993:197-202). Thus, the concept of the ethnic nation—in contrast to the democratic nation—implies from the start its own theory. This theory is based on the following three assumptions:

1. Mankind is by nature and historical evolution divided into different and easily definable 'peoples' or ethnic groups. These groups have the moral obligation and natural right to preserve and to cultivate their specific identity.

2. The defence and development of their identity is only possible inside their own state. Yet this state has, in most circumstances, first to be fought for and this collective and often heroic undertaking implies the transformation of the ethnic group from an objective entity into a self-conscious, subjective force.

3. It is this transformation of a people into a nation which precedes and facilitates the conquest of its own nation-state and it is, finally, in and through this nation-state that the ultimate realization of a nation's culture and destiny will be achieved (Kedourie 1961:9, 58, 32-50).

Liberalism necessarily conceives mankind as an aggregate of individuals. It takes account of biological and social diversity but superimposes on this diversity the freedom of individuals to accept or reject it and to form or transform it. It derives the legitimacy and functions of the state from the democratic consent and interests of its individual members, not from the defence and self-realization of a primordial community. From these two different concepts of nation there follow different views of what are and are not nations, and different 'maps' or 'political landscapes' for open and closed nations.

The same distinction can be found in three additional concepts which are all derived from the central idea of nation. These are the historical, the cultural and the linguistic nation. For the proponents of an open and democratic nation, history is not pre-ordained, it is an adventure, acted out by self-determined individuals. It creates, in the words of Ernest Renan, a group of people who are bound together by what they have experienced and by what they have forgotten. In the closed, ethnic nation, on the other hand, we find the idea of history as destiny; a history in which a primordial group heroically and often tragically confronts its pre-determined fate (Renan 1882/1993:309/294). There is a comparable contrast in the meanings and functions attributed to culture. On the one hand, culture is seen as an individual achievement; an open ended and unpredictable process of individual creativity where new means are constantly employed for new ends. On the other hand, we find the idea of culture as the constant rediscovery, manifestation and cultivation of a national genius, where new artistic means are to be employed only for pre-established cultural ends (Finkielkraut 1989:41-54).

Finally, there is the idea of language as an essentially practical, open and changing medium for communication and, in contrast, the idea of language as a repository of ethnic uniqueness and as a means of demarcation. While, on the one hand, the need for one language is stressed because of its social and political usefulness, on the other, the preservation of a specific language is stressed because it is conceived as a unique substance. Similarly, while in the one case literature is seen as an element of culture, in the second, it is seen as the unique and 'natural' product of a specific language (Kedourie 1961:62-71).

Given these fundamental differences, it is not surprising that, while the proponents of both the open and the closed nation attach the greatest importance to education, they attribute radically different functions to it. For the proponents of an open nation, education should impart to the young the historical knowledge, political competence and language skills which will enable them to participate in social life and which will simultaneously enable them to form an attachment to their nation. In contrast, proponents of a closed nation regard education as a means to mould the yet unfinished individual in accordance with the fixed concepts and canons of the group's unique history, tradition and culture (Fichte 1807/1909:19-37; Gellner 1991:58-62). Although both groups of 'nationalists' take pride in their respective histories, cultures and languages, there is a fundamental divide in the roles which history, culture and language play in these two concepts of the nation. The concepts of the open and the closed nation are not only incompatible but are also in constant competition.

Competition between the two concepts of nation

It is certainly right, as many observers have pointed out, that the concept of the open nation and nation-state arose first. It arose among Western European states during and after the process of democratic reform and revolutionary change, while the concept of the closed and ethnic nation expanded virtually unchallenged in Central and Eastern Europe, in the absence, or through the suppression, of democratic reform (Kohn 1964: 21-54). Apart from this East-West divide, there was and is a constant competition between these two mutually exclusive visions of society and state. As repeated and often unpredictable surges of xenophobia and racist politics demonstrate, ethnic nationalism does not automatically vanish in the process of modernization and democratization (Horowitz 1985:96-105). At least at the beginning of democratization and modernization, the liberal concept of the nation is in a weak position. As already mentioned, it cannot advance its own specific theory but rests on abstractions derived from the theory of liberalism: the sovereignty of the individual, democratic self-determination and constitutionalism. It is confronted, however, with a concept that can seemingly marshal the forces of empiricism, historicism and realism (Smith 1981:87-107). It is only to the extent that these abstractions have been transformed into new and decisive social ideals and values that the theoretical underpinnings of the liberal concept of the nation seem convincing and those of the ethnic concept of the nation seem questionable. Although it is, in principle, easy to refute the all-encompassing claims of the theory of the ethnic nation, this critique presupposes the emergence of that open society and open debate which are the results of a long process of democratization. Democratization is thus the prerequisite for the implementation, the demonstration and theoretical defence of the liberal concept of the nation-state. Yet this process, which transforms abstractions into productive illusions and, finally, into new structures of society and the state, is often obstructed by, and can (at least in the initial stages) even contribute to, the further development and growth of ethnic nationalism.

In the contemporary world, and especially in the Third World and the new one emerging from the former Soviet Union, we are confronted with a situation which is quite different from that which prevailed in the nineteenth century. Whereas, in the century of European nationalism, two different concepts of the nation evolved and spread more or less independently of each other, these two movements have now converged. All over the world we find formally democratic or democratizing states which have, at least outwardly, bound themselves to the implementation and maintenance of a liberal concept of the nation and nation-state (Huntington 1991:13-26). Yet in many of these states—especially in multi-ethnic ones—we find proponents and partisans of the ethnic concept of the nation and nation-state. In contrast to the predictions of the theorists of modernization, ethnic nationalism does not seem to vanish. Indeed it may even emerge as the unexpected result of ill-conceived attempts to 'build' a liberal nation-state (Horowitz 1985:306-339).

Two originally separate concepts of the nation have thus entered the same arena of political competition and ideological debate, where the proponents of each try to monopolize the term nation. A liberal nation and nation-state is seen as utopian and irresponsible and its opponents substitute for it the terms 'open society' and 'multi-cultural state.' An ethnic nation and nation-state is seen as dangerous and fascist and its opponents often refer to it as a 'racist society' or 'ethnic' state. In this battle for a semantic monopoly, the partisans of an ethnic nation-state are often the most insistent. Refusing to use the term nation or a liberal conception of society, they proceed to 'expatriate' their opponents from political debate and start to describe them as 'anti-national.' To the extent that the adherents of an ethnic nation attempt to distance themselves—whether out of conviction or convenience—from the now discredited idealization of race, they shift the emphasis from common descent to common history, culture and language. Radically different and contending visions and interpretations of history, culture and language are then advanced, in the name of the ideal historical, cultural or linguistic nation (Oberndörfer 1994b). We should not, however, concentrate on the ideological confusion which results from the competition between these two different concepts, but on the conflicts which must necessarily arise from the doctrine of ethnic nationalism—irrespective of the existence of a liberal tradition of the nation.

The political results of the two concepts of the nation

Ethnic nationalism postulates the existence of separate ethnic groups but, as its own logical inconsistencies and our historical experience show, such groups cannot be easily defined. Most of the criteria contradict each other. To this general difficulty must be added the intrinsic difficulty of establishing 'objective' differences—of descent, religion, culture, language and history—by which these groups are to be differentiated and defined (Rothschild 1981:87-94). Then there are the dangers of prescription. Ethnic nationalism is not content with the mere perception of ethnic differences but claims the right to exacerbate them through the cultivation of ethnic identities. It tends, therefore, to create those very ethnic differences and identities which form the basis of its claims (Horowitz 1985:70-73). Various and contending ethnic nationalisms, therefore, not only emphasize but also produce mutually exclusive patterns of ethnic division.

Ethnic nationalism, furthermore, claims to be able to determine unequivocally which individuals belong to the ethnic group and which do not. It can thus deprive the individual of his or her right to decide to which group, society and state he or she wants to belong. It can thus claim the allegiance and loyalty of distant members of its own group, even if these individuals or groups reject the claim. And it reserves the right to expel, marginalize or forcefully assimilate all those individuals who are not members of the ethnic group (Gellner 1991:10). Since ethnic groups do not normally inhabit an area entirely on their own, ethnic nationalism is not only a divisive but also an aggressive, expansive and suppressive force.

Finally, and in contrast to its theoretical assumptions, which simultaneously define and celebrate ethnic diversity, ethnic nationalism demands but seldom concedes tolerance. As experience has demonstrated, ethnic nations are not content to extol their own descent, religion, culture, language and history; they also tend to discredit the claims of others. Instead of an acceptance of ethnic diversity, we see different and antagonistic gradations of ethnic culture and attempts to impose cultural homogeneity (Oberndörfer 1994a:27-33).

Ethnic nationalism, therefore, is not disinterested theory, attempting to define, explain and justify the diversity of mankind. It does not take part in intellectual debate and it does not discuss nations in the plural. It enters the political arena and advances the claim of one nation, its own, against others. It is interested in ethnological, historical or philological scholarship only to the extent to which these sciences can substantiate its ideological assertions and further its political aims. It exacerbates arbitrary divisions and acts as an aggressive and intolerant force. It sets off a chain reaction of counter-claims and of further attempts at ethnic nation building. To the extent that these attempts succeed, they can lead to the fragmentation of the state, to ethnic incorporation, to the aggressive expansion of the state, to enforced ethnic homogenization or to the expulsion, marginalization or assimilation of minorities (Rothschild 1981:41-60). The concept of the closed and ethnic nation, therefore, necessarily gives rise to intra- or inter-state conflict. What are the political consequences of a liberal concept of the nation and the nation-state?

As my description, and that given by Ernest Renan a century ago imply, the liberal idea of the nation cannot, by its very nature, lay down exactly how to produce a self-sustaining allegiance to the nation-state. Nor does it have a clear-cut prescription for action when groups of various denominations or strength reject the 'daily plebiscite' of national consensus and democratic coexistence and start to demand various degrees of political autonomy (Renan 1882/1993:309-11). In addition, the liberal concept of the nation and nation-state cannot by itself prevent the emergence of old or new ethnic groups as ethnic 'vote banks,' parties and 'nations.' It cannot by itself avoid the marginalization of minorities through ethnic majority voting. And it is not immune to ethnic nation building disguised as modernization, centralization or democratization.

But whereas widespread ethnic conflicts, ethnic violence and ethnic civil war are the predictable consequences of ethnic nationalism, they are not the unavoidable consequences of a liberal concept of the nation and nation-state. There are various means, by which ethnic nationalism can be contained and the concept of the liberal nation and nation-state upheld.

Ethnic conflicts and their solution

In recent years, ethnic conflict, once seen as a passing phenomenon by the theorists of modernization, has grown in significance and in viciousness. In the post-colonial Third World as well as in the new one which is emerging from the break-up of the Soviet Union, ethnic conflict has contributed to the erosion of states and led to regional and international confrontations (Gellner 1993; Smith 1981:1-25). Given the ethnic complexity of most of these states, the number of conflicts might seem comparatively small, yet their destructiveness leaves little room for complacency. Instead of focusing on the (sometimes long-existing) causes of these conflicts, I will focus, in a more pragmatic way, on three interrelated points.

Firstly, by contrasting ethnic violence and civil war with conventional, inter-state warfare, I shall comment on the self-sustaining momentum of these conflicts, which makes them so singularly difficult to contain or to resolve. Secondly, I shall show that political means nevertheless exist, not only to prevent but also to control ethnic conflicts. Finally, I shall try to demonstrate that democracies, despite the fact that they may operate as catalysts for ethnic conflict, are still our best hope of implementing broad-based and self-sustaining political arrangements to prevent or resolve them.

Ethnic conflicts and civil war

An ethnic group sees itself as constituted by the real or imagined bonds of common descent, religion, language, culture or history. Ethnic conflict involves (at least according to the groups' leadership) the survival or other non-negotiable interests of the group (Rothschild 1981:9, 86-96). I shall describe as ethnic conflict a three stage process in which ethnic antagonism first becomes political competition, secondly gives rise to a spiral of ethnic violence and, thirdly, escalates into civil war. I shall focus on these three stages because it is through the politicization, radicalization and militarization of ethnic conflict that ethnic groups acquire the self-awareness and organization, cohesion and bitterness and, finally, intransigence and cynicism which make a peaceful settlement increasingly difficult to negotiate.

Democracies are, in theory, based upon parties which address a state-wide electorate on general issues concerning the national interest in order to maximize their votes beyond sectarian, regional or ethnic divisions. In many post-colonial democracies, however, we find political parties which restrict their efforts at vote-maximization to addressing the parochial interests of various ethnic groups (Rothschild 1981:33-66). In many cases it is a second generation of political leaders which has tried to turn minority or majority ethnic groups into ethnic vote-banks and parties. When such ethnic entrepreneurs have succeeded, against the spirit of democratic debate and against the logic of vote-maximization, in constituting a coherent ethnic party, they have often been able to erode or destroy a democracy. The electorate and the political debate now splits along ethnic lines, a process which intensifies the already existing ethnic cleavages. Election campaigns now turn into a threatening display of ethnic rhetoric and folklore and the election itself degenerates into a racial or ethnic census. In majority dominated states, election results can be foreseen and minority groups may turn to political apathy or militancy. In those states where no clear-cut ethnic majorities exist, multiethnic coalition governments form, recombine and split because they cannot satisfy the growing and incompatible demands of their various ethnic clienteles. Mounting political alienation in minority groups as well as mounting political competition between equally balanced ethnic groups can lead to ethnic violence and will often tempt the military to intervene (Horowitz 1985:340-64; Rösel 1990:219-36). I want to concentrate not on the demise of democracy, but on the structure of ethnic violence.

According to the American anthropologist Stanley Tambiah, there is a cognitive, an intellectual and a social predisposition to ethnic violence (Tambiah 1990). Fear and resentment grow to such an extent that members of an ethnic group routinely perceive any unfortunate incident involving their own group as an intentional and, therefore, ethnic attack perpetrated by a hostile ethnic group or state. But, to the extent that individual incidents are taken out of their contexts, a new interpretation sets in. The sleight is now explained with the help of the group's self-proclaimed image. It is interpreted as an attack on the group's achievements and ordeals, its status, pride and rights. The particular sleight now re-emerges as part of a general and growing dossier of the ethnic group's suffering and the bad intentions of its enemies. The cognitive predisposition to decontextualize and to dichotomize, and the intellectual predisposition to reinterpret and to enhance, inevitably lead to the point where mounting ethnic solidarity demands not only compassion, but also retaliation.

The ethnic group, often distributed over distant territories and composed of vastly different people, now resembles a giant war-drum which resonates as a whole with every single beat on its surface. Attacks against distant community members are not only instantly recognized, but are also protested against. A new form of compensatory revenge takes place in which distant attacks on one's own group are avenged by attacks against the local members of the enemies' group. To the extent that both communities indulge in this cycle of compensatory retribution, a spiral of ever-widening and self-sustaining aggression and violence emerges. This violence serves the interests of political and economic profiteers; it creates its own martyrs, rituals and routine; and it forces all members of the respective communities to subscribe to their own group's identities and demands. The particular dangers of ethnic violence are its capacity to escalate, to develop its own rationale and to discredit or destroy those intermediaries who try to contain it.

There is first the danger that the conflict will escalate to the point at which each party concludes that the other seeks its total destruction. In interstate wars, this unrelenting escalation of fear, hate and ambition will normally be checked by external forces. In the framework of an established state system, in which there are third parties, a balance of power and diplomatic calculations, a single state cannot hope completely to destroy another. In ethnic civil wars these safeguards do not necessarily exist. They are often waged in the 'backyard' of states. They are often 'silent' wars, which emerge and intensify without the knowledge or interference of the established state-system. Fear, and a strategy of total destruction, can therefore run their full course and negotiation becomes extremely difficult (Kriele 1980:47). A second result of civil war, furthermore, may be a fragmentation of political leadership which can destroy the institutional basis for negotiation.

The escalation of civil war often leads to a change in the group's leadership and to the emergence of political and militant factions. In the shadow of civil war, terrorist groups, militias and warlords acquire new positions of power, income and prestige, while the old-established political élite is intimidated or driven into exile. Escalation of conflict, however, implies escalating pressure to make difficult decisions and take new risks. Under this pressure, the new leadership often splits up along tactical, ideological or sectarian lines and it becomes increasingly difficult to determine which ideological segment has what political mandate and the authority to participate in negotiations. Whereas warring states always retain diplomatic institutions and remain in diplomatic contact, parties to civil wars either lack such institutions or lose such contact (Wight 1986:137). While the escalation of fear and hate ensures that the parties to an ethnic civil war do not want to negotiate, a third result of civil war, its mere persistence, often convinces the militant factions that they *need* not negotiate.

Persistent civil war destroys jobs, farms, offices and factories. It empties schools and universities, and it can alienate whole generations from the authority of parents, the constraints of education and the discipline of work. Yet while civil war enfeebles the established fabric of society, it simultaneously offers new and attractive alternatives: the unrestricted freedom of life in a militia and access to arbitrary power, illegal income and unexpected prestige. A negotiated settlement and the return to normal life will threaten faction leaders and followers with a new vulnerability, poverty and insignificance. It is therefore in their best interests to wage war against mediators and peace-keepers as well as enemies (Rösel 1993). This again contrasts with the development of war between states, where war cannot completely erode the fabric of civil society and where the political and economic advantages of war are constantly balanced against the anticipated advantages of peace.

The regulation of ethnic conflict

After what I have just written, it is easy to agree with Stanley Tambiah that "ethnicity is a persistent, boisterous and many-headed beast" (Tambiah 1990:741). How then, given the unpredictable intransigent and self-perpetuating nature of ethnic conflicts, can they be prevented or solved? There can be no clear-cut and universally applicable solution to a phenomenon which is always adapted to its local contexts, but it is possible to state some relevant insights, or even moral precepts.

The first of these is that there is nothing pre-ordained about ethnic conflicts. They do not derive from the supposedly primordial structure of ethnic groups. As my description of conflict escalation implies, there are always specific thresholds to be crossed and there are always political profiteers—ethnic entrepreneurs, ideologues and warlords—who will exploit the opportunities which result from political failure and political mistakes. If we view ethnic conflicts not as tragic confrontations between primordial groups but as the result of bad politics, we can at least reposition them in the political realm and thereby recognize that they are amenable to prevention, negotiation or control (Rothschild 1981:33-8). The recognition that there may be ethnic groups, but not necessarily ethnic conflicts, suggests that a multi-ethnic state cannot afford to ignore the existence of ethnic groups. Nor should it be intimidated by the existence of such groups. Rather than either rejecting or exploiting ethnic diversity, it should acknowledge and accommodate it.

This proposal, or moral precept, narrows down considerably the options which political systems in multi-ethnic states can, in the long run, successfully pursue, if they want to maintain their hold on power while avoiding ethnic conflict. It excludes those regimes in which a dominant ethnic group simply ignores the existence of any other ethnic groups and tries to maintain its ethnic exclusiveness as well as its monopoly on power. It excludes those regimes in which a dominant ethnic group, intimidated by the existence of other ethnic groups, embarks on a programme of forced assimilation, a programme which first transforms the dominant ethnic identity into a supposedly national identity and then forces it on all the remaining ethnic groups. It excludes those regimes in which a dominant ethnic group, or a non-ethnic, supposedly national élite, rejects the existence of any ethnic groups and embarks on an aggressive programme of nation-building, with the intention of replacing ethnic affiliation with a new image of the nation-state. Finally, it excludes all those regimes in which dominant ethnic groups, or non-ethnic national élites, try to rule by dividing opposing ethnic groups.

It is not difficult to see why such strategies will, in the long run, be counterproductive. Although circumstances may vary, it is quite unlikely that a dominant ethnic group will preserve enough cohesion and force to maintain permanently its separateness and its hold on power. It is equally unlikely that an expansionist ethnic group will have enough authority and power to embark on a programme of forced assimilation without encountering, or creating, ethnic resistance and conflict. The same holds true for those regimes which, in attempting to build a non-ethnic nation-state, not only reject the existence of ethnic groups, but also seriously underestimate their strength. Finally, those regimes which officially ignore but, in practice, co-opt and manipulate ethnic groups or parties, often encourage ethnic assertiveness, leading to conflicts which they are ultimately unable to control. While it is easy to see that these strategies will, in the long run, prove disastrous, it is equally easy to see that, in the short run and in the muddle of day-to-day politics, they serve the interests of various political actors and ethnic groups.

A traditionally dominant, well entrenched ethnic group may think it worthwhile to try to defend its hegemony under new political circumstances. It might even try to strengthen its position with new bureaucratic and technical means. Or it might be tempted to embark on the road of enforced assimilation, declaring its own history, culture and tradition to be that of the nation. In the same way, a dominant minority group, eager to disguise its small size and privileged position but deeply sceptical about the two options just mentioned, might use the newly-fashioned ideal of the nation-state as a perfect camouflage, and nation-building as a means to legitimate and preserve its position. And all these dominant ethnic groups will occasionally seek to exploit those ethnic groups which they normally reject, fear or ignore (Hanf 1989:322, 328).

In the short run, such groups pursue completely rational strategies to preserve or maximize their power. It is only in the long run that these strategies are likely to prove disastrous, and it is not necessarily the dominant ethnic group, or its leadership, which will suffer the consequences. The acknowledgement and accommodation of ethnic diversity imply power-sharing instead of power maximization. The depressing fact is that the benefits of this seemingly obvious strategy can only be appreciated by enlightened self-interest, or after civil war. This is what makes it difficult to implement such a strategy.

To acknowledge and accommodate ethnic groups is easier said than done. There is no clear-cut and universally applicable recipe, but I shall outline three strategies which will vary in their effectiveness according to the particular circumstances. In some circumstances, they might even prove disastrous. In order for these strategies—either in combination or in isolation—to achieve a minimum of success, they must rely on extraneous circumstances which are normally beyond the power of political scientists or actors to engineer. The implementation and success of these strategies normally requires a modicum of civic virtue and a minimum of trust, courage, humility and foresight, which only the wisdom of an independent political élite or sheer exhaustion and desperation following a protracted civil war can provide (Pohlmann 1988:31-4).

The strategies are 'consociation,' or the incorporation of ethnic groups into the political and administrative structure of the state; 'syncretism,' or the cultural representation of ethnic diversity accompanied by the *de facto* depoliticization of ethnic groups; and 'federalization,' or decentralization, implying the conceding of a certain autonomy to regional units, but often, in reality, to ethnic groups.

The first strategy acknowledges and accommodates ethnic groups by transforming the representative and administrative institutions of the state into a microcosm of the ethnic composition of society. Ethnic representation, on the basis of proportion or even parity, forces politicians to accept the need for compromise and consensus, and this new balance of ethnic power may be further balanced by giving the power of veto to each ethnic group (Lijphart 1977:25-52).

The second strategy acknowledges, but does not accommodate, ethnic groups. The different ethnic cultures are respected and represented as elements of a new syncretistic national identity. They are represented in a position of parity, they are seen as complementary and mutually compatible and they are valued as the basis of the nation's creativity and resourcefulness. But, parallel to this ideological revalorization, ethnic groups are denied the right to demand specific political, administrative or economic entitlements, whether in the form of ethnic parties, separate electorates, quotas or subsidies. This celebration of the culture and denial of the political ambition of ethnic groups contributes not only to the de-politicization, but also to the decline of ethnic identities. Ethnic groups can no longer complain of cultural marginalization, since they find their ethnic identity officially revalorized, even if only as one element of the national identity. From now on, not only the value of their tradition, but also their value as individuals is derived from the fact that they are integrated—and willingly integrated—into the syncretistic image of the nation-state (Hanf 1989:323).

The third strategy may neither openly acknowledge nor directly accommodate ethnic groups, but since they are often regionally concentrated, it can contribute significantly to the accommodation, integration and, finally, downgrading of ethnic identities. The attempt at spatial decentralization can assume many forms, depending on the size of the federal units and the amount and type of power, resources and prestige which are conceded. It is obvious that decentralization can also be used to undercut ethnic boundaries and to create new interests, affiliations and even identities. It is also obvious that federalization—as with the break-up of multi-ethnic states—will produce new minorities in its new constituent units (McGarry & O'Leary 1993:30-5). How can minorities, scattered over a whole region or even over the whole state, be accommodated and protected? One possibility is a non-spatial kind of decentralization, in which these dispersed ethnic groups would have the right to their own schools, their own language, their own traditions and sometimes even their own civil law (Hanf 1991:61-92).

As my description has shown, these strategies differ significantly. The first installs ethnic complexity at the centre of power; the second transforms it into cultural production and ideological representation; and the third transplants it to a newly-fashioned polycentric state structure. Although they differ, they can be combined, and although they can contribute to the solution of ethnic conflict, they can also result in the exact opposite.

This danger results from the fact that each strategy inevitably involves arbitrary political decisions—decisions about which ethnic groups should be 'consociated,' which should be officially and ideologically represented and which should be recognized as the major units of a federal structure. Although these strategies are intended to integrate, to reconcile and, in the long run, to downgrade ethnic groups, in the short run they give them a new official status, a new respectability and a new arena for their ambitions. Given the often diffuse, controversial and changing nature of ethnicity, it is difficult to arrive at a mutually acceptable definition of it on which the government of the state can be based. The implementation of these strategies, therefore, requires trust, courage, humility and foresight on the part of the political élite.

The acknowledgement or accommodation of ethnic groups is intended to weaken the absolutist claims which they advance against each other and which they all advance against new and competing alternatives of self-identification and loyalty. The political recognition of ethnicity is intended to begin a process in which the claims of single ethnic groups against each other, and the claims of ethnicity *per se*, are equally eroded. Having understood that these three strategies necessarily involve a sharing of power and that they can only succeed if they initiate an open-ended process of modernization and individualization, we arrive at the conclusion that democracy is a necessary precondition for the solution of ethnic conflict.

Democracy as the prerequisite for the regulation of ethnic conflict

I advance this proposition with considerable unease. As I have already indicated, it is often a democratic system which encourages the formation of ethnic parties and contributes to the escalation of ethnic conflict to which it finally succumbs. A democratic system of government is, nevertheless, our only hope of preventing or regulating ethnic conflict. This view is based upon the following three considerations.

1. The three strategies I have outlined imply a democratic form of government.

2. Although various non-democratic regimes may have shown an astonishing capacity to prevent or control ethnic conflict, in the long run they have been unable to erode ethnic loyalties.

3. Even if we regard democratic governments as the worst possible arrangement for the regulation of ethnic conflicts, we are still confronted with the fact that democratic systems of government are gradually acquiring a near-universal prevalence and legitimacy. We are thus forced to work out strategies which will allow for the prevention and control of these conflicts in democracies.

It is obvious that consociation, syncretism and federalism have been, and can be, practiced by democratic as well as non-democratic regimes. Yet for these strategies to succeed, they have to be turned from a political concession, dictated by the enlightened self-interest of some into constitutional rights to be owned, controlled and defended by all. This necessarily involves democratic controls and procedures, which alone can guarantee that these concessions cannot be withdrawn or manipulated.

It is undeniable that some non-democratic regimes have shown a great capability to adapt to ethnic diversity and to control ethnic conflicts. What they have never achieved is the creation of political structures and social processes which allow for the recognition as well as the secular decline of ethnicity and ethnic groups. As developments in the former Soviet Union so clearly demonstrate, the best these regimes can achieve is to 'deep-freeze' such conflicts and burden their successor regimes with a dangerous inheritance (Gellner 1993:30-44). This brings me to my final point and moral conclusion.

Given the new upsurge in democratic aspirations, it seems to me a futile exercise to try to stem this development with repeated warnings about the possible emergence of widespread ethnic conflict. It seems much more important to concentrate on introducing into the various transitions to democracy, strategies and safeguards which can contribute to breaking the vicious circle in which ethnic conflicts flourish because of weak democracies, and democracies become weak because of ethnic conflicts.

References

Fichte, J. G.
1909 *Reden an die Deutsche Nation.* Leipzig: Insel Verlag.

Finkielkraut, A.
1989 *Die Niederlage des Denkens.* Hamburg: Rowohlt Verlag.

Hanf, T.
1989 The prospects of accommodation in communal conflicts: A comparative study. In *Bildung in sozio-ökonomischer Sicht.* P. Döring *et al.* (eds.), pp. 313-332. Köln: Böhlau Verlag.
1991 Karl Renners Beitrag zur Frage der Konfliktregelung in multiethnischen Staaten. In *Staat und Nation in multiethnischen Gesellschaften.* E. Fröschl *et al.* (eds.), pp. 61-90. Wien: Passagen Verlag.

Gellner, E.
1991 *Nationalismus und Moderne.* Berlin: Rotbuch Verlag.
1993 Aus den Ruinen des großen Wettstreits. In *Grenzfälle - über neuen und alten Nationalismus.* M. Jeismann & H. Ritter (eds.), pp. 30-44. Leipzig: Reclam Verlag.

Horowitz, D.
1985 *Ethnic Groups in Conflict.* Berkeley: University of California Press.

Huntington, S. P.
1991 *The Third Wave, Democratization in the Late Twentieth Century.* Norman, Oklahoma: Oklahoma University Press.

Kedourie, E.
1961 *Nationalism.* New York: F. A. Praeger Publishers.
1971 *Nationalism in Asia and Africa.* London: Weidenfeld & Nicholson.

Kohn, H.
1962 *Die Idee des Nationalismus.* Frankfurt: Fischer Verlag.
1964 *Von Machiavelli zu Nehru, zur Problemgeschichte des Nationalismus.* Freiburg: Herder Verlag.

Kriele, M.
1980 *Einführung in die Staatslehre.* Opladen: Westdeutscher Verlag.

Lepsius, R.
1993 Nation und Nationalismus in Deutschland. In *Grenzfälle - über neuen und alten Nationalismus.* M. Jeismann & H. Ritter (eds.), pp. 193-214. Leipzig: Reclam Verlag.

Lijphart, A.
1977 *Democracy in Plural Societies: A Comparative Exploration.* New Haven: Yale University Press.

McGarry, J., & B. O'Leary (eds.)
1993 *The Politics of Ethnic Conflict Regulation.* London: Routledge & Keagan Paul.

Oberndörfer, D.
1994a *Der Wahn des Nationalen.* Freiburg: Herder Verlag.
1994b *Assimilation, multiculturalism or cultural pluralism? A normative approach to the quest for political identity.* Freiburg: Arnold-Bergstraesser-Institut.

Pohlmann, F.
1988 *Politische Herrschaftssysteme der Neuzeit.* Opladen: Westdeutscher Verlag.

Renan, E.
1993 Was ist eine Nation (Qu'est-ce qu'une nation? Paris 1882). In *Grenzfälle über neuen und alten Nationalismus.* M. Jeismann & H. Ritter (eds.), pp. 290-311. Leipzig: Reclam Verlag.

Rösel, J.
1990 Ethnische Konflikte im postkolonialen Staat. In *Macht und Recht.* H. Oswald (ed.), pp. 219-236. Opladen: Westdeutscher Verlag.
1993 Der Tamilen-Konflikt auf Sri Lanka. *Der Fremde* 6: 34-46.

Rothschild, J.
1981 *Ethnopolitics: A Conceptual Framework.* New York: Columbia University Press.

Smith, A. D.
1981 *The Ethnic Revival in the Modern World.* Cambridge: Cambridge University Press.

Tambiah, S.
1990 Reflections on Communal Violence in South Asia. In *Journal of Asian Studies* 49 (4): 741-761.

Wight, M.
1986 *Power Politics.* Harmondsworth: Penguin Books.

ETHNIC MOBILIZATION, WAR AND MULTI-CULTURALISM

HARRY GOULBOURNE

Centre for Policy and Health Research, Faculty of Business and Social Studies, Cheltenham & Gloucester College of Higher Education, Cheltenham, Gloucestershire GL50 4AZ

The mobilization of ethnicity as a basis for social and political action has become more evident in national and international affairs since the end of the Cold War. For some people this is a perfectly natural condition of human society and affairs but, for many others, the dramatic assertion of ethnicity is a bewildering development. In this chapter I seek to contribute to a better understanding of the phenomenon by establishing a relationship between ethnic mobilization and social and political conflict. A necessary starting point is to describe the concept of ethnic mobilization itself.

Ethnicity as a political currency

By ethnic mobilization I refer to situations in which leaders seek to transform characteristics deemed ethnic into a political currency in order to achieve diverse or specific ends. The notion of political currency is borrowed from Karl Deutsch's well known cybernetics model of politics (Deutsch 1963:118-27). Deutsch argues that, as in economic life, a political system has partly quantifiable currencies, such as the vote. He admits, however, that there are also factors that are less quantifiable, such as confidence in an economy or a government. To regulate economic life the state uses fiscal instruments such as paper money, gold, credit and taxation. Similarly, in the political system, the state assumes a general responsibility for the individual's security, and guarantees citizenship rights. Just as the state or a bank can guarantee to investors that a quantum of gold or paper money exists to underwrite vast borrowing, and just as the state can take action to stabilize inflation and limit potentially damaging effects upon economic activities, so too can the state utilize political currencies, such as force, to assure law-abiding citizens that the individual who jeopardizes the consensus of acceptable behaviour will be punished. In other words, the regularity of both economic and political life depends on acquiescence (or a disposition or willingness to obey the sovereign will, or the law, in Bentham's utilitarian terms) on the part of citizen Mary or citizen John. Deutsch makes the point most clearly when he argues that Governments, like banks, thus base their operations on the fact that the popular expectations favourable to them—that one ought to obey the law and the police—are highly coordinated, so that most individuals most of the time can count on everybody else to do as they do; while the opposite expectations—that one should withdraw money, or break the law—are usually quite uncoordinated, so that no individual could count on bringing down a bank or a government by starting a concerted run on the first, or a concerted revolution against the second (1963:121).

It has to be stressed that this observation is limited to what we may regard as ordinary day to day situations. After all, despite de Tocqueville's insightful observation that a political revolution is not the complete break with the past that revolutionists often think it is, there are nonetheless dramatic moments when individuals do act in concert to effect a run on banks, and do organize to change radically or significantly a given political situation. Deutsch's general point does, however, hold for most situations: otherwise there would be little or no regulated activity to speak of in society. This point can be admitted without accepting the underlying systemic and functionalist principles of his model, particularly if we accept that its value is not so much the model itself but its capacity for highlighting significant aspects of the phenomena being analysed. There are two important ways in which Deutsch's notion of political currency is relevant to the understanding of ethnic mobilization.

First, ethnic mobilization—understood as a currency in the broadly defined social marketplace—involves a range of political phenomena. If this were not so, there would be little or no need to refer to some kinds of activities as constituting moments of mobilization. Such moments occur when ethnic affinities are of prime importance in effecting outcomes. Of course, whilst socialization and ethnicity are not necessarily the same, the individual assumes an ethnic identity as soon as he or she is born. The identity acquired is not a matter of choice. It is ingenuous to believe that the individual rebel is ever able completely to turn against the shared fundamental elements of his or her primary socialization. More often than not, the rebel articulates the contradictions contained within the deep-rooted elements of his or her (ethnic) cultural baggage. And since it is supremely human for individuals to become open to the influences of other (ethnic) cultures, sometimes these may point to the strengths and limitations of his or her own (ethnic) culture, and this recognition may set off a creative reaction.

Aspects of Malinowski's work are highly suggestive here. In his critique of diffusionism, Malinowski argued that, in colonial Africa, Europeans did not simply diffuse, unhindered, their cultural messages and institutions: there were forms of calculated resistance by Africans. He therefore rejected the notion that culture change was "...a migration of elements or traits from one culture to another" (1961:18). He argued that the dynamic cultural changes which were taking place in colonial Africa, particularly in the urban and industrial areas, were not simply the result of the merging or fusion of elements from different cultures which could be "...easily invoiced back to (their) place of origin" (1961:21), that is industrial Europe or rural Africa. In other words, something new was occurring.

No doubt Malinowski exaggerated the extent of this newness by underplaying the importance of the *roots* of the elements of the new combination, particularly when he argued that no "...sorting of elements is possible; no invoicing back to a previous culture as an element of reality" (1961:24). Perhaps it is not so much a matter of sorting elements as identifying the most important factor in a developing, dynamic and new situation. Discussion about roots, or what Herskovits (1941) called "retentions" can hide the significance of Malinowski's point. Similarly, Barth's encouragement to fellow anthropologists to concentrate on boundary maintenance between groups (1969) may have shifted attention from culture-contact and change.

The significance of Malinowski's argument about culture-change is the recognition that the "...clash and inter-play of the two cultures produce new things" (1961:25). In this process of transformation, conflict is inevitable, because culture-change is not likely to occur without resistance. Malinowski was writing about a colonial situation in which conflict was overt, and frequently violent. There was a lack of democratic institutions and practices and, for the great majority of people in the colonies, the political regime was alien and dictatorial.

The second point I wish to make about ethnic mobilization as a political currency is that mobilization denotes an unusual level of activity. Ethnicity is not ordinarily activated; it is not normally high-pitched and rallying in its appeal. Under 'normal' circumstances a person's or a group's ethnicity is taken for granted. Those who share this affinity are secure in the knowledge of its quiet and certain continuation, its reproductive capacity and its repeatability in the lives of new members who are born into it. There are, of course, custodians of important aspects of what the group shares. Priests, writers, artists, musicians and many others participate in a division of labour which ensures the public reproduction of ethnic bonding and solidarity. They may also negotiate connections or links with other cultures, and therefore have a deep appreciation of the 'breaks' or 'greyness' in cultural boundaries. Primary institutions or agencies of socialization, such as the family and the household, provide the basis for the natural reproduction of the main patterns or characteristics of ethnicity. In 'normal' situations, however, none of these factors of ethnic bonding are mobilized for immediate action.

Mobilization conjures images of drama, fight, assertion, outrage, attack, defence and, ultimately, war. Ethnic mobilization demands that those who share, or perceive themselves to share,[1] ethnic characteristics should rouse themselves to unusual and extraordinary, action. The aims and purposes of

---

1 It is not important whether ethnic characteristics are in fact shared or are only perceived. Indeed, there are sound reasons to assume that, in many cases, ethnicity is perceived or is in the process of construction, consolidation or re-definition. Clearly, this is the case in contemporary Britain, where each ethnic group—including minorities and the

themselves to unusual and extraordinary, action. The aims and purposes of ethnic mobilization are therefore necessarily varied. Sometimes, the aim may be to defend the identity of a group against attacks from other ethnic groups; at other times, ethnic mobilization may be a deliberate attempt to promote an already dominant ethnic group.

Ethnic mobilization, then, is not the exclusive prerogative of minorities or majorities; its utility depends on the socio-political and economic circumstances in which groups find themselves in relationship to each other. As I have suggested elsewhere (1991:58), such action is both socio-economic and political to different degrees, and should be seen as varying across a spectrum, depending on prevailing circumstances. These may be such that a group is called upon to defend or to promote what members share, or believe they share. What they promote or defend may be largely cultural in nature and, far from involving conflict with other groups, may be mutually enriching. The pride some groups display in what are popularly called 'ethnic' cuisine, dress, and music, can benefit all groups which share a common territory and owe allegiance to a common political authority. At the other end of the spectrum of social action based on ethnic solidarity, there is a growing demand for community (people, ethnic group) to be coterminous with political authority (state). During the last two centuries, this combination has been partly achieved through the construction of what is generally called the nation-state (Goulbourne 1991). At both ends of the spectrum the relationship between ethnic mobilization and conflict is clear enough: at one end there may be no conflict at all, while at the other, the potential for open and even violent conflict is enormous.

The mobilization of ethnicity entails what Schattschneider called the *mobilization of bias.* His theory begins with the observation that "...the root of all politics is the universal language of conflict..." and that the "... central political fact in a free society is the tremendous contagiousness of conflict" (1960:2). A given situation of conflict involves actors and spectators, and it is a mistake to assume that only the former are participants and that they alone will determine the outcome. Indeed, the outcome of a conflict can sometimes be determined as much by the inside participants as by the observers, the crowd or the audience. This is because conflict is contagious and its scope is therefore likely to be elastic, spreading outward away from its original cause and centre. It is, of course, the task of politicians to contain or control this spread. With contagion comes the possibility of an increasing number of actors participating in the conflict so that the strong are no longer assured of certain victory. It is therefore nearly always in the interest of the weaker party to a conflict to broaden its scope and thereby

---

majority—is caught up in one or other of the processes entailed in construction, consolidation and re-definition.

involve more actors and a larger audience. Conversely, it is always in the interest of the stronger party to a conflict to limit the scope of the conflict.

Every new participant (as inside actor or part of the audience) brings a *bias* to the conflict and a resolution requires more compromises and, therefore, a deficit for the stronger party. To influence the outcome, each party to a conflict will want to mobilize those who hold the same bias or viewpoint. The strong will want to do so as a situation gets 'out of control'—usually, *their* control. The weak, or in Marxist terms the dominated, will want to mobilize bias and thereby make the cause of contention a public issue (and therefore contagious), rather than a private (and therefore contained) one. In an open, democratic system the potential for issues to become public is, of course, enormous. When this is linked to the problematic of ethnicity, which is ever so permeable and ever so emotional rather than rational, the potential for contagion is greatly enhanced.[2]

The action of arousing and organizing groups of people around their ethnicity is largely an attempt to participate more effectively in the political process. It is an attempt to secure or maintain scarce resources, either for the group or its leaders. This kind of mobilization of bias is, however, something of a two-edged sword, because there is always the risk of stimulating the mobilization of other competing ethnicities. This suggests that there is a limit to the usefulness of ethnic mobilization. Moreover, ethnic mobilization has the potential to ignore or belittle the most important fact about culture-contact and the creativity to which it gives rise, namely, change and development. The evolution of a 'new' culture, and change itself, are more than likely to disappear from the public agenda when ethnic mobilization is the rallying call to social and political action. In these circumstances, ethnicity, or ethnic solidarity, is used as a currency for political ends, and its attractiveness lies in the ease with which it can be mobilized, thereby spreading the scope of conflict.

The general situation

The international situation suggests that ethnicity is becoming increasingly used as a common, abundant and universally available currency, as groups and individuals struggle over limited, finite, resources. Whilst ethnic conflict is always pursued over tangible and visible material resources, once unrestrained conflict begins, its original cause nearly always disappears

2 There have been some important qualifications to Schattschneider's work by writers such as Olson, Baratz and Barach, and Crenson. The ability to conceal potential conflict, whilst recognized by Schattschneider, has been developed and explicated by the work of these writers.

from view. Thus, in a war between countries or, even more, between ethnic groups, deep-rooted questions of ethnicity, culture, religion and language surface as apparent reasons for the conflict escalating into open warfare. It is a paradox of the so-called 'new world order' that, whilst we no longer live under the threat of nuclear war, during the 1990s the world has been as heavily engaged in war as at any other time in recorded history.

The general reduction in military expenditure as a proportion of Gross Domestic Product does not of itself increase the prospects for world peace. In his study of military expenditures in 124 countries between 1972 and 1990, Daniel Hewitt (1993) found a fall of about 23 per cent (see also IMF/WB 1993:24-5). On average, a decline occurred in central government expenditure on the military in almost every part of the world. Of the 124 countries in the study there were decreases in 62, no change in 38 and only 20 experienced an increase in military spending. Cuts in military aid, the end of the Cold War, internal changes in countries in every part of the world and the ideological (and sometimes real) advances of democracy have been among the political reasons for these changes in overall military spending.

Encouraging as these dramatic changes undoubtedly are, global peace is still far from becoming a reality in the foreseeable future. We live in a 'world at war.' Between 1992 and 1993 there were around 28 wars being fought around the world, and threats of imminent war in 14 countries in Africa, Asia, the Caribbean, Central and South America, Europe and the Pacific. Only Australia, Greenland and North America appeared free of wars and threats of war. It should be noted, however, that in the Caribbean the main threats (in Cuba and Haiti) come from the United States defending its dominance in what it has regarded as its 'backyard' since the formulation of the Monroe Doctrine in 1817.

It is worth reminding ourselves of the kinds of violent conflicts which afflict the international community today and to consider the prominence of ethnic mobilization in them. In this decade, the war zones have included Columbia, Peru and Guatemala in Latin America; Angola, Zaire, Sudan, Somalia, Djibouti, Liberia, Western Sahara, and Rwanda in Africa; Iraq, Turkey, Lebanon, and Israel/West Bank and the Yemen in the Middle East; Bosnia-Herzegovina, Croatia, Moldavia, and Northern Ireland in Europe; Georgia, Armenia, Azerbaijan, the Russian Federation, Tajikistan, Afghanistan, Burma, New Guinea, Sri Lanka, and Cambodia in Asia; and the Philippines in the Pacific (*The Independent* 1994a, 1994b). The conflict has been going on since 1945 in the Philippines, since 1968 in Ireland, the 1960s in Colombia, New Guinea, Angola, and Western Sahara; and since the 1970s in the Lebanon, Peru, Iraq, Cambodia, and Afghanistan. Most of these conflicts started in the 1980s and increased dramatically in the later years of the decade and the early 1990s, particularly in Central and Eastern Europe and Asia. These conflicts may be sensibly categorized into those which have a predominantly *ideological* or *ethnic* bias. This is not a sharp distinction:

struggles for the change or maintenance of structures and practices which may be multi-ethnic or single-ethnic, but which place little or no emphasis on ethnic solidarity. In a situation of this kind the emphasis is placed on universal (dare I say, human?) factors such as equality, fairness, and justice. While these may be contradictory and conflictual, the consensus is that it is not through war but through discussion, protest, demonstration, propaganda and so forth that resolution will be achieved. Cuba, Guatemala, Haiti, Peru, Burma, Cambodia and the Philippines are dominant ideological situations in which either whole communities or organized groups are struggling over non-ethnic issues such as, for example, the best form of government and the distribution of wealth. The actual or imminent conflicts which are embedded in such situations may or may not have ethnic dimensions, but they tend to be muted where they occur. Colour, for example, is an important factor in Haiti and Cuba and, in the latter case, there may even be the potential for 'race' conflict in the near future. In general, however, specific conflicts within the world community are biased towards ethnicity, that is, towards the defence or promotion of the ethnic group. This is so in all the main conflicts in Africa, Europe, the Middle East and Asia.

It is significant that states in the Americas are less divided by ethnicity than by ideological considerations, whilst in the 'Old World' of Africa, Asia, the Middle East and Europe, ethnicity is the single most crucial factor. In the former areas, ethnicity is still contained within the established nation-state framework but, in the Old World, state-deconstruction and state-formation and building are continuous processes. The same processes could, of course, occur in the Americas, but at present this appears most unlikely. Only in French-speaking Quebec does the possibility of a new state beckon, even after the 1995 decision to stay in the Canadian federation. At least one of the major antagonisms of the Old World has failed to be transplanted wholesale to the Americas.

This is not, however, intended to underestimate the potential for large scale disruption and even war in the apparently tranquil and peaceful parts of the world. Significant ethnic divisions and ethnic mobilization exist in countries as diverse as Australia, Brazil, Canada, Fiji, Guyana, and Mexico. Moreover, I have not yet mentioned those countries in which civil (often separatist) wars or intra-state wars have been fought in recent decades. These include Spain (the Basques); India (the Sikhs, Kashmiris and others); Fiji (the indigenous and Indian-descended populations); Ethiopia (Eritreans, Oromos and Tigreans); Cyprus (the Turks and Greeks), Tibet, Bhutan, Macedonia, the Gulf, Kenya, Mozambique—and many others. Mobilization by Bretons in France, Welsh and Scots in Britain, 'ethnic' Germans in East and Central Europe, and minority Russians in the new republics which emerged out of the former Soviet Union, are further examples of the popularity of ethnicity as a political currency. The break-up of former Yugoslavia and Czechoslovakia and the potential break-up of some African popularity of ethnicity as a political currency. The break-up of former Yugoslavia and Czechoslovakia and the potential break-up of some African states such as war-torn Somalia or peaceful Tanzania, are further examples of the universality of ethnicity as a powerful political currency.

Multi-culturalism and the restraint on conflict

It is somewhere in the middle of the spectrum of social action based on ethnic considerations where difficulties arise for societies with relatively high levels of democratic participation, established institutions and conventions. There are severe conflicts in these societies over such issues as sexual preference, gender and colour discrimination, but there is a determination to resolve such conflicts within a framework of peace.[3] Here ethnic mobilization may involve such crucial issues as the use of language, the protection of religion, schooling and the control of the young, particularly females, within the family.

Most of these are issues about which the modern state will seek to make decisions binding on all individuals within its jurisdiction, irrespective of the ethnic groups to which they may belong. In democratic societies which are experiencing cultural change as a result of comparatively recent migration and settlement (or strong culture-contact), the debate about ethnic mobilization is taking place mainly within the context of what is described as the 'multi-cultural society.' In some of these societies multi-culturalism is viewed as a kind of panacea for social ills and a defence against social disorder; in others, the recognition of multi-culturalism is seen as a precursor of the disintegration of the traditional nation-state. Fortunately, however, whilst individuals and groups may be very militant about ethnic issues and the equality they seek, they are unlikely to lead to physical, as distinct from verbal, war.

Before illustrating this point with respect to post-World War II British society, it is important to note that, unlike earlier forms of state or political authority, the modern state in all its variations tends to homogenize, rather than 'pluralize,' through the rule of law. Inevitably, therefore, ethnic mobilization over issues of the kind mentioned earlier, entails conflict. Sometimes these conflicts are between groups; at other times the conflict may be between a group and the state itself. In either case the state becomes a party to conflict rather than merely a referee, as in some liberal-democratic formulations of the proper relationship between the state and civil society. When, however, the state is expected to be a referee, it is likely to take the

3 Even conflicts over access to raw materials and markets are resolved by the Group of 7 most industrialized countries through the GATT treaties, rather than through war as in 1914 and 1939.

side of the stronger party in order to keep conflict out of the wider national or international political arena.

This is certainly so in Britain. Apparently benign and liberal, the British state has attempted to present itself as a champion of those who suffer racial discrimination and exclusion from the mainstream of society. Nowhere is this more clearly demonstrated than in the passing of legislation (1968, 1976) to outlaw discrimination on the basis of a person's colour or 'race,' and the setting up of a statutory body (the Commission for Racial Equality) to oversee the working of the law, seek redress when necessary, and make recommendations for further changes in the law. At the local level, many city councils throughout the country have developed specific policies to counter colour or racial discrimination in the vital areas of housing, education, health and other services. Very many public bodies and employers who advertise vacant posts in the media now state that they are an 'equal opportunity employer.' For some British people the law does not go far enough in discouraging or outlawing racial discrimination; for others the law has gone too far in limiting the individual's presumed freedom. In general, however, it would appear that, for the great majority of people, public behaviour informed by racial or colour discrimination is unacceptable in a democratic and just society. It is, of course, difficult to measure this sentiment, but the fact that the extreme right-wing in British politics have not won significant support in either national or local elections is a strong indication that the electorate supports a liberal consensus around this issue. At the very least, this is placed lower on their list of priorities than are other questions relating to the country's economy, defence, infrastructure, health and so forth. In other words, ethnic mobilization by the majority ethnic group or groups in Britain has not, so far, been of the kind that calls for the total exclusion of new minorities, as advocated by Enoch Powell, the Monday Club and various neo-nazi or neo-fascist groups.

This does not mean, however, that the central state has been slow to use what ethnic mobilization there has been within the majority population. Whether the government is Conservative or Labour, in Britain the state has been quick to convert actual and perceived majoritarian ethnic mobilization into effective political currency. At nearly every general elections since 1964, there has been the Conservative politician willing to mobilize majority ethnic feelings against new minorities.[4] The major measures taken by the state in this area have been the discussion and enactment of the 1962 Commonwealth Immigration Act, which sought to limit black immigration (but on the contrary stimulated it between 1958 and 1962); the 1971 and

---

4 In the 1992 general elections the Social & Liberal Democrats were also willing to mobilize on this basis. They won the Cheltenham seat in the House of Commons from the Conservatives after declaring that its candidate was a 'local man,' when his Conservative opponent was a black barrister, John Taylor, from Birmingham.

1981 British Nationality Acts, which required people from the Commonwealth to register their British citizenship and redefined it (especially in 1981) along lines of blood or descent rather than the ancient Anglo-Saxon tradition in which citizenship was defined by place of birth. These measures were taken to reassure the majority white population that their governments were concerned to preserve 'the British way of life' which some saw as being under threat from so-called 'hordes' of brown and black immigrants from the Indian sub-continent, East Africa and the Caribbean.

Through both immigration and natural growth, the population of Britain has nonetheless changed during the decades since World War II. From being a relatively homogeneous population—at least in terms of colour, religion and language—Britain has become, since 1948, a society characterized by both European and non-European cultural patterns and rich in the variety of colour tones, religions and languages. The 1991 national census returns confirm this. With a population of 54,860,200 Britain's new ethnic minorities— people with backgrounds in Africa, Asia and the Caribbean—accounted for 3,006,500 or 5.5 per cent. Of the total population, 1,467,900 or 2.7 per cent were of South Asian backgrounds; the largest group within this category were Indians at 840,800, followed by Pakistanis at 475,800, who were in turn slightly less than African-Caribbeans at just over 499,000 (Owen 1992). Most of the new minorities live in the South East and the West Midlands, where they are concentrated in the nation's two largest cities, London and Birmingham respectively.

Partly because Britain is a relatively small island, densely populated and with long established national institutions, Christian denominations, relatively unified mass media and common myths, the high concentration of new ethnic minorities does not necessarily limit their nation-wide impact. The presence of African, Asian and Caribbean minorities is not, of course, new to British society. Before 1948, however, migration and settlement patterns were largely male and sporadic, resulting in cross-colour and cross-cultural marriage and other relationships. Often such migrants concentrated in specific industries, such as the merchant navy. The pockets of mixed black and white populations in Cardiff and Liverpool were formed largely out of these experiences. Earlier, the founding of the British Raj in the Indian sub-continent, particularly after the 1857 Mutiny, and the spread of the Union Jack in Africa after the Berlin Congress of 1884, provided the basis for an Asian and African presence in metropolitan Britain. Earlier still, from the sixteenth century, the exploration and exploitation of Africa and the Americas, the expansion of the slave trade and the production of commodities for the then world market on plantations, had resulted in Britain becoming a regular destination or transition point for Africans and members of what emerged as the African diaspora.

The multi-colour or multi-ethnic character of British society is not, therefore, as new as it is often thought to be. And whilst migration and settlement have not resulted in the large influx of Africans, Asians and Caribbeans that was feared by some people, nonetheless their presence has been qualitatively significant. The apparently homogeneous cultural landscape has changed, with the presence of a variety of religions such as Hinduism, Sikhism, and Islam from the Indian sub-continent and Africa. Caribbean Christians have brought their own evangelical, and sometimes radical, traditions. Rastafarianism from Jamaica has found fertile ground among the off-spring of Caribbean settlers. Asians have brought a number of languages such as Urdu, Hindi, Gujerati, Punjabi to the streets of Britain; a wide range of West African languages are also spoken, as are a number of Caribbean Creoles based largely on English and to a lesser extent French and remnants of West African languages. Jamaican reggae and Trinidadian steel-bands have become an established part of the popular music scene, with the annual Notting Hill carnival becoming, since the 1960s, the single largest street event in Western Europe. Track and field sports are now dominated by British-born black young people, who are also strongly represented in football, cricket and a number of other sports. Asian families have wrought something of a revolution in the ownership and running of traditional British corner shops, general retailing and wholesale.

From the 1980s, individuals from the new ethnic minority communities have asserted themselves in the political arena, both at local and national levels. The elections of 1987 returned three black and one Asian Labour candidates to the House of Commons and, in 1992, these individuals retained their seats, with one Asian being returned for the Conservatives. During the late 1980s, three London local authorities (Brent, Lambeth and Haringay) were led by black politicians and several had Asian and black mayors. With respect to the traditional professions, law and medicine have responded favourably to pressures for change from black and Asian young people; interestingly enough, the greatest resistance to progressive change (especially with respect to the employment of academic staff) has come from the universities. Whilst there are some Asians employed in natural science and economics departments, there is a glaring unwillingness on the part of universities (particularly the older ones) to employ academics of African and Caribbean backgrounds despite the declaration by each university that it is an 'equal opportunity employer.' Here is a situation that the late M. G. Smith (1974) would have described as the 'differential incorporation' of new minorities into British society. The racial discrimination and exclusion from certain crucial areas of British life experienced by people of African, Caribbean and Asian backgrounds, as well as the experiences of colonialism, have produced a high degree of unity amongst these communities. This was particularly strong from the late 1960s to the mid-1980s. However, with the remarkable success of some Asians in economic activities and the professions, this unity is being seen as an obstacle to their further progress, and has therefore been largely abandoned by significant élites.

For some, these developments are a welcome enrichment of British life, but for others they are a cause for disquiet. An example of each of these positions will illustrate this general point. On the far right of the British political spectrum, what I have called the cultural-conservatives have denounced change, because they see cultural pluralism within the nation as a threat to the very fabric of the national community. At the beginning of the 1990s Norman (now Lord) Tebbitt, a former member of Margaret Thatcher's cabinet, a former chairman of the Conservative party, and a fervent anti-European federalist, complained that

> ...almost an age of innocence is ending. Our gentle nationalism, more a sense of nationality, was never built on any sense of racial purity. After all, the early history of these islands was of successive waves of immigrants mixing Celts, Britons, Angles, Saxons, Romans, Norse and Norman French. Later Flemish, Huguenot and Jewish immigrants were integrated to such an extent that only the Jewish community remained identifiable and that only by a religion on which the culture of the whole nation is largely based. But in recent years our sense of insularity and nationality has been bruised by large waves of immigrants resistant to absorption, some defiantly claiming a right to superimpose their culture, even their law, upon the host community (1990:78).

This longing for an insular, homogeneous Britain which absorbs cultural differences, ignores the imperial, world-wide past of which Margaret Thatcher boasted in her now famous speech in September, 1988 in Bruges (Thatcher 1988). Tebbitt, reflecting the attitudes of the far right, also ignored the fact that whilst British society has been able to absorb other Europeans, the real test of the country's ability to assimilate or integrate others has been whether peoples from outside Europe (i.e., Africans and Asians) have been able to become part and parcel of the British social fabric. Evidently, they have not.

It is this situation that many liberal-minded people, ranging from left to right of the political spectrum, have been concerned to address. Roy (now Lord) Jenkins, when Labour Home Secretary in the 1960s, stressed that it would be fairer for Britain to abandon its policy of "a flattening process of uniformity" and, instead, nurture "cultural diversity and mutual tolerance" between peoples from different cultural backgrounds (Rex & Tomlinson 1979:170). The same point has been picked up in a number of statements by local and national governments and in papers by authorities dealing with education and health. But few would deny that it was the Swann Report of 1985 which best presented the aims, objectives and contradictions of the 'multi-cultural' society in Britain. Entitled *Education for all,* the report asserts that

> ...a multi-cultural society such as ours would in fact function most effectively and harmoniously on the basis of pluralism which enables, expects and encourages members of all ethnic groups, both minority and majority, to participate fully in shaping the society as a whole within a framework of commonly accepted values,

> practices and procedures, whilst also allowing and, where necessary, assisting the ethnic minority communities in maintaining their distinct identities within this common framework (1985:5).

The report sought to encourage a vision of British society as "...both socially cohesive and culturally diverse," but also a society in which individuals would share "common aims, attributes and values" (Swann 1985:7). There is little doubt that these aims and objectives are contradictory, but this should not distract from the report's essential principle of asserting that it should be possible for people of different cultural backgrounds to live together peacefully under the same political authority.

The question then arises as to what societal patterns would be necessary to make Swann's kind of multi-cultural or plural society a possibility. Clearly, if all groups were exclusively to live according to their own values and customs—which are sometimes irreconcilable—then we may expect the result to be what J. S. Furnivall and M. G. Smith have described as social and cultural pluralism. That is to say, people may live under the same political authority on a common territory and "meet and mix" in the market place but may not "combine" (Furnivall 1948; Smith 1965). I have argued elsewhere (1991) that there are societies in which some of the best elements of diversity have been combined to effect a relatively just social order. In such societies there is an acceptance of hybridism or syncretism as a norm of social existence. Before this can become commonplace, we need to accept what Malinowski saw as an inevitable result of culture-contact—culture-change.

Such an acceptance would contradict Swann, who recommended state assistance for minority ethnic groups to maintain their "distinct identities." The change that results from culture-contact does not require this kind of state interference. The state should neither seek to preserve extant cultures nor seek to privilege any one cultural group over another. What may be required of the state, however, is a guarantee to individuals that they will enjoy all the freedoms and liberties won in protracted struggles during the course of the founding of the state itself in its liberal-democratic form. If it is accepted that the mobilization of ethnicity has become as important to many contemporary élites as religion once was, then, just as it was important in specific instances for the modern state to place constraints on clericalism and promote secularism for the good of the greater number, so today it is becoming important for the state to put to one side the emerging hegemony of ethnicity. It is important for there to be democratic participation in the debate about how to promote a just and fair society in which ethnic difference is neither a matter for promotion nor defence, but one of the components in a secure and fair social order. In such a society, ethnic mobilization may become a less attractive option for political élites caught up in competition over scarce resources.

resources were to become abundant and fairly distributed, would war, like Frederick Engels' state, 'wither away,' or would groups struggle over other, more personal, issues such as sexual preference? Are apparently democratic societies always better equipped to tackle the problems of cultural pluralism? Has the nation-state now become an outmoded socio-political association incapable of accommodating legitimate difference? Is the multicultural or plural society a constraint on the resort to war, or merely a stopgap? Can cultural hybridism or creolism minimize differences to the extent that they become a pole around which unity can be achieved, as has occurred in many societies in the Caribbean and the Americas? Clearly, the search for a resolution of conflict between groups in an international environment of nation-states is likely to remain a way of life for the world community for some time to come. As Clausewitz observed, the "...result in war is never absolute" (1968:108).

References

Barth, F.
1969 Introduction. In *Ethnic Groups and Boundaries: The Social Organization of Culture Difference*. F. Barth (ed.), pp. 9-38. Boston: Little, Brown & Co.

Clausewitz, C. von
1968 *On War.* Anatol Rapoport (ed.). London: Penguin Books.

Deutsch, K.
1968 *The Nerves of Government*. New York: The Free Press.

Furnivall, F. S.
1948 *Colonial Policy and Practice.* Cambridge: Cambridge University Press.

Goulbourne, H.
1991 *Ethnicity and Nationalism in Post-Imperial Britain.* Cambridge: Cambridge University Press.

Herskovits, M.
1941 *The Myth of the Negro Past.* Massachusetts: Peter Smith.

Hewitt, D.
1993 Military expenditures 1972-1990: the reasons behind the post-1985 fall in world military spending. *IMF Working Paper, WP/93/18.* Washington: IMF/WB.

1993 Military expenditures: will the post-1985 decline be sustained? *Finance and Development* December, pp 24-25.

The Independent
1994a The dark horses of 1994. *The Independent* 1 January, pp. 4, 7.

1994b A year for making peace or war? *The Independent* 1 January, p. 5.

Malinowski, B.
1961 *The dynamics of culture change.* Westport: Greenwood Press.

Owen, D.
1992 *Ethnic minorities in Great Britain: settlement patterns.* National Ethnic Minority Data Archive 1991, Census Statistical Paper No 1. Coventry: Centre for Research in Ethnic Relations, University of Warwick.

Rex, J., & S. Tomlinson
1979 *Colonial Immigrants in a British City.* London: Routledge & Kegan Paul.

Schattschneider, E. E.
1960 *The Semi-Sovereign People.* Hinsdale: The Dryden Press.

Smith, M. G.
1965 *The Plural Society in the British West Indies.* Berkeley: University of California Press.

1974 *Corporations and Society.* London: Duckworth.

Swann, M.
1985 *Education For All: Report of the Committee of Inquiry into the Education of Children from Ethnic Minority Groups.* Cmnd. 9453. London: HMSO.

Tebbitt, N.
1990 Fanfare of being British. *The Field* May, pp. 78-79.

Thatcher, M.
1988 *Britain and Europe.* Text of the Speech Delivered in Bruges by the Prime Minister on 20 September 1988. Conservative Political Centre.

CLAN CONFLICT AND ETHNICITY IN SOMALIA: HUMANITARIAN INTERVENTION IN A STATELESS SOCIETY

IOAN M. LEWIS[1]

Department of Anthropology, London School of Economics and Political Science, Houghton Street, London WC2A 2AE

War and famine; peace and milk
(a Somali saying).

Since Boutros-Ghali delivered his famous jibe that, in comparison with ex-Yugoslavia, Somalia was a poor man's crisis, the situation has changed dramatically. The UN operation in Somalia was by 1993 the largest (28,000 personnel) and the most costly in the world ($1.5 billion annually, more than twice Yugoslavia). In this paper I explore how the crisis arose, how the international community has become so deeply involved, and the remarkable series of new departures in international behaviour which have arisen in the process. I will also consider weaknesses in the international response which should be addressed for future action. In the final section I look more generally at forms of communal conflict in the Horn of Africa and what light they shed on the general question of ethnicity and war.

It will be as well to begin by briefly highlighting these new departures in international activity. In responding, very belatedly, to the challenge of mass starvation and famine in a country torn apart by wars, whose statehood had lapsed, and whose economy and public services had collapsed, the UN found itself in the unexpected position of administering what was virtually an undeclared trusteeship (known as UNOSOM II). This astonishing development, bizarrely retracing Somalia's history as a UN trusteeship from 1950-60, has been largely triggered by the equally surprising initiative of the United States in mounting, with hasty UN legitimation, the heavily armed 30,000 strong operation, Restore Hope, to force food supplies along roads regularly menaced by trigger-happy Somali militias. Security Council Resolution 794, of 3 December 1992, authorized the US-led Unified Task Force (UNITAF), whose operations were directed by Mr. Oakley, a retired US ambassador to Somalia, to employ "all necessary means to establish as soon as possible a secure environment for humanitarian relief operations in Somalia."

1 This is a modified and up-dated version of a paper presented to the 1993 Forum of the Centre for the Study of Global Governance, London School of Economics on "Rethinking Global Institutions," held 10-12 September 1993 at Chewton Glen, New Milton, Hampshire. A record of events subsequent to those discussed here can be found in the *Horn of Africa Bulletin*, a bi-monthly journal published by The Life and Peace Institute, Uppsala Sweden.

If this was the first instance of unilateral UN military intervention in a (theoretically) sovereign state, this development had been pushed even further by the successive UN, and more directly, military administration which took over in May 1993 as UNOSOM II, with even wider powers to act against any faction violating the [warlords'] cease-fire and disarmament agreements. Very much in contrast to the situation in Yugoslavia (the Somalis have no military aircraft and are much poorer in equipment and organization), in its efforts to secure the implementation of the disarmament agreements the UN has been drawn into extended military action against the most formidable of the Somali warlords, General Aideed. A further significant development, however poorly handled, was to accuse Aideed of war crimes, to proclaim him an outlaw, and offer a reward for his arrest, to which the Somali warlord responded by issuing similar threats to the commander of UNOSOM II. It is, of course, somewhat ironical that all this should lead the UN to be criticized for intervening militarily in Somalia and for not doing so in Yugoslavia.

After the clashes in Mogadishu between US crack Delta force soldiers in October of 1993, which led to an unacceptably high level of American casualties, US/UN policy was drastically changed. Military actions against Aideed's militia ceased, negotiations with him were resumed in a desperate effort to secure peace, and the withdrawal of US troops commenced with the goal of complete American evacuation by the end of March 1994. The Germans, Belgians, French and Italians also started withdrawing and it was left to the Secretary-General to try to muster replacements from the Third World to join those contingents already in Somalia. UN resolution 897 of February 1994 provided for a force of up to 22,000. Officially, the operation would still be under Chapter 7 of the UN mandate, but the emphasis would be on delivering relief supplies, reconstruction, and peace-keeping rather than peace-enforcement. There would be no more coercive disarmament and UN troops would not necessarily intervene in battles between Somali groups. This striking reversal displayed the limits and precariousness of international intervention, since leading member states of the UN have shown that they cannot tolerate battle casualties incurred in attempting to control and compose conflicts far from home and in default of any national interest. Thus the New World Order floundered and perhaps foundered in the mean streets of Mogadishu.

In the course of these unforeseen and unintended consequences of seeking to deliver humanitarian aid effectively, the US for the first time conceded that its national forces could serve in a multi-national force formally under UN (rather than US) command. The second in command was an American, and UNOSOM II as a whole was directed by an American admiral, a former US Security Advisor, who was the Secretary-General's Special Representative in Somalia until January 1994. In responding to the appeal for international co-operation, Germany similarly made a unique, and controversial, concession in committing a military unit to provide technical services in the UN force—a landmark decision to post military personnel outside Germany for the first time, the legality of which has inevitably been contested in the courts.

Somalis and the world

Traditionally, the Muslim Somalis (about 5 million) are, for the most part, nomadic herdsmen, moving with their camels, sheep and goats (and sometimes cattle) over the inhospitable semi-deserts and arid plains of the Horn of Africa. In this region of scarce resources, where exploration for petrol has proceeded apparently unsuccessfully since the 1940s, Somalis are accustomed to fight for access to pasture and water. Prior to European colonization, they did not constitute a state and their uncentralized political organization was based on what anthropologists call a 'segmentary lineage system' in which political identity and loyalty were determined by genealogical proximity or remoteness (Lewis 1982; 1994). The ideological principle here was the same as that embodied in the famous Arab Bedouin political axiom: "myself against my brother; my brother and I against my cousins; my cousins and I against the world." With their lack of chiefs and absence of centralized government, the nineteenth century English explorer and Arabist, Richard Burton, who understood them well, characterized the Somalis as a "fierce and turbulent race of republicans." Had he been a modern travel writer, he might have added that, with their constantly shifting political loyalties, the Somalis lived in a state of chronic political schizophrenia, verging on anarchy. Instead, Burton rightly noted as a redeeming positive feature, the extraordinary prominence of poetry in Somali culture (Andrzejewski & Lewis 1964), although he neglected to emphasize the crucial role of poetic polemic in politics and war (Samatar 1982).

So constituted, as a proudly independent people with a strong sense of ethnic exclusiveness in terms of language[2] and culture—despite their myriad internal divisions—the Somalis have for centuries lived outside, or on the margins of world history. They have, rather characteristically, usually impinged on the outside world in contexts of conflict. The first extensive reference to the Somalis in written history is a sixteenth century document[3] recording their role on the Islamic side in the religious wars of the period

2 The Somali language, which contains a number of Arabic loan-words associated with Islam, belongs to the Cushitic family which includes other languages spoken in south-eastern Ethiopia.

3 This is a famous account by the Muslim Chronicler of the period written in Arabic between 1540 and 1560.

between Christian Ethiopia and the surrounding Muslim principalities. This describes the Somali warriors as being especially expert in road ambushes, a tradition they have maintained up to the present! Just after the French, British, Italians and Ethiopians had carved up the Somali nation at the end of the nineteenth century, a fiery Somali fundamentalist sheikh who was also the most brilliant poet of his age[4] (Andrzejewski & Lewis 1964:70-4) mounted a *jihad* against the Christian colonizers which lasted for 20 years. This rebellion required four major British military expeditions and the first use of air bombardment in Africa before it collapsed when Sayyid Mohamad—dubbed by the British the 'Mad Mullah' (a term unused by Somalis)—died of influenza. During this period, the Somalis frequently figured in English newspaper headlines. So, for example, the terrible battle of August, 1913, in which the British camel constabulary was routed by the Dervishes with heavy losses on both sides, was announced on the London news stands as "Horrible Disaster to Our Troops in Somaliland."

This long-drawn out conflict was concentrated in the north of the Somali region, mainly in the British Somaliland Protectorate and eastern Ethiopia, inhabited by the ethnically Somali Ogadeen, the clan to which the Dervish leader himself belonged. Further south, the Italian colony of Somalia was largely unaffected. Somali conscripts, however, were drafted into Mussolini's armies for the conquest of Ethiopia and the Italo-Ethiopian war of 1935-6, which was part of the run-up to the Second World War, developed from a minor confrontation between Ethiopian and Italian forces at the oasis of Walwal in Ogadeen territory, claimed by Ethiopia. The defeat of the Italians in 1941 brought their Somali colony together with those of Ethiopia and Britain under a single British military administration which encouraged Somali nationalism, directly and indirectly, especially the famous Bevin plan which proposed that all the Somalis should be administered as a single state and prepared for independence. This proved incompatible with the wider interests of the big four (Britain, France, Russia and America) and the Somali territories resumed their former status with the exception that the Italian colony of Somalia became a UN trusteeship, administered by Italy, with a ten year mandate (1950-60) to independence.

The next Somali intrusion on the world scene was in 1977-8 and again involved the Ogadeen clansmen. With the overthrow of Haile Selassie in Ethiopia in 1974, General Mohamad Siad Barre, who had come to power in a successful coup in Somalia in 1969, came under increasing pressure to support his kinsmen in the Ogadeen in their struggle against Ethiopian rule.[5] He waited until 1977 when Ethiopia seemed to be falling apart and then

---

4 One of the most famous of the Sayyid's poems is a chilling polemic commemorating the killing of the camel constabulary leader, Richard Corfield, on 9 August 1913.

5 Siad's mother came from the Ogadeen and that clan came to play an important role in his regime.

pitted his forces behind the Western Somali Liberation Front (Ogadeen) guerillas in their uprising against the weakened Ethiopians. The ensuing Ogadeen war precipitated a remarkable super-power somersault. The Americans, Ethiopia's traditional allies, had already distanced themselves from the revolutionary regime in Ethiopia creating an interesting opportunity for the Soviet Union which had been supporting and arming Somalia but balked at Siad's dangerous adventure in the Ogadeen. So the Soviets moved out of Somalia into Ethiopia, reputedly taking with them details of the structure and ordinance of the Somali armed forces.

Forced to concede defeat and pull out of the Ogadeen, Siad desperately sought American help, claiming now (rather suddenly) that he was bravely confronting the menace of communism in the Horn of Africa and dangling the bait of the former Soviet port facilities at Berbera in the north. So grudgingly, the US began to add western equipment to Siad's Soviet arsenals. Additional EEC arms supplies, sometimes paid for by Somalia's local super-power patron, Saudi Arabia, added to the stockpiling of weapons which kept Siad in power through the 1980s as he strove to suppress insurrection by clan guerilla movements in the north (former British Somaliland which had joined Somalia on independence in 1960) and north-east. Widespread disaffection against his increasingly tyrannical rule had developed in the wake of the Ogadeen debacle, and his survivalist, divide-and-rule tactics relied heavily on the unreliable expedient of bribing and arming friendly clans to attack the clans of his opponents. The ferocious fighting in the north powerfully eroded the strength of Siad's forces which became dominated by his own clansmen and other kinsmen.[6] Like the rest of the state, these forces depended heavily on supplies of food aid, officially for the huge refugee population (estimated at over 500,000) which had followed the retreating Somali army from the Ogadeen in 1977. The official economy, heavily dependent on the export of livestock from the war-torn north, was collapsing and had been eclipsed in importance by the informal sector based on livestock trading and migrant labour (what Somalis called the muscle-drain) in the Gulf States. The Civil Service, still paid at essentially the same rates as in the 1960s, before the years of hyperinflation, had virtually disintegrated by the end of the decade.

The final descent into chaos

As a functioning economic and political enterprise, the Somali state had already fallen apart before the actual overthrow of the dictator Siad in

6 Although Siad's regime was officially based on 'Scientific Socialism' (wealth-sharing based on wisdom—in Somali), in reality the core of his power structure depended on his own clan, his mother's clan, and the clan of his son-in-law who headed the national security service. His rule was thus, essentially, a family business as was well-known to most people in Somalia.

January 1991. Human rights pressure on Western governments, appalled at the ferocious internecine conflict in the north (*Africa Watch* 1990), had led to the virtual stopping of aid by 1990 when Siad's authority was increasingly circumscribed to the area adjoining the capital, Mogadishu. Thus, when he was finally dislodged from an already severely battle-scarred Mogadishu by United Somali Congress (USC) forces (of the Hawiye group of clans) led by General Aideed, Somalia had already disintegrated into its traditional component units.

A vivid illustration is provided by the experience of a friend of mine, a former Interior Minister who belongs to a northern clan. He and a group of relatives and friends decided to leave Mogadishu and return to the north. They formed a convoy of over 70 vehicles and took two months to complete a journey which, in time of peace, required little more than 24 hours. The convoy had its own paid armed escorts and was also forced to hire local guides and protectors while traversing the different clan territories. Four vehicles were looted *en route*—one by the convoy's armed escort when it had completed its mission. Other vehicles had to be abandoned along the way, and only 51 reached their destination. 18 people died on the journey and 30 were injured; however, nine babies were born.

This situation, of loosely articulated clan political units, was exactly the same as that described by Burton and other nineteenth century foreign explorers in the course of their travels in the Somali hinterland. The only significant difference today is the superabundance of modern automatic weapons which have long replaced the traditional spear. Visiting parts of the Somali interior in March 1992, every man and youth that I encountered was very visibly armed with a Kalashnikov, or American equivalent, and there appeared to be plenty of heavy weapons in the background. Additional supplies, including tanks, in which there is a lively trade, have flowed across the border from the arsenals of the former Ethiopian dictator, Mengistu Haile Mariam, whose American-supported overthrow in 1991 did not include any properly managed arrangements for the disbanding of his huge army, much of which disappeared with its weapons into the countryside. Other more recent supplies of arms have come into Somalia from Kenya—despite an official international arms embargo.

The deepening crisis

Having overthrown Siad, the USC Leaders, Aideed and Ali Mahdi (a prominent business man) started fighting over their respective positions, Ali Mahdi having already set up an elaborate phantom 'government.' This conflict which literally split Mogadishu into two armed fortresses polarized along clan lines, soon engulfed what was left of the city in a protracted blood bath in which (between November 1991 and February 1992) 14,000 people are estimated to have been killed and 27,000 wounded (*Africa Watch* 1993:5) often by indiscriminate artillery fire and anti-tank missile fusillades.

Fighting was not limited to Mogadishu and spread devastation and starvation throughout southern Somalia. The USC Hawiye had engaged in 'clan-cleansing' Mogadishu, butchering or driving out the remnants of people belonging to Siad's own clan or associated clans (the Darod). The latter regrouped in their home region south of Mogadishu under the leadership of another of Siad's former generals, 'Morgan.' Each side laid waste the agricultural region between the rivers which is Somalia's bread basket, killing and terrorizing the local cultivators who are less bellicose than the pastoralist Somali. As the conflict widened, Aideed struck up an alliance with Colonel Umar Jess's militia against Morgan who, in turn, joined forces loosely with another of Siad's former generals, General Adan Gabio and his militia. With the two factions in Mogadishu, these were the most heavily armed and aggressive militias fighting for control of what was left of Somalia, or key regions in the south. All were based primarily on traditional clan groupings held together by the attractions of the spoils of war. The main leaders, the so-called 'warlords,' were all dubious figures from the Siad regime.

In addition to this relatively organized violence but on a smaller scale, trigger-happy gangs of Qat-chewing[7] youths spread mayhem, looting and killing randomly in Mogadishu. With agricultural production devastated and livestock herding also severely affected, famine spread, particularly amongst those who could not protect themselves against the ravages of the warlords' attacks. The UN estimated a death toll of 300,000 from starvation, and 700,000 Somalis sought refuge in Kenya, Ethiopia and, on a smaller scale, in Europe, Scandinavia and North America. The death toll in the north in the earlier conflict between the Somali clansmen there and Siad's army of occupation added further to the terrible human cost of the Somali tragedy associated with the dictator, Siad.[8]

In this woeful picture there were, however, two rays of hope. In marked contrast to the chaos in the south, in the north-east and north-west, the reversion to clan structures shows the positive side of traditional politics—all the more striking in the absence of significant UN or other external intervention. In the north-east in the organization of the locally based Somali

---

7 Qat (*Catha edulis*) leaves, which look like English privet, are chewed raw, traditionally on religious or social occasions, when a group of men meet to talk in the evening. They are now chewed much more widely by individuals during the day and generate a strong craving for this stimulant in which the active ingredients are benzedrine-type compounds. The young urban gunmen who have adopted looting and killing, virtually as a way of life, are known as *mooryaan* in Mogadishu. One of their most popular role models is apparently Rambo.

8 *Africa Watch* estimates that between 50,000 and 60,000 civilians were killed by Siad's forces in the north.

Salvation Democratic Front (SSDF), traditional clan and modern political leadership has blended seamlessly to produce effective local government. The north-west, the former British Somaliland, where the Somaliland National Movement (SNM) guerillas had defeated Siad's forces in 1990, faced with the chaos in the south, declared unilateral independence from what was left of Somalia in May 1991. Although the region is more heterogeneous in clan structure than the north-east, its clan elders have proved remarkably persistent and successful in establishing and maintaining peace, to such an extent indeed, that they have forced the SNM 'government' effectively to disband and reconstitute itself through their traditional assemblies.

In a short field study commissioned by the British NGO Actionaid, a Somali social anthropologist has demonstrated how in such a war-weary population, peaceful relations within and between groups have been slowly built up over a period of two years by the local clan elders employing traditional nomadic diplomacy (Farah with Lewis 1993). In this process women have acted as go-betweens and have also been exchanged as brides in peace-settlements. Poets and religious leaders have played major placatory roles. Economic factors have also acted as a spur to pastoralists seeking to recover their wide-ranging movements accross areas occupied by hostile clans and to regain access to urban and farming settlements from which they had been expelled in outbursts of 'clan-cleansing' (as Somalis call it, adapting the terminology employed in Yugoslavia). They also sought to restore inter-clan trade and trade routes. Although, like all the pastoralists of the Horn of Africa, automatic weapons are pervasively distributed amongst the region's population and problems of controlling young 'freelance' militias are acute, Somaliland benefits from the absence of major warlords competing for power on the devastating scale current in southern Somalia. The result is a precarious and somewhat fitful peace. But, however imperfect and provisional, it has been achieved without the extensive foreign intervention, military and political, which in the south has achieved so much less.

International intervention

The pervasive conflict and the absence of any recognizable successor government to Siad's discouraged humanitarian intervention. Foreign embassies were withdrawn (or fled) and UN organizations followed suit, virtually abandoning Somalia to its fate. Only the Red Cross and a handful of NGOs, including Save the Children and Médecins Sans Frontières continued to work heroically in appalling conditions, having to employ armed guards to protect their houses, offices, stores and hospitals. Even the International Committee of the Red Cross (ICRC), for the first time in its history, found it necessary to hire armed escorts for its vehicles. Following much criticism and pressure and several false starts, aborted through attacks on UN staff, UNICEF reopened its offices in Mogadishu at the end of 1991. In early March 1992, Ali Mahdi and Aideed agreed to a ceasefire in Mogadishu which reduced the heavy artillery shelling which caused such terrible civilian casualties. This lull lasted for several months, with only sporadic outbreaks of fighting.

Although humanitarian aid was still far from adequate, it began to increase, highlighting the growing problem of looting. Much of the subsequent fighting in 1992 resulted from attempts by different factions to obtain or maintain control over the ports and distribution routes through which food and other supplies passed. Control of relief food was very lucrative for the warlords and their merchant allies. A faction who controlled a port (above all Mogadishu, as Aideed did) levied exorbitant taxes on cargoes, as well as taking direct cuts of 10 or 20 per cent of the incoming food aid (some of which was sold outside Somalia) and also providing trucks with machine guns (the Somali 'technicals') to 'protect' food deliveries. To add insult to injury, as we have seen, convoys were frequently robbed by those hired to defend them. Expatriate humanitarian organizations, despite the support of local Somali NGOs, thus found themselves caught up in a web of clan protection rackets and became part of the warlords' political economy. They were inevitably contributing to the problem whose most compelling symptoms they sought to assuage.

Relief agencies had already begun to warn that over a million Somalis were at risk of dying of hunger. From July 1992 onwards, the media took up the story and television relentlessly presented gruesome images of starvation and death in Somalia. It was yet another African 'famine' in which Somalis featured as helpless victims and objects of inexorable natural forces over which they had no control. This extremely powerful but misleading media coverage had the positive effect of catapulting the Somali crisis dramatically up the international political agenda to join Yugoslavia at the top. This even jolted the British Foreign Secretary and his EEC colleagues into making a hasty visit to Mogadishu to get some impression of the devastation at first hand, thus joining the throng of international dignitaries and film stars who touched down briefly on photo-opportunity missions.

Some of those who knew that Somalia was in the grip of a desperate man-made disaster felt that, since part of the fighting was over access to food, the solution was to flood the country with food. They, therefore, added their voices to the demand for massive food aid. Responding to a great deal of pressure for action, President Bush, in August 1992, assigned US military aircraft to transport bulk food relief for distribution to the interior where the devastated farmers were dying of starvation. Grain was also auctioned at reduced prices on the open market in Mogadishu in an unsuccessful effort to by-pass looters. Abundant food was certainly now available to Somalia: the problem was to get it to the hungry and dying, particularly in the agricultural villages between the Juba and Shebelle rivers. More and more NGOs were active in the country.

The UN had now begun, in a faltering way, to plan a stronger role which began inauspiciously with an inept attempt at mediation in January 1992 by Assistant Secretary-General, James Jonah. Security Council Resolution 751 of 24 April 1992 agreed in principle to the deployment of a UN security force to enable aid workers to operate effectively and safely. But this was sabotaged by the White House which did not want to raise the profile of foreign policy issues in an election year (*Africa Watch* 1993:10)[9] and it was only with Resolution 767 of 27 July that the deployment of a peace-keeping force of 3000 was authorized. It was not actually until the end of September 1992 that a contingent of 500 lightly armed Pakistani blue helmets arrived in Mogadishu, and it was two months later before they were able to assume guard duties at Mogadishu airport. The only really positive development in this dismal saga was the short-lived appointment (April-October) as UN Secretary-General's special envoy, of Ambassador Mohamed Sahnoun, an extremely energetic and shrewd Algerian diplomat with first-hand knowledge and understanding of the Horn of Africa. In the six months that he held the post, he showed enormous skill and initiative in negotiating with all sections of Somali society—not just the military leaders—and successfully persuaded them to agree to the deployment of UN troops to safeguard food delivery and distribution. Failing to receive the military support which the Security Council had authorized and extremely frustrated at the long delays and bureaucratic muddles involved in reactivating the various UN relief agencies in Somalia, Ambassador Sahnoun became strongly and publicly critical of the UN. He was forced to resign in October,[10] ironically in the same month in which the UN launched a vast '100 day Action Programme'[11] for Somalia which was a tribute to his efforts.

Lacking adequate protection, of the kind requested by Sahnoun, the increased flow of humanitarian aid and the greatly expanded NGO presence were inevitably accompanied by a general upsurge of looting and protection rackets. CARE, the agency responsible for bulk delivery of food supplies, was apparently spending $100,000 per month on bodyguards (Hillmore

---

9 My own contacts in the Defence Department in Washington tend to corroborate this.

10 Mohamed Sahnoun was a personal friend of Boutros-Ghali and seems to have felt betrayed when the bureaucrats in New York sabotaged his efforts and Boutros-Ghali failed to support him. His successor is generally considered, in Somalia, to have been unsuited for this post.

11 Donor countries pledged $150 million towards the estimated budget of $180 million to be spent on relief and development.

1993).[12] Some agencies claimed that the level of looting and organized pilfering was such that 70 to 80 per cent[13] of relief food did not reach its destination. ICRC ships delivering aid were often shot at by militia gangs. With wide media coverage and continuing reports of militarily weak Somali groups starving to death in the hinterland, calls for some form of UN military intervention became compelling. Boutros-Ghali reported to the Security Council in November 1992 that the UN Somalia policy had become 'untenable' and that fundamental UN principles might need to be reconsidered to find a solution. The outgoing US President, George Bush, began to review US options with his security advisers. Now that the elections were over, Bush evidently felt that he had nothing further to lose by a foreign policy initiative which might add to his international esteem. On 25 November 1992 he proposed that US troops should lead a UN operation in Somalia. This was quickly accepted by Boutros-Ghali and endorsed by the Security Council on 3 December by Resolution 794, approving UN intervention with the use of "all necessary means to establish as soon as possible a secure environment for humanitarian relief operations in Somalia." For the first time in its history, the international community had approved unilateral UN intervention, with offensive military force, in a (theoretically) sovereign state. A few days later, the advance parties of 'Operation Restore Hope,' which was to involve over 30,000 US and other troops, were landing in Mogadishu in a carefully staged photo-opportunity exercise before the eyes of the world (Lewis 1993a; *African Rights* 1993).

From 'Operation Restore Hope' to UNOSOM II

The Americans saw their primary objective as being to distribute food and humanitarian supplies securely to the worst affected areas of southern Somalia. They were, understandably, extremely anxious to avoid casualties (especially in the run-up to Christmas) and thus proceeded cautiously and with maximum (though often ill-conceived) publicity (Lewis 1993b), relying on their sheer numbers and technical superiority to overawe the Somali population. In this spirit, the operation was directed by an experienced diplomat, Robert Oakley, who had served as Ambassador in Mogadishu and knew some of the protagonists personally. He had also the delicate task of co-ordinating the work of his Unified Task Force (UNITAF) with the United Nations Operation in Somalia (UNOSOM) which was now led by the Iraqi diplomat, Ismat Kittani, who had replaced Mohamed

12 Other sources reported that, very reluctantly, the ICRC was spending £132,000 per month for the same purpose.

13 This was the figure reported to the Security Council on 25 November 1992.

Sahnoun as Boutros-Ghali's special representative. One of the main tensions here arose from UN pressure for UNITAF to enlarge its role to include disarmament, and thus aid the process of negotiation and reconciliation among the main armed groups. The Americans for their part were apt to raise the spectre of Vietnam and stressed the limited and short-term character of their intervention, which included an expanding circle of contingents from other countries—notably France but *not* Britain.

Most observers concluded that after a few weeks with a minimum of incidents, UNITAF had succeeded in opening up the supply routes and getting food through to most of the needy areas in southern Somalia. This entailed establishing military garrisons in key regions to quell oppressive militias and impose peace and control conflict—not always completely successfully. It also meant trying to re-establish a Somali police force in the war-torn capital, Mogadishu, where relations between the two local warlords, Ali Mahdi and Aideed, remained tense despite the truce negotiated by Ambassador Oakley as a precursor to the American intervention. Both sides hastened to welcome the powerful new force and to take as much advantage of it as possible. Heavy weapons and military trucks ('technicals') disappeared from the streets—some were hidden locally, others were moved into the interior. While many of the desperate citizens of Mogadishu and elsewhere unrealistically saw the Americans as saviours who would restore normal life and rebuild their country, others felt that the tyranny of the warlords was now sufficiently curtailed to allow them to voice independent views. Outside Mogadishu also, the US military presence enabled local elders, previously terrorized by the militias of the rival warlords, to regain some of their traditional authority as community leaders.

The re-empowering traditional community leaders, the importance of which had been consistently urged on UNOSOM by the Uppsala advisory group,[14] had been initiated by Mohamed Sahnoun, but was pursued only in a token fashion by his successor. With the usual Eurocentric preoccupations with hierarchical political structures totally different to the Somali system, the UN leadership in Mogadishu was more inclined to concentrate on the high profile warlords who, though their military strength was now held in check, had gained in legitimacy through their extensive dealings with

---

14 Based at the Horn of Africa Centre at the Life and Peace Institute, Uppsala, this small group, which I helped to establish, consisted of social scientists with specialist expertise on Somalia drawn from a number of countries and included three social anthropologists. With aid from the Swedish government, which is financing a number of peace-making projects in Somalia, four meetings have so far been held jointly with the senior officials of the political division of UNOSOM. The first two meetings were attended by the UN Special Envoy, Ambassador Mohamed Sahnoun. The group has consistently advised UNOSOM to follow a 'bottom-up' regionalist approach, with as much decentralization as possible. The response, in practice, has often seemed rather different. The Life and Peace Institute publishes the informative *Horn of Africa Bulletin*.

Ambassador Oakley—despite his efforts to prevent that. Taking advantage of the precarious lull in the fighting, produced by the huge but transitory military presence, Boutros-Ghali pressed ahead with his conception of the reconciliation process and, despite a hostile reception when he briefly visited Mogadishu, opened a peace conference of the faction leaders and their henchmen in Addis Ababa in early January 1993. Agreement in principle on a cease-fire was reached, although the terms remained to be settled. Aideed and his allies wanted an immediate cease-fire to consolidate their territorial gains, with reconciliation postponed to a later date. The other groups wanted the militias to return to their traditional clan areas and then proceed immediately to reconciliation. Eventually, formal cease-fire and disarmament agreements were signed, with the handing over of heavy weaponry to a 'cease-fire monitoring group' to be completed by March when a further and more comprehensive reconciliation conference would be held.

Clearly, the expectation was that UNITAF would not be involved in disarmament in one way or another. In fact, the uneasy calm which had been the initial reaction to the American intervention, had already begun to break down with renewed and sometimes sustained outbreaks of fighting in Mogadishu as well as in the southern port of Kismayu. The deteriorating security situation jolted the UNITAF troops into patrolling more aggressively, disarming townsmen openly carrying weapons, and raiding one of the most notorious arms markets in Mogadishu where they seized quantities of weapons. One of Aideed's encampments was destroyed and a contingent of General Morgan's attacked to prevent it gaining control of Kismayu. Given the vast quantities of weapons in the country and their constant replenishment from Kenya and Ethiopia, such action hardly constituted disarmament, although this was what Ambassador Oakley now vividly described as his policy of 'bird-plucking' disarmament—feather by feather. There were similar erratic shifts in dealing with the tricky question of the employment by NGOs of privately recruited armed guards—theoretically these freelance security agents were supposed to be unnecessary with the presence of UNITAF. In practice arms permits were issued to various categories of NGO guards, as well as NGO personnel, but the rules kept changing.

Thus, although Somalia was far from fully sanitized, the twin organizations of UNITAF and UNOSOM had established an unprecedented level of UN intervention in a previously sovereign state. The terms 'peace-making' and 'peace-keeping' hardly adequately covered the wide range of activities undertaken. Efforts were being made, especially by UNITAF, to involve local traditional community leaders—the elders—in aid distribution and preparations at local level for reconstruction. Embryonic police forces were being recruited, and while the UN prepared for the March Addis Ababa meeting of warlords, some symbolic disarmament was taking place. At the

UN, preparations were similarly in train for the establishment of UNOSOM II which would take over when UNITAF was withdrawn at the beginning of May 1993. Security Council resolution 814 of 26 March 1993 provided for a multi-national force of 20,000 peace-keeping troops, 8,000 logistical support staff and some 3,000 civilian personnel. The US undertook to make available, in addition, a tactical 'quick-reaction force' as required. The whole operation was to be directed by Admiral Howe, the new UN Special Representative, who had been a security adviser to George Bush. The armed forces would be under the command of a Turkish general with an American second-in-command, obviously an important appointment in view of the continuing US tactical support facility.

On the Somali political front, the UN was continuing to maintain its pressure on the leaders of the movements. The third UN co-ordination meeting in Addis Ababa in March on humanitarian assistance which received donor pledges of $142 million for relief and rehabilitation, was attended by a wide range of Somali peace groups who stressed the upsurge in violence in Somalia and the urgent need for improved security. This was highlighted by the brazen incursion of Morgan's forces into Kismayu—under the noses of the UN peace-keepers—which occurred during the national reconciliation conference which followed on. The agreement signed on 27 March by the leading warlords and representatives of sundry clan movements (some of dubious status) committed the parties to 'complete' disarmament, with the help of UNITAF/UNOSOM, urging that the latter should apply "strong and effective sanctions against those responsible for any violation of the cease-fire agreement of January 1993." In a new departure, very much in line with the UN's understandable but misguided desire to cobble together a Somali government as soon as possible, the agreement also provided for the establishment over two years of a 'transitional system of governance.' This included a Transitional National Council (TNC) with representatives from the 18 regions which had existed during Siad's regime, where Regional and District Councils would be established—a concession to the 'bottom up' approach advocated by the Uppsala advisory group and others. The TNC was also to be 'a repository of Somali sovereignty,' a particularly unfortunate reference, since the delegation from the self-proclaimed 'Somaliland Republic' in the relatively untroubled north-west, who had attended the Addis Ababa conference, had left before the agreement was signed and quickly disassociated themselves from these provisions. This insensitive approach to the achievements and aspirations of the people of the north-west was unfortunately characteristic of UN policy since the departure of Sahnoun, and critics quickly warned Admiral Howe to be cautious, since a heavy-handed UN troop deployment in the north-west would risk importing the chaos of the south into a region which had managed to control its own affairs surprisingly successfully. More generally, the agreement in Addis Abeba that UNOSOM II forces should deal firmly with infractions of the reiterated cease-fire provisions accorded well with the robust terms of Security Council Resolution 814.

UNOSOM II took over formally from UNITAF/UNOSOM I on 1 May 1993. With, initially, a considerably reduced complement of UN troops, drawn from a large number of countries, and with Aideed and the other militia leaders showing little signs of laying down their arms or disbanding their followers, it seemed likely that the resolve of the new UN force would soon be tested. This happened on 5 June when 24 Pakistani blue helmets were killed as their contingent prepared to inspect some of Aideed's ammunition stores in Mogadishu (The Pakistanis were despised by the arrogant Somalis, largely because the original UN detachment, which had neither the resources nor authority to do much more than ceremonial escort duties, had been Pakistani). This incident, significantly, occurred near Aideed's radio station which some of his militia apparently thought the UN was about to seize. It was in fact wastefully destroyed a few days later in the course of the powerful UN retaliation which included aerial rocket attacks on Aideed's bases, producing civilian as well as militia casualties. Aideed, who had gone to ground in Mogadishu but still gave press conferences, was proclaimed a wanted outlaw who had committed serious war crimes (*Africa Watch* 1993; *Amnesty International* 1993). Despite the many errors that were made in handling the situation, while it may have made tactical sense to deal with Aideed first, Somalis were naturally waiting to see what would happen to the remaining warlords if they continued to fail to implement the disarmament agreements.[15]

Sudanese support for Aideed, who suddenly became a champion of Islam, and the subliminal Muslim xenophobia of Somalis, encouraged commentators to opine that the UN risked inadvertently igniting a jihad against Western imperialism. The spectre of Aideed as a new 'Mad Mullah' seemed, however, a rather unlikely development. What was much more predictable was that Aideed's clansmen would close ranks behind him and, unless and until UNOSOM reached agreement with their elders, engage in guerilla attacks on UN troops. Meanwhile, UNOSOM embarked on more constructive action, responding in July 1994 to the invitation of the SSDF (Majeerteen) clan leadership in the north-east region where their help was sought in rebuilding wells and communications as well as demilitarization.

It was likely to be more complicated to initiate similar projects in the north-west (Somaliland Republic) where the newly elected president,

---

[15] After failing to defeat Aideed and his supporters and sustaining unacceptably high US casualties in the process, the UN changed tactics. US forces were withdrawn and UNOSOM used all its diplomatic efforts to cajole Aideed and the other war-lords to reach agreement, through a succession of expensive 'peace-conferences.' When these failed, the UN finally decided to give up, dismantling its operation completely by March 1995.

Mohammed Haji Ibrahim Igal (Somalia's last civilian prime minister), indicated that he would welcome UN help in establishing police forces, demobilizing irregular militia groups, and removing the hundreds of thousands of mines left behind by Siad's forces in 1988-89. The problem for the north-western Somalis is to obtain this help in such a way that it does not upset the delicate balance of relative tranquillity which the clan elders have worked so hard to achieve. Nor must it jeopardize their aspirations to retain, at least for the present, their self-declared, separate status as the 'Somaliland Republic.'

The wider political economy of conflict

There is an Islamic fundamentalist interest in events in Somalia which in the Sudan, Iran and to a lesser extent, Saudi Arabia, are seen as encouraging Western penetration of a Muslim region—a view promoted by Somali factions seeking Islamic military aid. Sudan, particularly, supports proselytising fundamentalist groups—with food and, by all accounts, military aid—which have exerted a destabilizing influence in the north-west and north-east. The Sudanese appear to have given Aideed a portable radio and other comforts. Various Gulf States have supported Aideed's rivals, as have until recently the Italians, who are very eager to regain influence in their former colony.

More immediately, the neighbouring states of Djibouti (with its aging Somali president) and Ethiopia and Kenya (both with substantial ethnic Somali populations), have very direct political and economic interests in Somalia. Following earlier Djibouti initiatives, the new Ethiopian government, which includes several Somali ministers, has played a leading role in peace-negotiations, as have also the Eritreans. During their struggle for independence against the previous Ethiopian regimes the Eritrean and Tigrean guerillas received support from Somalia including the provision of passports and diplomatic assistance. Since then, of course, both Ethiopia and Kenya have received huge influxes of Somali refugees and associated skirmishes between rival militias have spilled over the ethnically porous frontiers. Kenya has recently also joined the international peace effort. Neither country, however, has found it possible to take serious measures to enforce the international arms embargo and reduce the continuing flow of weapons into Somalia. This would not be easy, but with the sophisticated US equipment available, something could have been done. Any fruitful initiatives here would have to take account of the fact that the Kenyan Chief of Staff is a Somali with clan connections to some of his leading protagonists in Somalia. Of course, both Kenya and Ethiopia have experienced all too acutely the destabilizing impact of irredentist Somali nationalism in the past. This would tend to encourage some politicians in these countries to feel that the present Somali tragedy is not an unmitigated disaster in terms of their national interest.

Supplying arms is closely linked to the other major cross-border trade which brings daily cargoes of Kenyan and Ethiopian-grown Qat to the militia fighters, who chew it to keep alert, and other consumers. Qat flights from Kenya have regularly landed in Somalia when it was impossible to get food relief into the country. It is believed by Somalis that the Qat planes fly back into Kenya carrying illicit hard drugs and other contraband, which can be readily redistributed using Somalia as a staging-post, given the present chaos there. Given the links between former Italian governments involved in Somalia and the Mafia this seems not improbable. In any event, it has been estimated (Stevenson 1992) that the Kenya-Somalia Qat trade yields more than $100 million annually to wholesalers, transporters and street dealers and that its import value exceeds that of any other imported commodity, including food and arms. One of the main merchants is a close associate of General Aideed and acts as his finance minister. (During the active phase of UN operations against Aideed he was arrested for a time but released when the policy changed to include Aideed in attempts at national conciliation).

Thus the Qat trade (which is not immune to subtle pressures) is one of the mainstays of the political economy of the warlords and their militias. Other important contributions come from clansmen overseas and, as we have seen, interested foreign governments. Ironically, an important element which is hard to quantify derives, as noted above, from stealing humanitarian supplies and from protection money directly or indirectly paid by NGOs. The provision of transport and accommodation to NGOs and the various branches of UNOSOM is also a very lucrative trade which has been cleverly exploited, largely by entrepreneurs with close clan links to the principal warlords. In many cases this involves the rent of property stolen from the legitimate owners by warlords, and exorbitant rents are also paid to some of the most notorious ex-ministers of the Siad regime. It would have been much better, obviously, to have paid such rents into a national fund to be utilized in the future reconstruction of Somalia. But here, as in the other respects in which it had acted unwisely and carelessly, UNOSOM seemed unconcerned.

International intervention in Somalia: retrospect and prospect

In the 1980s Somalia had ceased to be a banana republic and had become virtually dependent on refugee aid. The withdrawal of aid as human rights criticism increased, paved the way for the collapse of the Somali state which finally disintegrated into its traditional clan components with the downfall of the dictator Siad. The struggle for survival in this nation of opportunists then became particularly acute. A heroic band of well-intentioned, but not necessarily well-informed NGOs entered the field and helped the media alert the world to the Somali calamity, presented as essentially a natural, rather than man-made famine. The UN was gradually cajoled into following suit and, spearheaded by Bush's publicity-seeking Operation Restore Hope (after his unsuccessful election campaign), has become more and more involved and now acts, to an unprecedented degree, as administering authority. Unlike the earlier (1950-60) UN trusteeship which was to prepare Somalia for self-government, the aim now is to enable Somalia (plus or minus the north-west) to become self-governing again. By any calculation based in reality, this is going to be a long and uphill task in which the primary condition of civil order has still to be established. As the erratic course of UN involvement to date shows clearly, there is a basic mismatch between the slow cradling which Somalia ideally needs and the short-term stop-go lurches which characterize UN policy formation and budgeting through *ad hoc* Security Council resolutions whose outcome depends on the interests or disinterests of member states.

There is nothing surprising about this. The UN is at present simply not constituted to assume such a complex and costly role in a lapsed state pushed to the forefront of the world's conscience by the suffering of its people in a crisis which is, in terms of military technology, more amenable to treatment than Yugoslavia. There is, of course, at present no UN standing army let alone effective military command structure with its own appropriate logistical support. Moreover, member nations, which are prepared to contribute to UN multi-national forces, always do so on an *ad hoc* basis and subject ultimately to their own public's views on their involvement in a particular crisis, views which naturally, may change over time and in the event of UN casualties. As the much publicized Italian attempt to make political capital out of their traditional association with Somalia illustrates, states which commit troops to UN operations may have their own private agendas and, at the very least, are apt to feel that committing troops entitles them to influence UN policy itself. On the other hand, governments which, like Britain in the case of Somalia, do not contribute military personnel, lack direct access to, and forfeit influence over, the daily conduct of operations. To that extent they are left out in the cold even if, as in the case of the UK, they are members of the Security Council and pay something like 10 per cent of the total cost of UNOSOM.

Given these intrinsic failings in the UN as currently constituted, and the notorious inefficiency of its cumbersome competing bureaucracies so evident in Somalia, if the UN is to continue to exercise its present role there (and elsewhere), it would seem to be more cost-effective to sub-contract the task of tutelage to an appropriately qualified single country. This, after all, is what happened in Somalia before: but it would not be advisable to award such a contract to Italy this time! Multi-national administration and military forces, coupled with UN careerism, offer conditions which competing

Somali interest groups will mercilessly exploit to the full. By the same token, in situations such as Somalia—and perhaps even Yugoslavia—it might be cheaper and more effective to sub-contract UN military operations to an appropriate state. (The ideal force in the Somali case, given their experience in neighbouring Djibouti, might have been the Foreign Legion).

Of course, if these procedures had been followed it does not in any way guarantee that the glaring errors of US/UN action in Somalia would have been avoided. Still, it might have been easier for such an operation to have taken appropriate measures to be better informed about the cultural specifics of the Somali context and correspondingly less naive in its dealings with Somalis. It would certainly not have been difficult to have been better advised about the intricacies of rival Somali political interests in Mogadishu and elsewhere, and to have appreciated from the beginning, the critical importance of radio broadcasting as the key to influencing Somali public opinion.[16] Here the bizarre image of American helicopters dropping leaflets, couched in pigeon Somali[17] onto Mogadishu's primarily oral population fittingly encapsulates the style of an over-grandiose Western intervention which is high on technology but low on culturally appropriate human understanding.[18]

Conclusion

This critique of well-intentioned but poorly designed and executed UN intervention in Somalia highlights the mismatch between such high-tech humanitarian intervention and local social and cultural conditions. Although, from time to time, lip service has been paid to a 'bottom-up' approach, enlisting the support of local community leaders (as in the formation of

---

16 Most Somali nomads have transistor radios on which they listen to all stations broadcasting in Somali—local and international. Their favourite is the BBC Somali programme which they listen to every afternoon with at least the same attention they give to their daily Muslim prayers. At the beginning of UN operations in August 1992, I and others urged the critical importance of effective broadcasting in the presentation of UN aims and policies. It took almost a year before UNOSOM did anything about this.

17 In the first leaflets dropped at the beginning of Operation Restore Hope, the words "United Nations" were, unfortunately, rendered as "Slave Nation." According to US military sources, much time and trouble went into the preparation of the leaflet and its printing at Fort Bragg. Apparently, the only Somali with the requisite military clearance for this delicate task was someone who had left Somalia for the US when he was 12 years old and whose command of Somali was "a bit rusty"!

18 The UNOSOM operation was officially abandoned in March 1995 by which time all UN troops had departed Somalia. An uneasy truce between the main militia groups followed until October 1995 when General Aideed's forces seized control of the autonomous Rahanweyn-Digil region (Lewis & Mayall 1995).

district and regional councils), greater effort has been expended in negotiation with the warlords and faction leaders selected by UN officials, sometimes rather arbitrarily, as Somali 'representatives' for the expensive, high profile international conferences in Addis Ababa and elsewhere. This partly reflects the structure of the UN, its budgeting organization and constraints, and its unsatisfactory short-term recruitment pratices governing the employment of civilian personnel, who are often poorly qualified and ill-prepared for effective service in Somalia. The inherent complexity of operating such an enormous multi-national military organization has already been sufficiently stressed. But it is perhaps worth emphasizing the exponentially increased complexity of a US-dominated UN military enterprise. It is difficult not to conclude that the huge UN budget could have been better spent on a smaller, tighter-controlled, and longer-term operation, including some form of trusteeship, and more in accord with local Somali timetables and processes. An essential feature here would have been a really effective UN special envoy with the negotiating skills and patience all too briefly brought to UNOSOM by Mohamed Sahnoun. That might have meant, although not I think necessarily, risking more foreign lives to stop Somalis fighting each other.

Let us now leave the UN and turn to consider further the nature of the conflicts which have destroyed the Somali state. These are, of course, not strictly ethnic conflicts—though sometimes misleadingly so described. More accurately, these are conflicts mobilizing clan and lineage allegiances in a society where, as we have seen, fighting and feud are deeply entrenched and highly valued in this essentially martial culture. The systemic character of the blood-feud is reflected in the institutionalized system of settling disputes by paying blood-compensation collectively. Clan conflict, typically over resources—traditional or modern—is thus based not on linguistic, cultural or other visible differences between people, but simply on invisible differences of ancestry. Peoples' origins are crucial. Descent as recorded in the patrilineal genealogies Somalis cherish (orally), is the crucial determinant of identity and political loyalty. People feel different from, and potentially hostile to, those who do not share their genealogy. As we have seen, aggravated by the fire-power of modern weapons, this can produce extremely bitter fighting, rape and pillage, and 'clan-cleansing' in settlements and towns.

Thus in Somali society today, as in the past, communal identity based on kinship has the same explosive potential as identity based on religion, ideology, or culture (including language) elsewhere. In my view, all these group identities belong to the same genus as 'nationalism': call them 'micro-nationalisms' if you wish. What is involved here is essentially collective solidarity, group cohesion. Whether or not one accepts Durkheim's distinction between organic and mechanical solidarity, it is beyond doubt that internal segmentary structures weaken national or ethnic cohesion at the highest level of grouping. The Somali dictator Siad, while practicing clan politics, professed to be constructing an organic nationalism, based on literacy and the destruction of the traditional segmentary system. But that is not what actually happened. So, it is not surprising that ethnic Somali nationalism, reactively stimulated but not created by the experience of colonialism, in its most expansive phase, found expression in the 1977-78 Somali-Ethiopian war which sought to achieve self-determination for the Ogadeen region of Ethiopia ('Western Somalia') to enable it to join the Somali state. In opposition to Ethiopian identity, Somali unity stressed cultural, linguistic and religious cohesion—their 'ethnic' identity in contrast with the (misleading) stereotype of 'Christian' (Amhara-dominated) Ethiopia. Today, however, the Somalis are conspicuously no longer mobilized at this level, and have fallen apart (for the present) into their component clans and lineages with the Ogadeen Somalis participating in the multi-national state of contemporary Ethiopia which, following its earlier centralization under a succession of autocratic regimes, has many analogies with Yugoslavia—as Yugoslav political scientists used to recognize. With the pervasive distribution of modern automatic weapons and the current policy of ethnic regionalism, that could naturally be a fateful parallel. Let us hope not.

Although all these identities and divisions of humanity—nations, ethnic groups, clans and the rest—present themselves as 'natural' categories, automatically determining sociability, they are, of course, nothing of the kind. This is conveniently illustrated by the English term for acquiring British citizenship—'naturalization.' Although they have the appearance of genetic origin, Somali genealogies are as arbitrary and man-made as culturally constructed ethnic or national identity. They are social not natural products. What they offer are natural-seeming, and hence indisputable bases for belonging and communal action, which are so easily manipulated by politicians and used by them for their own purposes to confuse and complicate social interaction by seeming to simplify it. While as the British (or was he South African, or Israeli?) social anthropologist Max Gluckman long-ago stressed, cross-cutting ties—economic, political and religious—may provide some measure of restraint on nihilistic communal violence, it would appear that social relations are likely to be most harmonious where material resources and opportunities are felt to be equitably distributed within a system of shared, pluralistic values. As I have tried to emphasize, the nature of political culture—which can be modified—is an important consideration. The self-help segmentary political processes of the Somali are profoundly antagonistic to the stable, and peaceful mobilization of wider national identity. Despite the obvious tendencies towards disintegration along ethnic lines, Ethiopia enjoys the positive factor of a long tradition of political centralization. The crucial aggravating factor of the ready supply of deadly modern weapons in Somalia, in ex-Yugoslavia and, for that matter, in northern Ireland, is too obvious to require further mention. More grandiosely, as I have suggested elsewhere (Lewis 1992:259; cf. Maffesoli 1988:209), at a global level, modern mass society seems by its scale and anonymity to extend the bounds of patriotism beyond acceptable, viable limits. This appears to encourage alienation at the local level, so distant from the centres of power, promoting a renaissance of the 'little tradition' of familiar communal identity.

References

Abdi Sheik-Abdi,
1993 *Divine Madness: Mohammed Abdulle Hassan.* London: Zed Books.

African Rights
1993 Somalia operation 'Restore Hope': a preliminary assessment. *African Rights* May: p. 60.

Africa Watch
1990 Somalia: A government at war with its own people. *Africa Watch* January: p. 269.
1993 Somalia: Beyond the Warlords. *Africa Watch* March: p. 5.

Amnesty International
1993 Somalia: update on a disaster - Proposals for Human Rights. *Amnesty International* April: p. 10.

Andrzejewski, B. W., & I. M. Lewis
1964 *Somali Poetry.* Oxford: Clarendon Press.

Crosslines
1993 Somali peacekeepers: precedent, altruism or public relations. *Crosslines* April: pp. 4-8.

Farah, A. Y. (with I. M. Lewis)
1993 *The Roots of Reconciliation.* London: Actionaid.

Hillmore, P.
1993 *The Observer*, 27 June.

Lewis, I. M.
1982 *A Pastoral Democracy.* New York: Holmes & Meier.
1988 *A Modern History of Somalia.* Boulder, CO: Westview.
1992 *Social Anthropology in Perspective.* Cambridge: Cambridge University Press.
1993a Restoring hope in a future of peace. *Cooperazione* (Rome) March: pp. 43-45.
1993b Misunderstanding the Somali crisis. *Anthropology Today* August: pp. 1-3.
1994 *Blood and Bone: The Call of Kinship in Somali Society.* New Jersey: Red Sea Press.

Lewis, I. M., & J. Mayall (eds.)
1995 *A Study of Decentralised Political Structures for Somalia.* London: London School of Economics for the European Union.

Maffesoli, M.
1988 *Le temps des tribus.* Paris: Meridiens, Klincksieck.

Samatar, S.S.
1982 *Oral Poetry and Somali Nationalism.* Cambridge: Cambridge University Press.

Stevenson, J.
1992 Krazy Khat. *New Republic,* 23 November.

ETHNIC WAR AND INTERNATIONAL HUMANITARIAN INTERVENTION: A BROAD PERSPECTIVE

MARK DUFFIELD

School of Public Policy, University of Birmingham, Edgbaston, Birmingham B15 2TT

The changing nature of humanitarian intervention

Between 1991 and 1993 more aid workers met their deaths due to war and insecurity than during the whole of the preceding decade (Jean 1993). Through being inadvertently caught up in fighting, some have died or been injured. A few have been deliberate targets. Others have been killed following criminal attacks on aid convoys, or as the result of action by armed groups to undermine international attempts to maintain peace and security. In countries as far apart as Angola, Bosnia and Afghanistan, landscapes depleted of opportunity and resources have increased the stakes of physical and political survival for their inhabitants. The breakdown of conventional political organization under such conditions has produced situations where humanitarian aid, and the personnel involved in its delivery, have become targets of violence and forceful appropriation.

These developments have served to concentrate the attention of UN agencies and non-governmental organizations (NGOs) on the issue of providing humanitarian assistance in situations of insecurity and war (Minear & Weiss 1993). In many areas of the globe, such as Africa and parts of the former Soviet block, the decay of formal economies and relations has prompted the emergence of unconventional and aggressive political formations (Duffield 1993; Schierup 1992). The spiral of violence and fragmentation that has often followed has laid waste to transport and communications infrastructures. Conflict has destroyed commercial networks and health system, and taken huge areas of land and natural resources out of production. It has devastated the human resource and skill base, blighted the educational aspirations of whole generations, and forced millions into abject poverty and exile. The social and political problems so caused will remain with the international community for decades, if not longer.

A shrinking resource base

The systemic economic crisis that has emerged in the marginal areas of the global economy provides a starting point for the analysis of ethnic conflict.

Following the end of the Cold War there has been a shift away from external causes in favour of examining internal factors. As formal economies have collapsed, the utility of subsistence assets has been emphasized.

Until the 1960s, African economies, for example, were typically undergoing modest yet real growth and development. During this period, India provided the world with its images of famine and poverty. During the 1970s, Africa and India have structurally and conceptually changed places. It is a shift that has gathered momentum as East Asia has begun a development curve that has thrown its regional economies into effective competition with an ailing West (Harris 1987). As for the former Soviet bloc, the 1970s was also the decade in which modest but real achievements began to slow and reverse (Arrighi 1991).

Africa's response to the global crisis of the 1970s was to dismantle its generally protectionist and internally oriented economies in favour of more open, external and Western oriented productive regimes. The irony was that, at the same time, Western countries began to disengage. The global economy had begun to concentrate within and between the emerging North American, Western Europe and East Asian economic blocks (Oman 1994). As the economies within these blocks underwent an historic technology and materials revolution, the response in Africa was to intensify the production of those same raw materials that it had traditionally farmed and mined.

Intensification was a failure in several respects. Increasing investment and borrowing encouraged the growth of Africa's debt problem as the terms of trade for African exports declined. Perhaps more important, intensification has accelerated environmental decline, asset depletion and the erosion of the subsistence base. This has led to increasing impoverishment and food insecurity. In Africa's market economies, intensification often took the form of the expansion of mechanized agriculture (Duffield 1991). Vast tracts of land have been lost to pastoralists simply to be farmed to exhaustion. In the former planned economies, intensification took the form of large-scale population movements in villagization and relocation programmes. The resulting asset loss has similarly promoted the spread of poverty, rapid urbanization and growing ethnic tension over remaining resources.

The political economy of violence

As Gantzel shows in this book, over the last three decades there has been a steady increase in the number of ongoing wars: from ten in 1960 to around fifty. This growth has been due to the burgeoning number of internal as opposed to inter-state wars. Internal war is particularly associated with ethnic conflict. Of the hundred or so wars fought since 1945, it has been estimated that around half have an ethnic dimension (Welsh 1993). The process of state formation reflects this. Between 1945 and 1989, only a couple of new states were established through ethnic secession. Between 1990 and 1993, however, ten new states emerged in this fashion (Smith 1993). As a result, ethno-nationalism has become a growing force in international relations (Kaldor 1993).

Several common strategies have emerged for pursuing ethnically structured internal war. Sectarian governments have pursued counterinsurgency tactics that have typically singled out specific groups for attention. Areas have been depopulated in an attempt to corral populations and deny opposition movements any source of potential support. Depopulation has been achieved through a variety of means. The commercial and transport infrastructure in opposition areas has been destroyed. Troops have sown agricultural areas with mines, poisoned wells and killed livestock (*Africa Watch* 1991). Members of particular ethnic groups have been intimidated and terrorized. Food aid and other essential supplies have also been denied.

In the past, opposition movements typically pursued nationalist or socialist wars of liberation. As with Eritrea and Tigray (Bimbi 1982), such movements attempted to be inclusive in the furtherance of their wider aims. Today, however, opposing political movements and factions have increasingly followed more limited and divisive strategies (Caratsch 1992).

In Sudan, Angola, Mozambique and Bosnia, for example, not only are political movements ethnically defined, they have commonly adopted a predatory attitude to unrelated groups that fall under their control. In Southern Africa, opposition movements have targeted the educated middle class in government areas for elimination. The physical destruction of economic infrastructure and symbols of political authority is also common (Gursony 1988). Predatory relations towards non-kin groups in controlled areas have usually hinged around systems of taxation or appropriation. These range from direct seizure to the establishment of tributary peasant plantation systems.

Predatory regimes and movements signify the emergence of autonomous, ethnically defined war economies. These structures are based upon the control and development of parallel economic activities, internal taxing, asset appropriation and the manipulation of relief aid. They enable political movements to function beyond the bounds of conventional relations (Duffield 1993). To a large extent the dominant groups within these economies are sanction proof. War economies have emerged in parts of Africa, East Europe and Eurasia. They are partly a response to the collapse of the formal economy outlined above. Lacking legal means of survival, extralegal structures have emerged.

Internal ethnic war has become today's main challenge for international relations and humanitarian policy. It has also radically changed the terms in which conflict and its effects are analyzed. Famine in Africa, for example, is increasingly understood as resulting from ethnically structured competition between dominant and subordinate groups encouraged by a shrinking resource base (Keen 1994).

The transformation of social relations

The pattern of ethnic violence is rarely spontaneous. It usually builds on earlier trends. In Africa, for example, the intensification of raw material production that began in the 1970s initiated a profound transformation between social and ethnic groups. Many so-called 'coping strategies,' by which rural producers attempt to deal with economic stress, are responses to these changes (de Garine & Harrison 1988). The increasing commercialization of agriculture, for example, has polarized relations between rich and poor. The resulting growth in labour migration has helped to undermine the position of elders as the youth have found new sources of wealth and influence (Duffield 1981). Family and gender relations have also changed. New burdens have been placed on women as family units have split. Relations between ethnic groups have become more antagonistic as a shrinking resource base has reinforced the value of subsistence assets and increased local tension.

Growing insecurity and the manner in which internal wars are fought, including the employment of modern weapons, has accentuated these earlier trends. Armed militias and the income available through banditry have further eroded the position of elders. The appearance of child soldiers denotes an extreme form of the inversion of familial relations. Shorn of the sanctions of kinship, moreover, rape and the sexual exploitation of women has become a common adjunct to ethnic violence (Helsinki Watch 1992). Following the breakdown of normal relations between groups, in several places in Africa slavery and debt bondage has reappeared (*Africa Watch* 1990). Growing competition over scarce resources has greatly increased the political vulnerability of subordinate groups. In the case of Rwanda, this led to an organized attempt at genocide (Huband 1994).

The cost of ethnic war

In the past, few attempts have been made to gauge the cost of internal war. For Africa, what work there has been has usually dwelt on assessing the physical damage to infrastructure and loss of GNP through trade and educational disruption (Green 1987). While important, the danger in this approach is that it sees the effects of war mainly as physical destruction and material shortage. In the light of this wastage, conflict is made to appear irrational. The logic and political economy of internal war are largely missed. The corresponding relief strategies that have developed in relation to the irrational view of violence have concentrated on short-term physical inputs, for example, basic shelter, drugs, water equipment and, especially, food aid. In other words, the international humanitarian response to ethnic war is based on a natural disaster model.

The social, civil and political costs of ethnic war, however, are immense. Unlike natural disasters such as droughts or floods, orchestrated insecurity and violence can destroy the very relations that form the foundations of conventional society. It can erode the subsistence, human resource and skill base of a region. Not only is the result a growing pool of displacement and impoverishment but also the loss of skilled and educated classes causes the institutions of civil and public administration to collapse. Ethnic violence attacks networks and social systems. The danger is that unless the singular character of internal war is allowed for, humanitarian aid prescribed according to a natural disaster model simply becomes part of the political economy of violence.

The response of NGOs to ethnic conflict

Many regimes and movements in the marginal areas of the global economy have a predatory and non-reciprocal character. Such structures are, themselves, disaster producing. The economic and political survival strategies of the dominant and contending groups have produced unprecedented levels of displacement, dislocation and impoverishment for the losers. Part of the complexity of today's political emergencies relates to this factor. This is further compounded by the relative autonomy and sanction proofing that parallel war economies have developed. In this situation, international humanitarian aid has itself become a factor to be controlled and manipulated by the warring parties (Scott-Villiers *et al.* 1993). Consequently, insecurity and violence have become a personal reality for aid workers.

While there are many earlier precedents, the involvement of NGOs in Africa as an historical force dates from the mid 1980s. By this time, the Cold War on the continent was all but over (Clough 1992). Despite the developmental mandate of most NGOs, their expansion in Africa has largely been associated with the limitations of governance, restricted UN mandates and the effects of internal war and ethnic violence. Enhanced NGO involvement in protracted political emergencies is an important part of the post-Cold War re-working of North-South relations.

Since the Biafran civil war in the late 1960s, NGOs had, of necessity, to find ways of working in ongoing conflict and insecurity. Lacking a mandate or means to end violence and faced with the limitations of the UN system, NGOs have been at the forefront of developing ways of delivering humanitarian aid to contested areas. New organizations dedicated to working across lines, such as the French NGO, Médecins Sans Frontières, have emerged. NGO consortia have also been formed (Davis 1975). These were often church based. During the Cold War, many of these operations were helped by the comparatively greater organizational cohesion of the movements and factions involved (Jean 1993).

It should be emphasized, however, that non-mandated attempts to feed the victims of ongoing structural violence represented an essentially new response to Third World conflict. Until the end of the 1980s, most of the relatively few UN peace keeping missions demanded a ceasefire arrangement before the international community intervened (Goulding 1993). The ability to mount humanitarian operations in war situations became one mark of NGO flexibility during the Cold War period.

Despite the innovative achievements of some NGOs, the cumulative evidence from the Horn and Southern Africa raises a major concern. Since the mid 1980s, the general effect of NGOs willingness to work with violence has been to institutionalize conflict and support the growth of war economies (Keen & Wilson 1994). Although there have been a few cross-border operations into non-government or rebel areas, most NGO safety-nets have operated in government controlled areas (Clay 1991). From such locations, relief operations have often been an indirect support for the counterinsurgency tactics described above. Where governments and movements have depopulated areas, for example, NGOs have usually taken on the role of supplying food aid to the displaced population. They have fed and watered the camps.

Since the 1970s, emergency relief has also been a source of indirect or diverted assistance for governments and movements alike. Apart from the more visible appropriation of food aid, as for government finance, large scale relief operations have been a useful source of foreign exchange for regimes at war. One aspect of this concerns the pegging of the exchange rate for aid programmes in favour of the state. Sudan, Ethiopia and Iraq are examples (Duffield & Prendergast 1994).

NGOs have often been reluctant to speak out about human rights abuse in areas in which they work. The reason usually put forward is that the agency is protecting the wider programme. To speak out and encourage government hostility would jeopardize the aid that is getting to its designated target. In the former Yugoslavia, for example, while many NGOs have criticized the Serbs for human rights violations, there is less said about Croat activities. Owing to the international pariah status of Serbia, the Serbs are a relatively safe object of criticism. Conversely, during the Gulf War, NGOs were reluctant to take up the issue of the effect of allied bombing on Iraqi civilians due to the involvement of Western military forces.

While the general effect of NGO intervention has not been to lessen conflict, but to learn to work with it, this has not been an uncritical process. Some have attempted to develop programmes independent of large-scale relief operations. These programmes, however, have been unable to prevent the growth of ethnic instability.

The new UN: the emergence of 'negotiated access'

During the Cold War, UN action was constrained by two main considerations. First, non-interference in domestic matters and respect for nation-state sovereignty was a cornerstone of international relations. Second, the frequent use of the super-power veto on the Security Council effectively paralyzed the UN at key moments of global crisis. Since the end of the 1980s, these factors have been greatly reduced. With some justification, some commentators have argued that a so-called new UN, more interventionist than the old, has emerged (Higgins 1993). Between 1987 and 1992, for example, there were 13 UN peace-keeping missions. The same number as in the previous 40 years (Boutros-Ghali 1992).

The emergence of a new more interventionist UN marks an historic turning point. As mentioned above, during the Cold War a precondition of UN involvement in conflict was the securing of a prior ceasefire agreement (Goulding 1993). Increasing UN activity was tantamount to it following the lead established by NGOs and accepting the need to work in unresolved war situations.

The predominance of ethnically structured internal war has helped define the organizational character of humanitarian intervention. What can be called 'negotiated access,' the attempt to reach agreement between warring parties and factions about the movement of relief assistance, developed towards the end of the 1980s. In some places, this development was described by the UN as creating 'corridors of tranquillity' or 'corridors of peace.' Examples include, Operation Rainbow (1986) and Operation Lifeline Sudan (1989) in South Sudan, the Special Relief Programme for Angola (1990) and the Northern Line in Ethiopia (1990) (Duffield 1994; Duffield & Prendergast 1994; Minear 1991).

Due to its operational character, negotiated access served to expose the lack of implementation capacity within UN agencies. Responding to ethnic war has also encouraged a new UN/NGO relationship to emerge. Intervention in what the UN now calls 'complex emergencies' has been effected by a developing division of labour between the UN and NGOs. The UN obtains access and provides coordination while the NGOs implement the relief programmes. The safety-net is based, essentially, on a series of subcontracting relationships presented as a neutral mechanism for delivering basic survival commodities and services.

Negotiated access also denotes the emergence of an integrated UN response to internal war. That is, besides a UN/NGO relationship, such programmes frequently establish a division of labour between the UN specialist agencies with one taking a coordinating lead. In South Sudan, for example, UNICEF is the lead agency while in Bosnia it is UNHCR. More recently, the coordinating role in several complex emergencies has been assumed by the UN's Department of Humanitarian Affairs.

The limitations and achievements of 'negotiated access'

The initial phase of UN 'negotiated access' has been a failure in many ways, but especially where the underlying objectives that informed these early programmes are concerned. Negotiated access denoted a growing politicization of 'neutral' relief aid. 'Corridors of tranquillity' were founded on the underlying belief that humanitarian aid could promote peace by providing a platform that could bring warring parties together. Sudan and Angola are good examples (UNICEF 1991). It was an attitude symptomatic of the initial post-Cold War euphoria that overtook Western policy makers before the Gulf War.

This paternalistic approach failed to understand the inner dynamics of ethnic conflict. Its biggest failing was the implicit assumption that warring factions share with the international community similar humanitarian concerns. In ethnically structured resource wars, one cannot take this for granted. Agreements on the movement of humanitarian aid without a general ceasefire are notoriously fragile (Goulding 1993). Moreover, in these situations the assessment of needs becomes part of the negotiating process rather than an objective exercise. In this manner, 'corridors of tranquillity' have played an important role in further integrating relief aid into the political economy of internal war (Scott-Villiers *et al.* 1993).

Where the initial phase can be regarded as a success is in the organizational maturation of humanitarian intervention. The NGO operations of the mid 1980s were usually based on informal contractual relations with donors (Duffield 1992). With the development of negotiated access, by the end of the 1980s relations were becoming more formal, with written contracts and dedicated coordinating institutions (Minear & Weiss 1993). This maturation has been matched by another development, since the 1980s, the total volume of development assistance has begun to stagnate and decline. Simultaneously, that proportion devoted to relief assistance has been increasing (Borton 1993). Combined, these phenomena denote the emergence of a new North-South relationship.

The rise and fall of military humanitarianism

Building on the failures of the earlier period, current trends have been marked by the selective appearance of a more aggressive form of interventionism. Although negotiation has remained the cornerstone of the approach, a new element is the protection of the humanitarian programme by military force. This can relate both to vulnerable peoples and to the delivery of humanitarian aid. Contemporary military humanitarianism first appeared with the Safe Havens programme in Kurdistan (1991) following the Gulf War. It has subsequently been attempted in the former Yugoslavia (from 1992) and Somalia (from 1993) (Roberts 1993).

Where it has been attempted, military humanitarianism has usually aroused considerable controversy (Higgins 1993). Rather than a blue print for a New World Order, as many commentators believed it would be, military protection has proved difficult. Despite the high hopes following the Gulf War, the military is not well suited to protect aid in an internal or ethnic war. If military personnel use direct force, as in Somalia, there is a danger of exacerbating the situation. If, on the other hand, they show restraint, as in Bosnia, the military becomes a hostage of the warring parties and despised by the people it is supposed to help. In both areas the West has shown a growing unwillingness to commit military forces except under exceptional circumstances.

The growing sophistication of negotiated access

Despite a cooling of enthusiasm for military protection, negotiated access has continued to evolve. Within UN negotiated access operations, the emphases have been on further separating politics from humanitarian relief. The chief policy instrument for this has been the development of formal rule-based physical security and delivery systems. NGOs affiliate to the UN run operation based on agreed neutrality and codes of conduct. The operational core of negotiated access is the collective UN/NGO distribution plan. Such plans are usually drawn up on a weekly or monthly basis by the lead UN agency. They are cleared in advance with the warring parties and aid is delivered according to set times and corridors. This type of formal system is presently running in Angola, Bosnia and South Sudan (Duffield 1994). While having military protection as an appendage, Bosnia is essentially a negotiated access programme.

Another development is that the increased level of insecurity has called into question the UN/NGO division of labour as a model for intervention. The Gulf War and Bosnia have shown that international NGOs, rather than being flexible, have a great deal of inertia, especially those that have developed in Africa. They are unsuited to working in a high risk and fast changing situation. The absence of established field offices has often added further to operational difficulties. This has prompted two developments: a new generation of European NGOs that are already adapted to war conditions has begun to emerge in Bosnia; and, due to the limitations of

NGO implementors, multilateral and bilateral donors have themselves become operational. The establishment by the EU of the European Community Humanitarian Office (ECHO) in 1992 is a case in point (Pooley 1991). Following the Gulf War there has been a growing tendency for governments themselves to become humanitarian agents. This has further politicized the situation.

Issues in humanitarian intervention

Since the end of the 1980s, the UN has had to confront the nature and consequences of ethnically structured internal war. More specifically, it has had to address the emergence of political formations in the margins of the global economy that exist beyond the bounds of conventional relations. As formal economies have collapsed, alternative ways of survival have emerged. In facing this challenge the UN has shown major weaknesses. One of these relates to the legality of some relief interventions.

The humanitarian operations held to be the hallmarks of the new UN, such as, Kurdistan, Bosnia and Somalia, have all been based upon little more than *ad hoc* Security Council resolutions (Roberts 1993). Although negotiated access has given intervention a degree of uniformity, the specific institutional character of the relief system differs in each location. Relief operations are often an assemblage to pre-existing institutions. Despite attempts at integration, these safety-nets are characterized by weak coordination and fragmentary delivery.

Integrated relief programmes also invariably define the complex political emergencies in which they operate as only requiring the delivery of basic relief commodities. This is despite the fact that the defining characteristic of such emergencies is their ability to destroy the social, cultural and political foundations of society. In other words, the international community continues to respond to political emergencies as if they were natural disasters.

Relief programmes are built from a series of short-term assumptions and institutional arrangements. Funding and personnel structures are often *ad hoc*. Some relief programmes, such as that in South Sudan, have been operating in some form or other for a decade. Nevertheless, they are still supported by periodic ‘emergency’ appeals. This short-termism is also reflected in the new UN’s lack of political aim. Such operations display a serious predilection not to examine the underlying causes of conflict. The predominance of relief aid in certain areas of the world suggests that such places no longer have an economic or strategic importance for the West.

The challenge of ethnic war

The conflict and insecurity that presently shape many parts of Africa, Eastern Europe and Eurasia have deep seated structural causes. The emergence of proactive war economies in response to economic decline is an important aspect of the crisis. These economies often support predatory and autonomous political movements. This suggests that attempts to mediate between protagonists or impose democratization may not be enough.

A long standing solution must encompass reform of the global economy. The conventional economies in the now marginal areas have to be revitalized and given room to grow. Without this, many of them will have few alternatives but extralegal parallel activity and ethnic fundamentalism. Unfortunately, given the predominance of free market ideology, there is a real possibility that the world economy will continue to polarize.

Apart from global economic reform, the quality of relief institutions has to be considered. There should be a move from short- to long-term thinking. The systemic crisis sketched above will be here for sometime. Funding and institutional arrangements need to reflect this.

The organizational evolution of large-scale relief operations has taken place based on surprisingly little real information on the nature of the emergency they are dealing with. Since these safety-nets have occupied the space left by collapsing state capacity, the quality of relief institutions should be examined. In particular, there is little or no accountability in relief programmes. Since many have come to play a quasi-governmental role, this is a serious deficit.

While food aid will remain important, alternative programming in political emergencies should be considered. There are two possible directions. First, a move away from supporting what are seen as transitory populations of displaced people or refugees. Within an ethnic war, specific people are displaced for distinct reasons. Causes need to be reconnected with effects. In other words, much more proactive attention should be directed to the issue of political vulnerability. Second, rather than simply working with people in crisis, indigenous institutions should be supported. Ways have to be developed of helping institutions to adapt to protracted political and economic crisis. This should not be confused with 'development' as conventionally understood.

In seeking a long-term solution to ethnic war, the concept of neutrality needs a thorough critique. It represents the dominant philosophy informing work in conflict situations but, rather than neutrality, it is solidarity which our divided world most requires.

References

Africa Watch

1990 Denying the Honour of Living...Sudan: A Human Rights Disaster. New York: *Africa Watch.*

1991 Evil Days: 30 Years of War and Famine in Ethiopia. (September) New York: *Africa Watch.*

Arrighi, G.

1991 World income inequalities and the future of socialism. *New Left Review* 189: 39-65.

Bimbi, G.

1982 The national liberation struggle and the national liberation fronts. In *The Eritrean Case*. RICE (ed.), pp. 167-207. Rome: Research and Information Centre on Eritrea.

Borton, J.

1993 Recent trends in the international relief system. *Disasters* 17 (3): 187-201.

Boutros-Ghali, B.

1992 June 17, General Assembly, Forty-Seventh Session, Item 10 of the Preliminary List (A/47/277). *An Agenda for Peace: Preventive Diplomacy, Peacemaking and Peace-Keeping*. New York: United Nations.

Caratsch, C.

1992 Humanitarian design and political interference: Red Cross work in the post-Cold War period. *International Relations* pp. 301-313.

Clay, J. W.

1991 Western assistance and the Ethiopian famine: Implications for humanitarian assistance. In *The Political Economy of African Famine*. R. E. Downs, D. O. Kerner & S. P. Reyna (eds.), pp. 147-175. Philadelphia: Gordon & Breach.

Clough, M.

1992 *Free at Last? US Policy Toward Africa and the End of the Cold War.* New York: Council on Foreign Relations.

Davis, M. (ed.)

1975 *Civil Wars and the Politics of International Relief.* New York: Praeger Publishers.

Duffield, M.

1981 *Maiurno: Capitalism and Rural Life in Sudan*. London: Ithaca Press.

1991 *War and famine in Africa*. Oxfam Research Paper No 5. Oxford: Oxfam Publications.

1992 Famine, conflict and the internationalisation of public welfare. In *Beyond Conflict in the Horn: The Prospects for Peace, Recovery and Development in Ethiopia, Somalia, Eritrea and Sudan*. M. Doornbos, L. Cliffe, A. Ghaffar, M. Ahmed & J. Markakis (eds.), pp. 49-52. The Hague: Institute of Social Studies.

1993 NGOs, disaster relief and asset transfer in the Horn: Political survival in a permanent emergency. *Development and Change* 24 (1): 131-157.

1994 *An account of relief operations in Bosnia*. Relief and Rehabilitation Network, Network Paper 3. London: Overseas Development Institute.

Duffield, M., & J. Prendergast
1994 *Without Troops or Tanks: Humanitarian Intervention in Eritrea and Ethiopia.* Trenton, NJ: Africa World Press Inc/Red Sea Press Inc.

Garine, I. de, & G. Harrison (eds.)
1988 *Coping With Uncertainty in Food Supply.* Oxford: Oxford University Press.

Goulding, M.
1993 The Evolution of United Nations Peacekeeping. *International Affairs* 69 (3): 451-464.

Green, R. H.
1987 *Killing the dream: The political and human economy of war in Sub-Saharan Africa.* Institute of Development Studies Discussion Paper 238. Brighton: Institute of Development Studies.

Gursony, R.
1988 *Summary of Mozambican Refugee Accounts of Experience in Mozambique.* New York: Department of State, Bureau For Refugee Programme.

Harris, N.
1987 *The End of the Third World.* Harmondsworth: Penguin.

Helsinki Watch
1992 *War crimes in Bosnia-Hercegovina.* New York: Human Rights Watch.

Higgins, R.
1993 The new United Nations and the former Yugoslavia. *International Affairs* 69 (3): 465-483.

Huband, M.
1994 Survivors name henchmen of Ruwanda genocide. *The Observer* 8 May: 15.

Jean, F. (ed.)
1993 *Life, Death and Aid: The Médecins Sans Frontières Report on World Crisis Intervention.* London: Routledge.

Kaldor, M.
1993 Yugoslavia and the New Nationalism. *New Left Review* 197: 96-112.

Keen, D.
1994 *The Benefits of Famine: A Political Economy of Famine and Relief in Southwestern Sudan, 1983-1989.* Princeton, NJ: Princeton University Press.

Keen, D., & K. Wilson.
1994 Engaging with violence: A reassessment of the role of relief in wartime. In *War and Hunger: Famine, Complex Emergencies and International Policy in Africa.* J. Macrae & A. Zwi, with M. M. Duffield & H. Slim (eds.), pp. 201-221. London: Zed Press.

Minear, L.
1991 *Humanitarianism Under Seige: A Critical Review of Operation Lifeline Sudan.* Trenton, NJ: Red Sea Press.

Minear, L., & T. G. Weiss
1993 *Humanitarian Action in Times of War.* Boulder: Lynne Rienner Publishers.

Oman, C.
1994 *Globalisation and Regionalisation: The Challenge for Developing Countries*. OECD Development Centre (January).

Pooley, P. (ch.man)
1991 *Task Force de la Commission pour l'Office Européen d'Aide Humanitaire*. European Community Humanitarian Office. Brussels: European Commission.

Roberts, A.
1993 Humanitarian War: Military Intervention and Human Rights. *International Affairs* 69 (3): 429-449.

Schierup, C. U.
1992 Quasi-proletarians and a patriarchal bureaucracy: Aspects of Yugoslavia's re-peripheralisation. *Soviet Studies* 44 (1): 79-99.

Scott-Villiers, A., P. Scott-Villiers & C. P. Dodge.
1993 Repatriation of 150,000 Sudanese refugees from Ethiopia: The manipulation of civilians in a situation of conflict. *Disasters* 17 (3): 202-217.

Smith, A. D.
1993 The ethnic sources of nationalism. *Survival* 35 (1): 48-62.

UNICEF
1991 *From Ceasefire to Elections (June 1991 - December 1992): Implications and Strategies of UNICEF/Angola*. Luanda: UNICEF.

Welsh, D.
1993 Domestic Politics and Ethnic Conflict. *Survival* 35 (1): 63-80.

POSTSCRIPT: CURRENT ISSUES IN THE STUDY OF ETHNICITY, ETHNIC CONFLICT AND HUMANITARIAN INTERVENTION, AND QUESTIONS FOR FUTURE RESEARCH

GIORGIO AUSENDA

Center for Interdisciplinary Research on Social Stress, 6 Contrada S. Francesco, San Marino (Rep. of San Marino)

I wrote this final chapter with two aims in mind which became clear during the discussion of the papers and, especially, the concluding one. The first was to provide a basis of historical knowledge concerning the meaning of 'ethnicity,' the role of NGOs in humanitarian intervention and the relationship of this role to ethnic wars; the second was to list the questions and problems which arose during the discussions, so that they can be taken up at the next San Marino meeting on the topic 'War and ethnicity.'

I noted, in fact, that whilst the concept of 'war' did not seem to pose any problem to the participants, 'ethnicity' gave rise to different interpretations and definitions. The same uncertainty was present when it came to humanitarian intervention and its complementarity with ethnic wars.

The chapter is accordingly divided into two parts. The first gives an historical overview of the most popular theories concerning the meaning of 'ethnicity' and the structuring of ethnic beliefs. The second analyzes the most recent developments in humanitarian intervention by NGOs in the face of the burgeoning number of ethnic wars and the many failures to cope with them on the part of international bodies, especially the United Nations and its various agencies.[1]

PART 1: CURRENT ISSUES IN THE STUDY OF ETHNICITY AND ETHNIC CONFLICT

History of the term

The word *ethnikòs* was used in the Greek translation of the New Testament to refer to populations which were still pagan (Bernardi 1995:52-3). Its Latin equivalent became the English 'gentile' and referred to the fact that those 'primitive' peoples, who were nevertheless considered worthy of redemption, still recognized themselves as grouped by *gentes* (clans). The

[1] The references are also divided into two parts, the first concerning 'ethnicity' and the second the evolution of NGOs in the face of ethnic wars.

Oxford English Dictionary picks up this traditional meaning by defining 'ethnicity' as "heathendom, heathen superstition" and gives the word 'ethnic' two meanings, (1) "nations" which are "heathen" or "pagan," and (2) "race" or "nation."

The French *La Grande Enciclopédie* (1896-98 edition) gives us a foretaste of ensuing difficulties with finding a common definition of *ethnikòs*.

> Ethnographie, ethnologie. Deux termes qui se rapportent au même genre d'études e qui servent presque indistinctement à désigner la science des "groupes humains" ou groupes ethniques (peuples, peuplades, tribus, etc.). Malheuresement, on n'est pas bien d'accord, non seulement dans les différents pays, mais même entre les savants d'une seule et même nation, sur ce qu'il faut entendre exactement par l'un ou l'autre de ces termes.

The same dictionary mentions a French scholar, W. Edwards, as the first to use the word 'ethnology' when he formed the Société d'ethnologie in 1839, although it was dedicated to physical anthropology. At the beginning of the nineteenth century 'ethnography' simply meant the classification of populations according to their language, but by the time the dictionary was published it had achieved its modern meaning, "the study of man as a social being."

The terms 'ethnic' and 'ethnicity' were used by Max Weber in his *Wirtschaft und Gesellschaft*, first published in 1922. Here he introduced the term "ethnische Gemeinsamkeit" (Weber 1964:307), translated into English as "ethnic membership" (Weber 1978:389) and distinguished it from the related "Gemeinschaft," 'community.' His definition has a very contemporary ring:

> We shall call "ethnic groups" those human groups that entertain a *subjective* [italics mine] belief in their common descent because of similarities of physical type or of customs or both or because of memories of colonization and migration (Weber 1978:389).

And further:

> Ethnic membership (Gemeinsamkeit) differs from the kinship [community][2] precisely by being a presumed identity, not a [community] with common social action (Weber 1978:389).

Max Weber's brilliant conceptualization was obscured during the interwar period by a worldwide surge of racial theories.

While the exact date will never be known with certainty, the expression 'ethnic group' began to be used in the 1950s by "sociologists and social anthropologists alike to identify culturally distinctive groups" (Barot

---

[2] The translation by G. Roth and C. Wittich has "group," but 'community' is a more literal translation. In fact, in the original the word "Gruppe" appears in the previous paragraph while "Gemeinschaft" is used in the following one.

1993:4). According to Joan Vincent, the term 'ethnicity' was first used by social anthropologist Lucy Mair in 1965 (Vincent 1993:127).

By adding up the titles of books and articles dealing with 'ethnic groups' and 'ethnicity' published every year and laboriously listed by G. Carter Bentley (1981) one obtains the following curve:

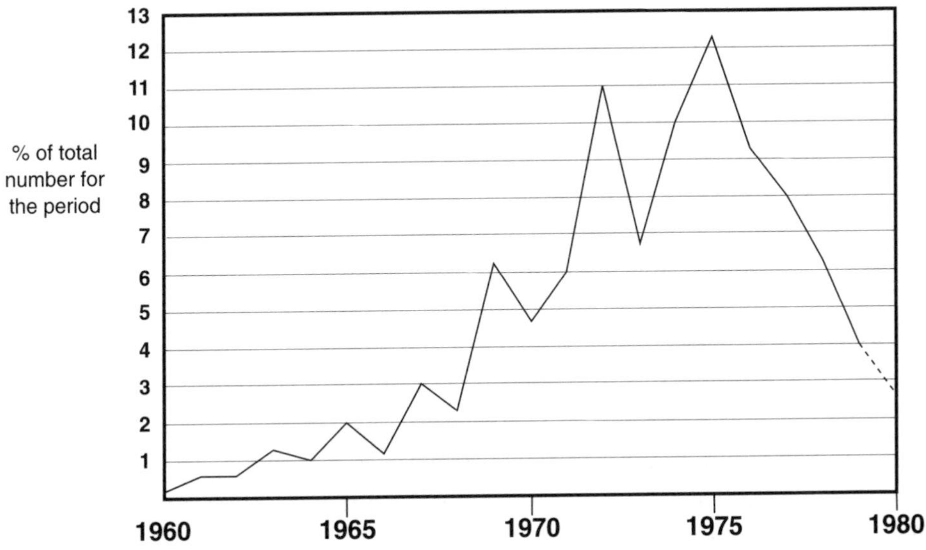

Fig. 10.1 - Frequencies of titles in English on ethnicity and nationality as annual percentages of total number for the period (data from G. Carter Bentley 1981).

The concept thus became popular in the sixties and reached the peak of its popularity in 1975, a phenomenon perhaps connected with the protest movement. The post-war popularity of the term was seen by some as a consequence of its being "simply a euphemism for 'race'" (Watson 1977:8). It is worthwhile, therefore, to compare 'ethnicity' with race and other related social categories.

Ethnicity and race

The consensus of opinion among scholars is that 'race' has a "biological base" (Parsons 1975:54), even though, because of the blending and intermixture of populations all over the world, "...if it were conceived of in purely biological terms, it would be a concept that could be applied to only a relative handful of people on a few small isolated islands in the oceans" (Sowell 1983:11). Even the term 'race' has been subject to semantic changes. Formerly, it meant descent or lineage and it was only during the nineteenth century that it acquired the meaning of a "fixed and permanent type" (Banton 1983:32-59).

The former sharp distinction between race and ethnicity is becoming blurred by the recognition that "genetic variation is important in human interaction only because it is often correlated with cultural, historical, and status differences" (Yinger 1985:155). According to Yinger, race and ethnicity are "overlapping concepts" since race is "one of the defining characteristics of ethnicity" (Yinger 1994:16-7). Race, however, is more easily definable in geographical terms, since 'place' is considered "a crucial element in all of our arguments about the social construction of 'race' and nation" (Jackson & Penrose 1993:13), while 'ethnicity' is more bounded, as will be discussed below. One talks about 'race riots,' but not about racial wars, while it is quite common to talk about 'ethnic wars.' It follows that 'ethnicity' applies to bounded groups, while 'race' does not.

Ethnicity and caste

Caste implies hierarchy, and an 'accepted' one at that. The defining criteria of caste, according to Pierre van den Berghe, are that it is "ascriptive, endogamous and hierarchized" (van den Berghe 1970:11). The fact that they are 'hierarchized' makes castes completely different from ethnic groups, in that this presupposes an accepted set of relations between castes which are not necessarily different ethnically. In Fredrik Barth's words:

> The cultures of the component ethnic groups in such systems are thus integrated in a special way: they share certain general value orientation and scales, on the basis of which they can arrive at judgements of hierarchy (Barth 1969:27).

Caste is a principle of social organization which characterizes a given social system. Ethnicity is, or can be, a source of social disfunction. Caste rests on accepted hierarchical or vertical relations whereas ethnicity rests on contiguous or horizontal and conflictual relations. We rarely hear of caste conflicts and not at all of caste wars. We may conclude that the two categories are perpendicular and do not influence each other.

Ethnicity and class

Class is similar to caste in that it is also a hierarchized social structure, but the hierarchy is not accepted (Jackson 1984:209). While caste is ascriptive class is not. Hence, while there is no mobility between castes, there is great and increasing mobility between classes (cf. Deutsch 1966:30-2). Historically, class conflict preceded ethnic conflict, not because classes existed while ethnic groups did not, but because classes became socioeconomically relevant with the beginning of industrialization (cf. Armstrong 1992:27) while ethnic groups became relevant later, mainly after the breakdown of medieval empires, beginning with the Austrian and Ottoman.

'Class' and 'ethnicity' are competing categories, in that both are instrumental to the social advancement of their members in a given nation-state. Some believe that "class solidarity" can "play a more important role...than ethnic solidarity across social barriers" (Panayi 1994:98), while recognizing that "ethnicity can cross class boundaries" (Panayi 1994:98). Others maintain that "ethnic solidarity [should be] easier to achieve than class solidarity and more rewarding as well" and that "ethnicity will predominate to the extent that the rate of interclass mobility exceeds the rate of interethnic exchange" (Hechter 1986:20). Another view is that "ethnicity has become more relevant because it can combine an interest with an affective tie" (Bell 1975:169). Concerning conflict, Stack writes:

> Ethnic conflict...seems to have become more effective in reaching and drawing upon the more emotional layers of the human and social personality than class conflict (1986:3).

Class, then, is seen as losing out to ethnicity in the fight for political priority. There have been no class wars since the Chinese communist revolution because 'ethnicity' is a more cohesive and powerful rallying cry. 'Ethnic groups' have proved more effective than 'classes' in furthering the socioeconomic (and not only material) interests of their members (cf. Glazer & Moynihan 1975:7; Guidieri 1988:20; Roosens 1989:9; Stack 1986:7), and Marxist sociologists have been quick to ascribe the 'invention' of 'ethnicity' to capitalist society (cf. Eduri 1984:10-1; Mullings 1984:21-3, 36).

Ethnicity and nationalism

It became clear during the discussion of several papers at the conference that 'nation' and 'nationality' tend to be seen as overlapping respectively with 'ethnic group' and 'ethnicity.' Indeed some participants considered them to be indistiguishable. The concept of 'nation' is, however, much older than that of 'ethnic group.' The word comes from the Latin *nasci*, 'to be born,' and meant a group of people born in the same place. Its modern meaning goes back to the French revolution, to the merging of the three estates in a *National* Assembly (*Intl. Encyclopedia of the Social Sciences*, 1968 ed.):

> ...a 'nation' is either synonymous with a state or its inhabitants, or else it denotes a human group bound together by common solidarity—a group where members place loyalty to the group as a whole over any conflicting loyalties (Rustow 1968:7).

This definition is taken from one proposed by John Stuart Mill substituting 'nation' for what he called 'nationality.' Later definitions are all variations on the theme. Among the most complete is:

> A nation is a group of people who feel themselves to be a community bound together by ties of history, culture and a common ancestry. Nations have 'objective' characteristics which may include a territory, a language, a religion, or common descent (though not all of these are always present), and 'subjective' characteristics, essentially a people's awareness of its nationality and affection for it. In the last resort it is 'the supreme loyalty' for people who are prepared to die for their nations (Kellas 1991:2).

The term 'nation' is often used for 'nation-state' which refers to a nation "living in a state of its own" (Deutsch 1966:17), and also for 'country.'

According to Yinger, it is not "wise to see 'nation' simply as a synonym of 'ethnic group'" (1994:12). Anthony Smith sees the nation, defined as "a compact territorial unit of population having a common history and culture, a single economy and common legal rights and duties" as "sociologically" close to an "ethnic community." This makes him consider "an understanding of the forms and role of ethnic identity" as a necessary preliminary to an analysis of "nationalism and multinational states" (Smith 1992:49). Even though 'ethnic groups' and 'ethnocentrism' are comparable to 'nation' and 'nationalism,' Kellas believes that they are differentiated "on several dimensions." Ethnic groups are "smaller," they are "based on a common ancestry" and they are "more pervasive in human history," in the sense that membership is limited to people who "share certain inborn attributes." Nations "are more cohesive and are culturally and politically defined" (Kellas 1991:14). According to Armstrong, who considers 'nationality' and 'ethnicity' as synonyms, 'nationality' "fits in a continuum of identity structures including at least religion and class" characterized by "the strength of boundary mechanisms...reassuring the group member of his identity and deterring him from defection" (Armstrong 1992:26).

I would add here differences in the motivations and results of ethnic conflict as compared to national conflict. More often than not, ethnic conflict gives rise to extreme consequences such as 'ethnic cleansing' and even genocide, as if the intention were not only the acquisition or retention of territory belonging to another group, but also their physical removal from the territory, in one way or another. I would, therefore, see ethnic conflict as potentially much more radical and violent than national conflict. Whereas the aim of national mobilization is the acquisition of territory regardless of the people who live there, the aim of ethnic conflict is the acquisition of territory free of any trace of competing ethnic groups. Thus, ethnic confrontations appear to be more radical than national ones. Ethnic confrontations seek 'final' solutions whereas the outcomes of nationalist confrontations can be modified and reversed by history.

The nature of ethnicity

Sociologists tend not to think of ethnicity as a thing in itself (Roth *et al.* 1968:389), but as a presumed identity (Weber 1978:389) merging the individual with the group (Stack 1986:3) and, therefore, as a powerful means of political pressure when groups are competing for the control of scarce resources (Bennett 1973:7; Watson 1977:9). Like all social groups, ethnic groups have a life span. They are born from "inter-group contact," which may be due to "trade, war, industry or mere chance" (Hechter 1986:14), they rise and, in due course, disappear.

Ethnicity is maintained by intra-group marriage, by residence in the same neighbourhood, and by religious and social activity (Panayi 1994:76-8). Ethnic sentiment is found not only in pluralistic societies, such as the United States and Russia, but also in apparently homogeneous countries, such as those of Western Europe (Greeley 1977:57). It has both positive and negative aspects. On the one side it promotes kinship and community and enriches the overall culture of a state, while on the other, it can promote conflict and violence (Greeley 1977:58). The 'markers' or 'indicators' of ethnicity include race, language, religion, customs and place of origin (cf. Barth 1969:11; Jackson 1984:206; Weber 1978:320-1).

The strength of an 'ethnic group' lies in its capacity to galvanize its members into effective political action towards the achievement of group aims. It follows that when such aims are no longer paramount, its strength wanes: "economic prosperity or education may weaken ethnic formations" (Jackson 1984:215). Furthermore, contiguous ethnic groups in pluralistic societies are subject to a relentless process of homogenization whereby "the cultural content of each ethnic group becomes very similar to that of others, even if the emotional...attachment to the ethnic group" persists (Glazer & Moynihan 1975:8).

Theories of ethnicity

The theoretical study of ethnicity began in earnest in the late 1960s and early 1970s (Roosens 1989:11), and has created "a social science sub-discipline with a large and expanding literature" (Jackson 1984:205; cf. Yinger 1985:152). One way of looking at this literature is to divide it between 'individualist' and 'structural' approaches or theories. Individualist theories include 'primordialism' and 'sociobiology' while structuralist theories include 'contextualist', 'material interest', 'core-periphery' and 'ethnic boundary' theories.[3]

---

[3] Different authors divide the field in different ways, e.g. Crawford Young (1993:21 ff.) lists "three conceptions of cultural pluralism," the "instrumentalist" corresponding to

Primordialism has been championed, among others, by Clifford Geertz, who saw a "primordial tie, the 'longing not to belong to any other group'" as the critical defining characteristic of ethnicity (Geertz 1963:109). Geertz here was following Max Weber, who remarked that ethnic groups are "groups that entertain a subjective belief in their common descent" (Weber 1978:389), but he went beyond Weber in stating, that "dormant ethnicity is a sociobiological constant or 'given'" (Geertz 1963:109; cf. Stack 1986:1). Such dormant ethnicity does not require any explanation "for it is simply always 'out there'" (Jackson 1984:216). Having taken ethnicity as a given, the explanation shifts to how it is mobilized or evoked. This approach has not had a great following, even though some consider it as constituting a "useful perspective from which to analyze the dynamics of ethnicity throughout the world" (Stack 1986:1).

Sociobiology is based on the theory of 'inclusive fitness' developed by W. D. Hamilton in 1964 and on the "universal presence of ethnocentrism [which] gives some support to the argument that it is genetically determined" (Kellas 1991:10-1). According to Hamilton, 'inclusive fitness' is achieved through 'kin selection.' 'Kin selection' is predicated on the development, through 'gene selection,' of favourable inherited attitudes, statistically limited to the kin group (Kellas 1991:10-1). According to Pierre van den Berghe (1981:80), since "ethnic and social sentiments are extensions of kinship sentiments" they must "conform to the principle of 'inclusive fitness.'"

While biology cannot be discounted in any phenomena pertaining to human beings, to construct a theory of ethnicity entirely on a biological basis is out of the question. The only relevant characteristic found in all human beings is suspicion and fear of alterity, be it racial, linguistic, or cultural. This fear is instinctive in all mammals and is probably adaptive, since it compels individuals to behave suspiciously and to be ready to act, either by aggression or flight, when confronted with a 'different' individual. This instinct is undoubtedly present in the formation of ethnic feelings, but it is not a major constituent. It seems certain that socially induced beliefs and behaviour are far more prevalent in the development of the behavioural complex which is called 'ethnicity.'

Contextualists argue that populations follow a "paradigmatic historical transition from 'community' to 'society' which Weber termed 'rationalization'" (Jackson 1984:212). With the advent of the nation-state, 'ethnicity' is replaced "with something which can become nationhood" (Kellas 1991:37). According to contextualists, then, nations develop from

those listed hereunder as 'contextualists' and 'material interest theories'; the "primordialist" which is listed below with the same title; the "constructivist" which is not discussed as an explanatory theory as it could belong to both other groups but will be discussed later as an interpretation of how ethnic feelings are developed and structured.

ethnic groups, although it is not easy to determine how or when the transition took place. The explanation is left to "theories which explain the emergence of nationalism in the modern world" (Kellas 1991:38), the most important and recent of which are, in chronological order, those of Karl Deutsch, Michael Hechter, Stein Rokkan, Ernest Gellner, Benedict Anderson, and Anthony Smith (Kellas 1991:38).

Material interest theories have been developed outside the Marxist tradition possibly because that tradition "has paid scant attention to ethnicity, except as a policy problem" (van den Berghe 1975:71). Several authors have argued that ethnic groups are, essentially, a means for the pursuit of the material interests of their members (cf. Bell 1975). Because ethnic identity transcends class distinctions, it can "help the members of an ethnic group to gain dominance in specific and relatively valued niches of the occupational structure (e.g. Irish policemen and Jewish diamond merchants in New York)" (Hechter 1986:20). Material interests are important, but rather than basing them on simple competition for scarce resources one should also look for the feelings, rightly or wrongly entertained, of being wronged or defrauded by members of another group. This is a defensive rather than an aggressive feeling.

According to *core-periphery theory*, in certain countries ethnic feeling builds up between the dominant core and the periphery because core groups occupy the best class positions (Kellas 1991:40). This does not apply to all situations, however, and, in particular, it does not apply in Britain where, for "example, Scots are not...relegated to inferior social positions" (Kellas 1991:40). Other authors, [such as Stein Rokkan with Derek Urwin] have worked on the problem of core-periphery relationships as they affect regionalism in Europe (Kellas 1991:41).

In *Wirtschaft und Gesellschaft* Max Weber remarked that:

> Any cultural trait, no matter how superficial, can serve as a starting point for the familiar tendency to monopolistic closure.
> ...But if there are sharp boundaries between areas of observable styles of life, they are due to conscious monopolistic closure, which started from small differences that were then cultivated and intensified (Weber 1978:388).

This *boundary theory* has been developed by Fredrik Barth. Barth recognized the importance of culture in ethnic group formation and argued that the maintenance and continuity of ethnic groups is predicated on the creation and maintenance of a boundary separating those who belong from those who do not (1969:14). He noted that the boundary "defines the group, not the cultural stuff that encloses it" (1969:15). According to Roosens (1984:12) Barth's work has been influential in the clarification of such concepts as 'culture group,' 'ethnic identity,' 'own culture'; while, according to Despres "the view [of Barth and his colleagues] that the genesis and persistence of ethnic boundaries, the incorporation of ethnic populations and the organization of non-ethnic relations are generally related to factors affecting the competition for environmental resources" is a "substantial contribution toward the advancement of comparative ethnic studies" (1975:2-3).

Constructivism

Crawford Young included this among theories of ethnicity (see page 223, note 3). In my view, however, constructivism helps to explain not ethnic feelings themselves, but the way they are shaped for common action. In other words, the underlying realities of ethnic activism. The most visible of these appears to be 'tradition.'

Recent studies have highlighted the doubtful 'inborn' quality of tradition. Contrary to 'custom,' which is seen as a baggage of relational habits and rules that a group inherits from its forebears and which changes gradually with circumstances, tradition is defined as "a set of practices...which seek to inculcate certain values and norms of behaviour by repetition, which automatically implies continuity with the past" (Hobsbawm 1983:1). While 'custom' is seen as gradually changing, 'tradition' is postulated as invariant, even though "the peculiarity of 'invented traditions' is that the continuity with [the past] is largely factitious" (Hobsbawm 1983:2). The validity of this analysis is confirmed by, for example, the "very recent (and highly inauthentic) emergence of such cultural features as the Scottish tartan and kilt or the Welsh love for music" (Sollors 1989:xii). As a result of this awareness, "analysts are increasingly wary of employing reifying conceptions of nation, ethnic group, culture, and tradition" (Handler 1994:27). Social science must widen its perspective in order to see these phenomena as the constructions they are, rather than as "bounded and unchanging entities" (Handler 1994:27).

A logical corollary to Hobsbawm's *Invention of Tradition* approach was Benedict Anderson's generalization of the 'deconstructionist' critique of the nation, seeing it as a kind of "imagined community" (Armstrong 1992:25). But while the deconstructionist approach is indisputably correct as a basis for the scientific analysis of ethnicity and nationalism,

> ...*any kind* of socialization transforms human existence into a relative "world closedness," artificial rather than biological in origin. ...closure...is...necessary to provide direction and stability for most human conduct, for "*all societies are constructions in the face of chaos*" (Berger & Luckmann 1966 in Armstrong 1992:25).

"Construction theory does not deny the need for some kind of categorization" (Jackson 1993:2), since categories are indispensable communication devices. "Construction theory only challenges the idea that some categories are more fundamental ('essential,' 'natural') than others"

(Jackson 1993:2). In future work on ethnicity we need to ask how, and in answer to which stresses, social tradition is 'invented.'

Ethnicity and religion

Religion is "one amongst a number of commonalities which are primordial in the human condition and which lead to consciousness of kind and group formation" (Geertz 1963 in Rex 1993:18). According to Yinger "religion today, as in the past, is one of the crucial defining characteristics in ethnic identity and one of the rallying points in ethnic conflict" (1985:168; cf. Barot 1993:7; Gellner 1992:245). Gellner notes that past empires, such as the Habsburg, Ottoman and Tsarist, were "legitimated by religion rather than ethnicity, even if each was also endowed by a dominant ethnic group" (1992:249). Armstrong further recognizes that "the categorical distinction between religion and ethnicity is slippery" (Armstrong 1992:27).

In the past, beginning with the 'Cathars' in the twelfth century and probably even earlier, conflicts which would probably now be called ethnic followed the boundary lines of religion and were labelled 'religious wars.' During the second half of the sixteenth century and the first half of the seventeenth there was a series of religious wars, or 'Wars of religion,' which culminated in the Treaty of Westphalia in 1648. The fact that ethnicity was not dominant at the time may be due to a completely different pattern of communications. The countryside was almost non-existent in the communication network and insignificant in the political arena. Furthermore, poor communications did nothing to enhance ethnic sentiment based on linguistic and cultural differences, so that religion remained the most immediate and obvious discriminating factor. In-depth historical studies are necessary to understand this phenomenon. Such studies may help to explain the resurgence of religious conflicts in so many parts of the world today.

Ethnicity and communication

Several scholars have recognized the important relationship between communication and ethnic phenomena, but it was Karl Deutsch who explored the topic most extensively (1966). According to Deutsch, a common language and culture engender "habitual preferences and priorities in men's attention and behavior, as well as in their thought and feelings" (Deutsch 1966:88). He went on to develop the concept of *complementarity*. A "community which permits a common history to be experienced as common, is a community of complementary habits and facilities of communication." Such complementarity is signalled by "communicative effectiveness" which is established by the aid of facilities for the "storage of information, such as libraries, statues, signposts, and the like" (Deutsch 1966:96 ff.). Deutsch sees populations as held together "from within" by "the complementarity of the communicative facilities acquired by their members." This cohesive force which he calls "ethnic complementarity" is not subjective, in that it may be measured by objective tests. It is also distinctive and additive (Deutsch 1966:98-9).

Deutsch distinguishes two main levels of complementarity. The "primary" level consists in "the complementarity of communication habits" and the "secondary" in "the complementarity of acquired social and economic preferences" (Deutsch 1966:101). Thus, culture and complementarity are inextricably interwoven. They "are not things apart from the rest of life" since "at every step we find social communications bound up indissolubly with the ends and means of life." Culture "is of interest to men and women" in that it goes "into the daily texture of their lives" (Deutsch 1966:106), while communication is the main vehicle of complementarity.

Plural societies

Plural societies were described by Barth and van den Berghe in the late 60s as "integrated in the market place, under the control of a state system dominated by one of the groups, but leaving large areas of cultural diversity in the religious and domestic sector of activity" (Barth 1969:16), and as being "segmented into two or more groups that have distant and duplicatory sets of institutions" (van den Berghe 1970:14).

Barth sees this interaction as (1) taking place through trade when ethnic groups occupy "clearly distinct niches in the natural environment," (2) as involving "politics along the border" when they monopolize separate territories, and (3) as being in close inter-dependence when they occupy "reciprocal and therefore different niches" (Barth 1969:19). Van den Berghe was less optimistic, since he recognized that attempts to institutionalize "more democratic forms of pluralism" were "often...disrupted by open conflict and plagued by instability" (van den Berghe 1970:14).

Ethnicity and conflict

It seems to be agreed that the number of ethnic conflicts in the world has increased since the 1960s (Glazer & Moynihan 1975:5; Guidieri 1988:7). Infrastructural conflicts are mentioned, such as those fed by "black nationalists in the United States," or "between nationalities in contemporary Yugoslavia," or "Afrikaaner nationalists" in South Africa (Brass 1991:43-4). According to Horowitz, the decline of 'overarching' systems, (such as the

Habsburg, Ottoman and Soviet empires) (1992:14), and the dissatisfaction of wealthy peripheries (such as the "Basque country and Catalonia in Spain") at the distribution of revenue between the collecting center and the disbursing periphery are the primary causes for the development of ethnic conflicts (1992:14-5). He concludes that "ethnic affiliations are a durable source of conflict in the modern world," that "ethnicity possesses some of the powerful conflict-producing characteristics which Marx erroneously attributed to social class," (1992:20) and that there "are more or less effective policies to increase or decrease ethnic conflict," especially "those that have nonethnic purposes" (1992:21).

Globalization and ethnicity

Thirty years ago Karl Deutsch wrote optimistically that "the chances of effective world organization depend...in large part on the ability of the social sciences to suggest answers...." (1966:15).

> ...the age of nationalism has grouped people apart from each other, and may for a time continue to do so. But at the same time it is preparing them, and perhaps in part has already prepared them, for a more thoroughgoing world-wide unity than has ever been seen in human history (Deutsch 1966:191).

In a more sober vein W. and M. Connor noted that "somewhat ironically, the spokesmen for most of the region's ethnic minorities have also been amongst the most avid proponents of an integrated Western Europe" because the 'overarching' presence of the European Community would tend to make national borders more permeable (1977:7). J. F. Stack, Jr. has noted how, during the 1980s, the confident predictions of liberalism that, as a consequence of the trend from a primitive, tribal stage to industrial complexity, "the primordial dimensions of ethnicity would simply become obsolete" (1986:6), were utterly contradicted. According to Yinger, "the political-moral agenda for decades to come is how to increase justice among societies, ethnic groups, races, classes, ages, sexes" (1994:vii). We may share Deutsch's confident prediction that humanity is heading "for a more thoroughgoing world-wide unity," with one qualification. This is that not only social scientists but also educators will have to impress upon their charges that diversity is an asset for all mankind and that unity should not be achieved at the cost of uniformity.

Restraining violence: overarching and non-governmental organizations

Ethnic wars have proved more catastrophic than nationalistic wars and their increasing frequency makes them much more dangerous. Future work on this subject should also aim at highlighting successful ways of intervening to reduce or check ethnic warfare and bring relief to affected populations. Research on ethnic conflict must, therefore, take into account the role of overarching international organizations, such as the UN, and regional ones, such as the Organization of African States and the Organization of American States, in checking violence, and the role of aid organizations, both governmental and non-governmental, in helping the affected populations.

The UN and regional organizations have taken over, under a 'democratic' veneer, the overarching role of former empires, with the obvious drawback that such organizations are not controlled by monolithic apparatuses but are answerable to a number of nation-states with independent armies and different, if not diverging, interests. The UN has intervened in many ethnic conflicts, with a measure of success. More often, however, its efforts have met with dismal failure. Regional organizations seem to have even less strength and unity of purpose and they have not been very active into the field. As far as aid to stricken populations is concerned, intergovernmental and non governmental organizations have been much more successful in achieving their aims.

It seems obvious that the only method of restraining ethnic violence is to utilize a power greater, even considerably greater, than that put in the field by ethnic factions. History seems to confirm this, since ethnic wars were almost non existent under the domination of empires. In ancient and recent history, empires had to quell nationalistic upsurges, but only rarely inter-ethnic strife. One might have expected the divide-and-conquer policy of empires to have fed ethnic enmities but, when revolts took place, they were mostly directed against the visible enforcers, i.e. the administration's police and army. The collapse of empires both continental and colonial, including the most recent collapse of the Soviet empire (but not yet of the Russian and Chinese) left several vacuums which were filled reluctantly by the United Nations and, more rarely, by regional organizations.

Operations sponsored by the UN are affected by a series of handicaps the most significant of which are: (1) diversity of intentions and motivations; (2) diversity of command; (3) uncoordinated behaviour of the various national forces called into the area; (4) lack of training and equipment for restraining operations rather than aggressive warfare; (5) high operational costs resulting from the previous points; and (6) direct responsibility of national governments for casualties sustained by their forces. In the former Soviet area, the Russian Federation has taken over the overarching role of the former Soviet Union, with the abysmal results we have seen in, for example, Chechnya and Tajikistan. This is a political problem which is incapable of solution until the Russian empire becomes a real democracy *vis-à-vis* all component ethnic groups.

It was suggested at this conference that an 'international legion' should be created. This would presumably eliminate handicaps (2), (3), (4), (5) and (6) by providing adequate training and equipment, by lowering costs in enrolling volunteers from all over the world and, finally, by eliminating the direct responsibility of each national government as the 'legion' would consist of volunteers from several countries, whose nationality would be overshadowed by their allegiance to the international body. It goes without saying that the setting up of such a task force would require careful and detailed study and a series of experiments before the operation could be launched in its final form. It does not seem, however, that other solutions are readily available.

Questions for future research

1. What 'ethnic' conflicts or wars may be discerned in past history? What were their types, outcomes and restraining factors?
2. Were empires overarching institutions that restrained ethnic wars?
3. Did empires end because of their excessive cost compared to the ethnic security they provided?
4. Did historical religious wars have an 'ethnic' component?
5. Has ethnicity superseded religion in recent conflicts? If so, is this because modern communications have spread political factionalism from the cities to the countryside?
6. Do ethnic feelings develop more strongly in cities or the countryside? Do they develop among élites and then spread to the rest of the population?
7. What triggering factors transform latent ethnic conflicts into out-and-out wars?
8. Can war be used as a background to explore the meaning of social differences in history because it is a strongly marked and, therefore, better researched phenomenon?
9. Do ethnic wars slow down globalization or facilitate it? What are the mechanisms by which they influence globalization?
10. What do the past successes and failures of UN intervention teach us about a more appropriate restraining organization for ethnic wars?

PART II: HUMANITARIAN INTERVENTION

As Gantzel shows in his chapter, the number of intra-state wars has grown exponentially since the 1950s and shows no sign of subsiding. The intensity of humanitarian interventions, by both public and private agencies, has been growing in parallel with the incidence of these conflicts. At the same time, private or non-governmental organizations (NGOs) have proliferated in a spectacular way, suggesting multi-faceted connections between the growth of ethnic wars and of those agencies. Therefore, it seems appropriate to examine the two phenomena together.

One reason, although not the primary one, for the extraordinary growth of humanitarian agencies is the peculiarity of ethnic, in contrast to traditional, wars. In ethnic wars the enemy lies not only on the other side of the battle lines, but may be part of the civilian population on both sides of those lines. As a consequence, the civilian population suffers as much or more than the opposing armies. This gives rise to floods of refugees and displaced people and a never ending chain of dislocations.

The supply of relief on such a large scale is a new phenomenon which may be connected to the end of the Cold War and the consequent waning of superpower engagement in developing countries (Minear & Weiss 1995:2). This considerable change in the pattern of international tensions also brought about a change in the orientation and motivations of governmental and non-governmental humanitarian operators. Until the 1970s, suspicious of each other's aims, they had followed different approaches (ODI 1995:1). Established governmental organizations are better suited to working with governmental counterparts whereas non-governmental organizations could move more easily in areas where government control and responsibilities are ill defined.

Governmental institutions are constitutionally slow-moving and hamstrung by international agreements, while private organizations can move more quickly and are more flexible. Governmental operators, furthermore, are expensive because they are weighed down by bureaucracy. As a consequence of this difference a fruitful cooperation began in the 1980s, whereby government organizations provided the high level contacts and NGOs delivered the goods to the affected populations.

> Till ten years ago, they [NGOs] worked within a confined 'humanitarian space' defined by governments in their own self interest: not a truly apolitical space but conventionally described as one. They had relatively small budgets, for all major programmes were handled by governments. In the UK, it was only in 1975 that NGOs first started receiving government funding, only in 1985 that they started receiving significant amounts of food for distribution (de Waal 1995:11).

In the meantime the 'operating environment' had also changed. At the receiving end, affected by so-called 'emergencies,' states had collapsed, while the power of the UN was progressively eroded, presumably by lack of funding and political will. The influence of the media became paramount in choosing the areas where aid should be directed; in the course of the last ten years funding by governments has become so indiscriminate that NGOs have been accused of behaving like a "rabble" in their competition for territory and visibility, while "all technical standards go to the wall" (Seaman 1995:4).

The changes in operating environment have caused NGOs to face up to the political aspects of their operations. This has entailed the acceptance of violations of national sovereignties in carrying out humanitarian operations. The examples set by NGOs have extended even to international organizations such as UNICEF. Because investment by Western donors in poor countries is declining, using NGOs for their relief programmes allows them to achieve a "high profile" with the media with little accountability (*African Rights* 1994:6).

In the last four years the international aid system has shifted its focus from long-term development to short-term relief assistance. This is partly due to the widespread failure of expensive long-term development projects and partly to the fact that short-term relief assistance is now considered the best possible response of the world community to armed conflict. This process began in the 1970s and grew considerably "in response to humanitarian emergencies...mainly in the Horn of Africa" (Adams & Bradbury 1994:27).

An obvious consequence of the mushrooming of the numbers and mandates of NGOs has been a decrease in the quality of interventions, as seen in the precedence given by the Geneva conventions to aid workers rather than civilians and in the deregulation of the "industry." Fifteen years ago, donors could only work through the ICRC in a war situation but now it is possible for any organization, by signing up with a locally recognized agency, to evade the already unsatisfactory standards of assessment and monitoring (Duffield 1995:15). As Minear and Weiss put it succintly:

> The humanitarian system labors under many strains. It is under fire from many directions, not just from the pressures of armed conflicts. Its creaks and groans are institutional and financial, political and moral. Strained or not, the system has abundant empathy, energy and experience, qualities that need to be reinforced and used effectively (1995:12).

Complex emergencies

In line with the 'soft' approach appropriate to humanitarian operators, armed conflicts entailing the most horrific excesses committed by opposing factions have been euphemistically termed 'complex emergencies.' The attribute 'complex' purports to portray the collapse of state structures while their functions are taken over by "warlords, bandits, arm dealers and so on" with whom NGOs are often forced to come to grips (de Waal 1995:19).

The adjective 'complex' distinguishes these violent conflictual situations in which "famine, food insecurity, nutritional stress and vulnerability" are the result of "political victimization," from emegencies due to natural causes (Adams & Bradbury 1994:5). People now recognize that war "is probably the single most significant factor explaining the persistence of famine in Africa today" (Adams & Bradbury 1994:18). Often violence reaches the ultimate peak of genocide, something that "human rights organizations" should be prepared to oppose with all their strength (*African Rights* 1994:29).

In recent years, the violence of these conflicts, already appalling even when 'primitive' weapons are used (witness the wholesale massacres in Rwanda), has been made even worse by the proliferation of automatic weapons, the dissemination of land mines and the curtailing of food to stricken populations. All these causes have increased civilian casualties to 90 per cent of war-related deaths as against 52 per cent during World War II (Sommerfeld 1990 cited by Adams & Bradbury 1994:4).

The background and development of humanitarian operations

The dictionary definition of 'humanitarian' as a "person promoting human welfare and social reform" (*Webster's New Collegiate Dictionary*), is insufficient to cover the activities of humanitarian agencies. No agreement exists even about the foundations of humanitarian intervention, whether it is the response of "organized institutional structures" or due to traits of "generosity and altruism," seen by some scholars as a human universal (Minear & Weiss 1995:18-20). This lack of precision is compounded by the phenomenal growth of the industry. To give a few figures, the United Nations, which started as a "modest" institution having only diplomatic aims, has increased from its approximately 50 original member states to the present 185. UN organizations headquartered in the major cities of the Western world are staffed with some 50,000 civil servants, and NGOs operating on the humanitarian scene now number in the thousands (Minear & Weiss 1995:13-5).

Recognition of humanitarian rules has grown from complete silence in the Covenant of the League of Nations, adopted after World War I, to a number of protocols signed by most major powers and even recognized by some insurgent groups. The legal status of persons who have fled their country was clearly stated in the 1951 international convention on the Status of Refugees. No such legal status is yet afforded to internally displaced persons currently more numerous than 'external' refugees who, at present, exceed 20 million. The next step required is a codification of international intervention in cases of "aggression, life threatening human suffering, and human rights abuses." 'Intervention' covers a broad spectrum of actions from a diplomatic note to military action (Minear & Weiss 1995:31-5). At present there is still considerable controversy about the meaning and scope of humanitarian intervention, which is seen by some as a contradiction in terms and opposed by many Asian and Middle Eastern governments as incompatible with the absolute sovereignty of states in "matters which are essentially within the domestic jurisdiction of any state" as per Article 2 of the UN charter (Minear & Weiss 1995:36-8).

Humanitarian actors must cope with formidable obstacles in coming to the aid of war stricken populations especially when involved in cross-border operations. They must pay attention to the social background of those populations in order to establish relations of mutual trust. The political implications and security aspects of humanitarian operations must be taken into account, both with regards to personnel and beneficiaries. All these aspects are subject to negotiations which invariably restrict "humanitarian space" (Minear & Weiss 1995:40-9).

Humanitarian actors can be categorized as either external or internal. Among the external ones are: (1) the agencies of the UN, prominent among them UNHCR, UNICEF and UNDP, however affected they are by poor coordination due to the "very limited" authority of the secretary-general and despite their "need of transparency and accountability" (*African Rights* 1994:37; Minear & Weiss 1995:46-7, 142-51); (2) governments providing humanitarian assistance directly to suffering populations which meet in a Development Assistance Committee affiliated with the OECD (Minear & Weiss 1995:47-8, 153-6); (3) NGOs, called 'private voluntary organizations' (PVOs) in the US, from the largest and long-established, such as Oxfam, Save the Children Fund, Catholic Relief Services, etc., to a miriad smaller and emerging "'mom and pop' operations that provide limited assistance to individuals affected by a specific war" (Minear & Weiss 1995:48, 157-63); (4) the all important International Committee of the Red Cross (ICRC) which acts as a standard-setting organization, "epitomizes humanitarian action at its most authentic" and is criticized by some for its "'gold-plated approach to relief operations" (Minear & Weiss 1995:49-50, 164-7); and (5) outside military forces, which have been increasingly called upon to perform humanitarian operations (e.g. in Somalia and Bosnia) but the ambivalence of whose operations (trying to keep the peace by exerting force and providing relief at the same time) raises "fundamental questions about using military forces to ameliorate war-induced suffering" (Minear & Weiss 1995:45-52, 142-178).

According to Minear and Weiss, the 'internal actors' include, (1) local governments and military authorities with which relief organizations must negotiate, insofar as their consent is required to carry out humanitarian operations (1955:53); (2) insurgent political and military forces whose consent is required for assisting the population in the contended territories (1955:53-4); and (3) local NGOs which, even though modest in scope and organization, can become useful partners in that they know best the habits and needs of the local populations (1995:54-5). Thus, humanitarian organizations range in size from the huge UNHCR, with 177 field offices, to "no frills agencies with anything but up-to-date communication systems and with staff who volunteer or work for subsistence wages" (Minear & Weiss 1995:57-59).

The military occupy a controversial, albeit important, position among humanitarian actors. They have been deployed on humanitarian missions under the UN flag in Bosnia and Somalia and under that of a single nation as, for example, the French in Rwanda. Their qualifications for disaster relief are that they

> ...possess strategic and local mobility—essential in inaccessible areas—and a wide range of specialised equipment: helicopters, aircraft, earth moving machinery, respirators, medical supplies, power and lighting equipment and under-water capability. More important, they are self-contained with their own rations and transport. They operate a command and communications system invaluable in liaising with the host government and other forces and agencies in the area (Field Marshal Lord Bramall at International Peace Academy 1986:1 in Walker 1992:154).

Nevertheless, civilian agencies are wary of cooperating with the military for several reasons. These include the need to keep the military from acting independently; the fact that military decision-making is centralized whereas NGOs devolve it to their officials in the recipient countries; the short-term nature of military operations which means that they have little effect on the more demanding long-term problems; and the fact that military resources are often more expensive than civilian ones (Walker 1992:156-7). In view of the particular qualifications of armed forces for disaster relief, however, it is worth pursuing the possibility of employing them. According to Walker "disaster relief can become a legitimate task for armies using appropriately designed techniques and purpose-built equipment, rather than hastily adapted military technology" (1992:159).

According to Minear and Weiss, humanitarian interventions should be informed by a number of "guiding principles": (1) "relieving life-threatening suffering" mainly among the 20 million 'formal' refugees, the 5 million refugees lacking 'formal' status and the estimated 25 million who "have been uprooted by violence within their own countries" (1995:60-5); (2) "proportionality" to the degree of suffering in directing interventions where they are most required, not where they fit the political ends of the donor countries (1995:65); (3) "non-partisanship," meaning not taking sides in administering humanitarian interventions (1995:58-73), also termed 'neutrality' by others (cf. Adams & Bradbury 1994:28-30); (4) "independence", i.e., the capability of obtaining from the controlling authorities permission to act without undue interference (1995:73-76); (5) "accountability" to both donors and beneficiaries (1995:77-83); (6) "appropriateness" to local circumstances, having taken into consideration local resources both in material and personnel (1995:84-9); (7) "discerning the context" by going to the root of problems and addressing the variables that affect them while at the same time making people aware of the need to respect human rights (1995:90-5); and (8) "keeping sovereignty in its proper place," by respecting sovereignty as long as it does not clash with humanitarian action (1995:96-8).

The complex functioning of humanitarian operations

> Markets are, in theory, regulated by consumer choice. In humanitarian emergencies, the 'consumers' are often destitute and are excluded from planning and coordination meetings. 'Choice', from the perspective of the intended beneficiary, is academic. If refugees and other disaster victims are unable to exercise consumer sovereignty, market-driven humanitarianism is certainly responsive to meeting the needs of other categories of 'consumers', such as major donors and army commanders (Stockton 1995:18-9).

The 'chain' of humanitarian response starts with "outside resources" which, as already seen, "are made available...through five major channels: intergovernmental organizations, the bilateral agencies or donor governments, NGOs, the ICRC, and outside military forces" (Minear & Weiss 1995:14).

NGOs have increasingly become the 'agents' or 'subcontractors' of donors in delivering humanitarian assistance to stricken populations when they do not obtain funding through their own channels. While both the gathering of funds and delivering of aid need special expertise, the latter is decidedly more difficult. According to the Overseas Development Institute the factors which have led donors to operate through NGOs include the poor performance of official donor programmes in the late 1960s and 70s, compared to the successful achievements of NGOs, the knowledge NGOs have of local difficulties and bureaucracy and their well defined constituencies of local beneficiaries (ODI 1995:2).

Despite their primacy, donors are not absolute in determining the aims and recipients of their humanitarian help because quite often they operate through other humanitarian actors, generally NGOs, whose policies are of necessity well defined and do not always coincide with those of the donors. In fact, several northern NGOs have been reluctant to accept official aid because of their "qualitatively" different approach and the fact that it would be likely "to compromise the integrity of NGO approaches to development" (ODI 1995:3). As a result, a 'reverse agenda' has taken shape whereby the "approach and methods of the NGOs are now influencing the activities and perceptions of donors." Most donors have widened their programmes to "include poverty alleviation, concern with the environment and enhancing the status of women as major aid objectives." Still, many of the long-established NGOs prefer to remain independent of official donors by collecting and managing their own funding (ODI 1995:3-4).

Stockton notes that the growth of NGOs was also aided by the need of northern donors to meet budgeting costs by using more efficient distribution networks. He also sees NGO success as obtained, in part at the expense of the "legitimacy of central governments" and comments on the possibility that "ethnically defined conflicts" may be fuelled in part by the success of NGOs in strengthening civil society while not being able to help people enhance their standard of living (Stockton 1995:17-8).

NGOs thrive on what has been termed the 'contract culture,' in that they have increasingly become the go-betweens, used by international and governmental organizations from the UN down, to convey aid to the field. This situation is condemned by Stockton who points to the "rapid expansion of humanitarian international aid and the simultaneous decline in refugee welfare and protection standards" (Stockton 1995:19). One cannot help feeling that the increasingly fierce competition between NGOs, once regulated by appropriate codes of conduct, will ultimately not be beneficial to the populations in need.

The main fuel of humanitarian action is, of course, funding. The Overseas Development Institute cites World Bank figures for 1992 which estimate total aid funds at $ 2.5 billion. Again, the ODI estimates that approximately "5% [more probably 50%] of all official aid is now channeled to NGOs" (ODI 1995:1). Financing is largely affected by the public and by pressure groups, hence the overwhelming importance of the media (Seaman 1995:3). The situation is described tersely by *African Rights*:

> Band Aid in 1984 was a watershed in international responses to disasters in Africa. It was a demonstration of the power of the media and international NGOs, who succeeded in reversing the policies of the major western powers, which had neglected Ethiopia's needs on account of Cold War realpolitik (*African Rights* 1994:11).

And further:

> Occasionally—repeatedly if unpredictably—the international media gives [*sic*] saturation coverage to a particular emergency that creates an unstoppable momentum for immediate supply of relief (*African Rights* 1994:8).

Media coverage has become so shrill in some cases that the "representation of misery" has been described as "a branch of entertainment" (Benthall 1995:7). There is no doubt that the future of NGOs will be greatly affected by television coverage and by the public's response.

To complete the picture of humanitarian operations one should mention local or "southern" NGOs which are destined in turn to take on a greater role. Indigenous NGOs have grown in numbers during the past 15 years from their early beginnnings in South and East Asia. Donors have been recognizing the merits of southern NGOs and increasing their share of fundings (ODI 1995:3). In one recent case, that of the Eritrean Relief Agency, the results achieved by the local structure paying attention to the needs of the entire community, including health and education, outstripped the traditional NGO approach (*African Rights* 1994:12; Minear & Weiss 1994:2).

Relief agencies have grown in experience and stature to a point where they "are now empowered to make important political judgements which go far beyond their traditional role" (*African Rights* 1994:2). As a result they are seen by international and national organizations as the *representatives* of needy populations and hence are increasingly protected by international conventions implemented by the UN Security Council and other organizations. They are seen, in other words, "as proxies for the suffering populations" whose rights may be consequently neglected (*African Rights* 1994:8; de Waal 1995:1).

Objectionable and useless practices in humanitarian intervention

To give an overall picture of the humanitarian industry one should also point out the failings and outright objectionable practices that its operations frequently entail (cf. Hancock 1989). The first and, one might say, structural objection is that, "having grown phenomenally in the wake of armed conflicts, NGOs may be becoming accommodated to them" (Adams & Bradbury 1994:27). The implication is that they may be fattening like vultures, on wars and distress.

A quite widespread practice of Western governments is the "cynical use of humanitarianism as a smokescreen, either for following a certain political agenda or for the absence of a political agenda" (*African Rights* 1994:8-9). Minear & Weiss call such governments "political wolves [masquerading] as humanitarian sheep" and point to Japan's invasion of Manchuria in 1931, Hitler's invasion of the Sudetic mountains to 'protect' their people, and Soviet Russia's invasion of Afghanistan in 1979 to 'protect' that nation against itself (1995:31-2). De Waal describes the UN intervention in Bosnia, as an attempt to conceal the "lack of political action" (1995:11).

> Humanitarian discourse is developing into a humanitarian hegemony, its language leaves virtually no room for dissent. It is difficult to question the motives or efficiency of the HI [humanitarian international] without appearing to advocate what they are opposed to, that is to say war and famine and suffering (de Waal 1995:11).

Among the objectionable consequences of humanitarian operations is the risk of aiding one or both factions. This may happen in several ways: (1)

providing material assistance to the authority controlling the area by, for instance, allowing a share of the provisions for the population to be diverted to one of the combatants; (2) providing strategic protection by, for instance, allowing strategic material to be shipped with convoys marked for aid shipments; and, most of all, (3) providing legitimation to the controlling authority (*African Rights* 1994:4-5). The very act of negotiating for access legitimates the controlling authorities (Duffield 1995:14). As Stockton notes, "Given the media profile that NGOs seek, it is obvious why aspiring insurgents prefer dealing with the international NGOs to the publicity shy ICRC" (1995:19).

Another objectionable aspect is the willingness of some NGOs to make compromises with the controlling factions in the interests of their own humanitarian venture (*African Rights* 1994:25). Critics have termed this 'fieldcraft,' in that it elevates *realpolitik* above concern for the abuse of human rights by the controlling authorities under the very eye of humanitarian operators. The common excuse is that the mere presence of humanitarian agencies prevents abuses, but this is not always true (*African Rights* 1994:26). The choice offered to NGOs witnessing human rights abuses is to remain silent, to speak up and be expelled or to side openly with the anti-government forces. In the present absence of clear standards of behaviour and mandates,

> ...the central dilemma is whether it is possible to supply humanitarian assistance under the auspices of a government authority that abuses human rights, without also giving undue assistance to that authority and hence doing a disservice to the people one is aiming to help (*African Rights* 1994:4).

De Waal puts himself in the shoes of the people receiving assistance in interpreting their perception of relief workers:

> They are not people who are making a sacrifice to assist the poor and vulnerable, but immensely wealthy foreigners who descend from aircraft, spending a short time consulting with local people, never in the vernacular. The questions HI [humanitarian international] people ask have more to do with politics and military questions than with what would normally be thought as charitable concerns. They frequently fail to display elementary courtesy to local elders, bishops and so forth, they give and withdraw assistance with apparent caprice, very rarely in accordance with comprehensible principles, and they very often fail to check to see whether their help is taken by the poorest or by the military. This behaviour gives rise to a variety of perceptions of the HI sometimes approximating to cargo cults. The viewpoint of educated southerners who work within the HI is, if anything, more cynical and ambivalent, they see racism, 'glass ceilings', corruption, incompetence, political bias, lack of trust of the Sudanese (1995:10).

In addition to the objectionable consequences of NGO operations and their workers' behaviour, it is necessary to look at two forms of outside intervention which are considered objectionable by some humanitarian operators.

Firstly, some observers see cease-fires as counter-productive in that they allow the forces of the dominant faction, usually the government-initiated repression, to re-deploy and utilize movements of material and aid for its own advantage inhibiting at the same time access to populations in insurgent controlled areas (Adams & Bradbury 1994:47; *African Rights* 1994:11-2). African Rights cites as an example the 1990-91 attempts to bring about a cease fire between the Ethiopians and the EPLF, "Fortunately, these peace efforts did not succeed...Mengistu would have been able to pursue a new war strategy...." (*African Rights* 1994:12; cf. Minear & Weiss 1995:25). Adams and Bradbury cite the Rwandan crisis where a cease fire would have prevented the RPF forces from putting an end to the blood letting, Sudan, where Operation Lifeline Sudan "has become integrated into sustaining the local war economy," and Bosnia where the "'peace havens' have arguably frozen the war offering little future for those in the havens, evidenced in the high rates of depression and suicide" (Adams & Bradbury 1994:49).

Secondly, peace-making efforts are a further target of criticism by some observers, on the grounds that: (1) they serve as a cover for preparations for more intense war; (2) they waste the time and distract the attention of the insurgent leaders from their own constituencies; and (3) the fact that these initiatives are handled by outside parties forces local leaders to cater to "the demands of these outsiders" rather than to the needs of their constituents (*African Rights* 1994:16). The critics are forced to concede that some good came out of the peace initiative by IGADD in Southern Sudan in that it forced the government to show its hand in refusing to yield to the human rights-based claims of the Southern Sudanese factions (*African Rights* 1994:16).

Organizational methodology for humanitarian operations

Minear and Weiss have proposed a list of steps to be taken by humanitarian actors before entering a war affected zone: (1) evaluating with the utmost clarity, "the nature and extent of human suffering" as "the basis for future humanitarian action" (1995:106-8); (2) negotiating access to stricken populations, bringing into the picture all the humanitarian actors involved (1995:111-6); (3) raising the necessary resources from the public or private sectors by publicizing the undertaking or having recourse to their own constituents (1995:116-8); (4) delivering relief and protecting human rights, perhaps the most difficult step in the sequence as it entails huge logistical problems in unsafe territory and problems of credibility both with the recipients and the controlling authorities (1995:119-22); (5) coordinating operations with all other agencies in the area so as not to work at cross purposes (1995:126-7); (6) making the supporting public and donor governments aware of the problems of the stricken populations—this step should probably be taken from the very beginning—so as to receive the necessary contributions (1995:129-31); and (7) paying attention to the long-term problems of the population so as to allow them to pull themselves out of the poverty caused by war—admittedly a difficult task for organizations hard pressed by the immediacy of complex emergencies (1995:131-4).

The last item is taken up by Adams and Bradbury, who note that the *endemic* duration of armed conflicts has blurred the "simplistic, and by now anachronistic, distinction between development and relief" (1994:35). In other words long-term programmes must stand up even during crises and short-term relief must be compatible with long-term development. Development policies must avoid the danger of exacerbating conflict by enhancing the difference between rich and poor (1994:37). Duffield points out that war should not be considered a development opportunity, a tendency growing out of an "accommodation with violence and protracted crisis" (1995:14). Minear and Weiss quote a Chinese proverb: "Give a starving man a fish, and he will need more fish; give him a pole and he will provide for himself" (1995:29). The humanitarian operator should not be overwhelmed by the immediate emergency, but consider also long-term measures: some relief operators have begun to provide seeds for future harvests to displaced populations and taught them how to organize their own medical facilities (Minear & Weiss 1995:29). The following remark aptly sums up the situation:

> Relief and development have come to be viewed as ends of a continuum, interacting rather than existing in static isolation (Minear & Weiss 1995:29).

Several authors underscore the importance of having recourse to the insights of local people, because their attitudes are different from those of Westerners and their participation is paramount in the preparation of plans to address their needs. Efforts should be made to facilitate communications with them by all available means (Adams and Bradbury 1994:53; Harrell-Bond 1986; Slim & Thompson 1993; de Waal 1989; Wallace 1990). At the same time, relief organizations should be careful not to raid the local structures for personnel. One can readily see how the activity of relief operators is based on a delicate balance between pursuing a logistical target and respecting the social environment.

African Rights goes even further, calling for "solidarity" which "although implicit in the philosophies of most development oriented NGOs...is rarely transferred to...the victims of oppression in times of disaster" (*African Rights* 1994:26). In addition to dedication to human rights, "solidarity" should entail "consultation with and accountability to the people...; shared risk and suffering with the people; concrete action in support of the people and their cause" (*African Rights* 1994:27).

Obviously the participation of highly qualified personnel is a primary factor for the success of humanitarian endeavours. Here again, in addition to the critical comments of de Waal quoted above (page 239), one must register the fact that the increasing level of danger discourages older and more experienced personnel from accepting employment in the field thus leaving such demanding jobs to young and inexperienced staff (*African Rights* 1994:7). Adams and Bradbury note that the composition of a team is fundamental to an effective relief operation and that this should be achieved by the proper balance of gender and ethnic provenance, in addition to thorough training of a multi-skilled staff supplemented by the necessary specialists. They further note that relief operators in emergencies tend to rely on expatriate staff entailing a high turnover and high costs and "the lack of an institutional memory." They stress the need for training a local staff and "equipping them with the skills, tools and confidence with such situations that will diminish the need for distance management" (1994:57-9).

Because populations in distress are made up of about an equal number of men and women, in addition to the fact that women care for children and, therefore, represent considerably more than one half of the population, it is essential that relief staff should include women, especially at the interface with the population receiving assistance. Adams and Bradbury point out that "the injustice and violence" suffered by women are more widespread than armed conflicts and that women's "material, physical, economic and psychological role is fundamental to the way in which people and communities survive and cope with armed conflicts" (1994:21). Because women traditionally work on the 'inside' of communities, they are all-important when the community is going through a crisis. In certain cases their community management roles have been recognized (Templer 1995:20). Dodd also notes that women, because of their affinal links with patrilineal groups, can sometimes act as go-betweens among warring factions (1995:21).

The future of humanitarian intervention and NGOs

The recent failures of humanitarian ventures in Sudan, Somalia, Bosnia and Rwanda have prompted some critics to conclude that "the HI [humanitarian international] has over-reached itself" and that its main concern is with "charitable work" so that "human rights concerns will be fudged or jettisoned" (*African Rights* 1994:36). The Overseas Development Institute foresees a dramatic increase in the use of southern NGOs by northern donors. It acknowledges the momentary decrease in private funding and the cuts in donor allocations and, correctly, attributes this to cuts in social aid across the board, brought about by the worldwide financial crisis (ODI 1995:4). More pessimistically, Mark Duffield foresees "a time without restraint or principle in international affairs" and, as a consequence, "a period of great opportunity for a deregulated relief and development industry." He sees an increasing "polarization" between 'haves' and 'have nots' which, on account of "the hegemony of free-market ideology," is not destined to decrease in the short term (1995:16).

Even though they acknowledge that the "structure for future humanitarian action requires substantial reform," Minear and Weiss are more hopeful, they suggest a set of "four actions." Firstly, reform of humanitarian operations should begin with more incisiveness by the UN leadership. It should give clearer mandates to its special representatives and obtain the "strong backing" of the major actors in a crisis. NGOs will certainly be the preferred channel—the major ones should provide educational initiatives in addition to "alerting the media"—and while expanding their scale of activities they should remain committed to "responsiveness and independence...preserving at the same time their special heterogeneity and autonomy" (1995:199-204). Secondly, there should be greater accountability *vis-à-vis* both donors and beneficiaries (1995:207-11). Thirdly, there should be interventions in areas where "disasters" are "waiting to happen," such as "in much of the former Soviet Union and in the Zaires of the Third World" (this seems a naive demand, as it does not take into account the possible destabilizing impact of such interventions in areas where strife has not yet exploded, because they would constitute a glaring proof that the local government no longer has the power and competence to face a possible emergency) (1995:211-4). Fourthly, the decision to use force should be judged carefully and, once made, should be followed through effectively. Short and ineffectual interventions should be avoided. "Hollow gestures can be worse than no action at all" (1995:214-9).

Questions for future research

1. Is it possible to evaluate the effectiveness of NGOs by identifying the relative costs per assisted person in a given theatre?
2. Is it possible to define criteria for the evaluation of NGO effectiveness in general?
3. Can one obtain more accurate estimates of global financing devolved to NGOs and directly utilized by official donors? (Note the fuzziness of the figures given by ODI [1994]. It is said on page 1 that the World Bank put the 1992 figure at $ 2.5 billion and that in aggregate about 5% [prob. 50%] of all official aid is now channelled to NGOs [approximately $ 125 million]. This is said to represent about 30 per cent of total NGO income which would then amount to about $ 400

million. On page 4, however, a figure of $ 5.4 billion is given for 1994, different from the previous figures even if 50% instead of 5%.

4. Can one classify NGOs according to levels of activity?
5. Which geopolitical or social factors cause the media to focus on particular areas of the world as being in need of relief operations?
6. What forms did humanitarian assistance take in the past?
7. What is the rationale for humanitarian assistance in the present?
8. Would it be expedient and possible to establish a code of conduct for NGOs and a monitoring organization to check conducts and apply sanctions to delinquent ones?
9. Is the British 'best network of NGOs' due to the coverage of world affairs by the BBC or to Britain's colonial history?
10. To what extent are relief operators the successors of colonialism?
11. Is it possible to draft a realistic agenda that can be applied to early preventive operations?

References in Part I

Armstrong, J. A.
1992 The Autonomy of Ethnic Identity: Historic Cleavages and Nationality Relations in the USSR. In *Thinking Theoretically About Soviet Nationalities: History and Comparison in the Study of the USSR.* A. J. Motyl (ed.), pp. 23-43. New York: Columbia University Press.

Arutiunov, S. A., & Y. V. Bromley
1978 Problems of Ethnicity in Soviet Ethnographic Studies. In *Perspectives on Ethnicity.* R. E. Holloman & S. A. Arutiunov (eds.), pp. 11-13. The Hague: Mouton Publishers.

Balandier, G.
1970 *The Sociology of Black Africa: Social Dynamics in Central Africa.* New York: Praeger Publishers.

Banton, M. P.
1983 *Racial and Ethnic Competition.* Cambridge: Cambridge University Press.

Barot, R.
1993 Religion, Ethnicity and Social Change: An Introduction. In *Religion and Ethnicity: Minorities and Social Change in the Metropolis.* R. Barot (ed.), pp. 1-16. Kampen (The Netherlands): Kok Pharos Publishing House.

Barth, F.
1969 Introduction. In *Ethnic Groups and Boundaries: The Social Organization of Culture Difference.* F. Barth (ed.), pp. 9-38. Boston: Little, Brown & Co.

Beissinger, M. R.
1993 Demise of an Empire-State: Identity, Legitimacy, and the Deconstruction of Soviet Politics. In *The Rising Tide of Cultural Pluralism: The Nation-State at Bay?* C. Young (ed.), pp. 93-115. Milwaukee: The University of Wisconsin Press.

Bell, D.
1975 Ethnicity and Social Change. In *Ethnicity: Theory and Experience*. N. Glazer & D. P. Moynihan (eds.), pp. 141-174. Cambridge, MA: Harvard University Press.

Bennett, J. W.
1973 Introduction: A Guide to the Collection. In *The New Ethnicity: Perspectives from Ethnology*. 1973 Proceedings of The American Ethnological Society. J. W. Bennett (ed.), pp. 3-10. St. Paul, MN: West Publishing Co.

Bentley, G. C.
1981 *Ethnicity and Nationality: A Bibliographic Guide*. Seattle: University of Washington Press.

Berger, P. L., & T. Luckmann
1966 *The Social Construction of Reality: A Treatise in the Sociology of Knowledge*. Garden City: Double Day.

Bernardi, B.
1995 Ethnicità e confini. Il fattore etnico. In *Etnia e stato. Localismo e universalismo*, pp. 49-68. Roma: Studium.

Brass, P. R.
1991 *Ethnicity and Nationalism: Theory and Comparison*. Newbury Park: Sage Publications.

Butt Philip, A.
1980 European Nationalism in the Nineteenth and Twentieth Centuries. In *The Roots of Nationalism: Studies in Northern Europe*. R. Mitchison (ed.), pp. 1-9. Edinburgh: John Donald Publishers Ltd.

Connor, W., & M. Connor
1977 Political Fusion and Ethnic Fission in Western Europe. In *Ethnicity*. A. M. Greeley & G. Baum (eds.), pp. 1-8. New York: The Seabury Press.

Despres, L. A.
1975 Introduction. In *Ethnicity and Resource Competition in Plural Societies*. L. A. Despres (ed.), pp. 1-7. The Hague: Mouton Publishers.

Deutsch, K. W.
1966 *Nationalism and Social Communication*. Cambridge, MA: The M.I.T. Press.

Edari, R. S.
1984 Introduction: Racial Minorities and Forms of Ideological Mystification. In *Racism and the Denial of Human Rights: Beyond Ethnicity*. M. J. Berlowitz & R. S. Edari (eds.), pp. 7-18. Minneapolis: MEP Publications.

Enloe, C. H.
1986 Ethnicity, the State, and the New International Order. In *The Primordial Challenge: Ethnicity in the Contemporary World*. J. F. Stack, Jr. (ed.), pp. 24-42. Westport, CO: Greenwood Press.

Geertz, C.
1963 *Old Societies and New States: The Quest for Modernity in Asia and Africa.* Glencoe, IL: Free Press.

Gellner, E.
1992 Nationalism in the Vacuum. In *Thinking Theoretically About Soviet Nationalities: History and Comparison in the Study of the USSR.* A. J. Motyl (ed.), pp. 243-254. New York: Columbia University Press.

Glazer, N., & D. P. Moynihan
1975 Introduction. In *Ethnicity: Theory and Experience.* N. Glazer & D. P. Moynihan (eds.), pp. 1-26. Cambridge, MA: Harvard University Press.

Grande Encyclopédie
1896-98 *La Grande encyclopédie: Inventaire raisonné des sciences, des lettres et des arts.* Paris: H. Lamirault et C.ie, Editeurs.

Greeley, A. M.
1977 Editorial Summary. In *Ethnicity.* A. M. Greeley & G. Baum (eds.), pp. 57-59. New York: The Seabury Press.

Guidieri, R., & F. Pellizzi
1988 Introduction: "Smoking Mirrors"—Modern Polity and Ethnicity. In *Ethnicities and Nations: Processes of Interethnic Relations in Latin America, Southeast Asia and the Pacific.* R. Guidieri, F. Pellizzi & S. J. Tambiah (eds.), pp. 7-38. Austin: University of Texas Press.

Handler, R.
1994 Is "Identity" a Useful Cross-cultural Concept? In *Commemorations : The Politics of National Identity.* J. R. Gillis (ed.), pp. 27-40. Princeton, NJ: Princeton University Press.

Hechter, M.
1986 Theories of Ethnic Relations. In *The Primordial Challenge: Ethnicity in the Contemporary World.* J. F. Stack, Jr. (ed.), pp. 13-24. Westport, CO: Greenwood Press.

Hobsbawm, E.
1983 Introduction: Inventing Traditions. In *The Invention of Tradition.* E. Hobsbawm & T. Ranger (eds.), pp. 1-14. Cambridge: Cambridge University Press.

Holloman, R. E.
1978 The Study of Ethnicity: An Overview. In *Perspectives on Ethnicity.* R. E. Holloman & S. A. Arutiunov (eds.), pp. 3-9. The Hague: Mouton Publishers.

Horowitz, D. L.
1975 Ethnic Identity. In *Ethnicity: Theory and Experience.* N. Glazer & D. P. Moynihan (eds.), pp. 111-140. Cambridge, MA: Harvard Univ. Press.
1992 How to Begin Thinking Comparatively About Soviet Ethnic Problems. In *Thinking Theoretically About Soviet Nationalities: History and Comparison in the Study of the USSR.* A. J. Motyl (ed.), pp. 9-22. New York: Columbia University Press.

Jackson, P., & J. Penrose
1993 Introduction: placing "race" and nation. In *Constructions of race, place, and nation.* P. Jackson & J. Penrose (eds.), pp. 1-23. London: UCL Press.

Jackson, R. H.
1984 Ethnicity. In *Social Science Concepts: A Systematic Analysis*. G. Sartori (ed.), pp. 205-233. London: Sage Publications.

Kellas, J. G.
1991 *The Politics of Nationalism and Ethnicity*. London: Macmillan.

Morris, H. S.
1968 Ethnic Groups. In *International Encyclopedia of the Social Sciences*. Vol. 5 & 6. London: Collier-Macmillan Publishers.

Mullings, L.
1984 Ethnicity and Stratification in the Urban United States. In *Racism and the Denial of Human Rights: Beyond Ethnicity*. M. J. Berlowitz & R. S. Edari (eds.), pp. 21-38. Minneapolis: MEP Publications.

Panayi, P.
1994 *Immigration, ethnicity and racism in Britain, 1815-1945*. Manchester: Manchester University Press.

Parsons, T.
1975 Some theoretical Considerations on the Nature of Trends of Change of Ethnicity. In *Ethnicity: Theory and Experience*. N. Glazer & D. P. Moynihan (eds.), pp. 53-83. Cambridge, MA: Harvard University Press.

Rex, J.
1993 Religion and Ethnicity in the Metropolis. In *Religion and Ethnicity: Minorities and Social Change in the Metropolis*. R. Barot (ed.), pp. 17-26. Kampen (The Netherlands): Kok Pharos Publishing House.

Riggs, F. W. (ed.)
1985 *Ethnicity: INTERCOCTA Glossary. Concepts and terms used in Ethnicity Research* (pilot edition). Honolulu: Dept. of Political Science, University of Hawaii.
1986 *Help for social scientists: a new kind of reference process*. Paris: UNESCO.

Rokkan, S., & D. Urwin
1983 *Economy, Territory, Identity: Politics of West European Peripheries*. London: Sage.

Roosens, E. E.
1989 *Creating Ethnicity: The Process of Ethnogenesis*. Newbury Park: Sage Publications.

Roth, G., & C. Wittich (eds.)
1968 *Economy and Society: An Outline of Interpretive Sociology*. New York: Bedminster Press.

Rustow, D. A.
1968 Nation. In *International Encyclopedia of the Social Sciences*. Vol. 11, pp. 7-14. London: Collier-Macmillan Publishers.

Sandberg, E.
1994 Introduction: The Changing Politics of Non-Governmental Organizations and the African State. In *The Changing Politics of Non-Governmental Organizations and African States*. E. Sandberg (ed.), pp. 1-31. Westport, CO: Praeger.

Smith, A. D.
1992 Ethnic Identity and Territorial Nationalism in Comparative Perspective. In *Thinking Theoretically About Soviet Nationalities: History and Comparison in the Study of the USSR*. A. J. Motyl (ed.), pp. 45-65. New York: Columbia University Press.

Sollors, W.
1989 Introduction: The Invention of Ethnicity. In *The Invention of Ethnicity*. W. Sollors (ed.), pp. ix-xx. Oxford: Oxford University Press.

Sowell, T.
1983 *The Economics and Politics of Race: An International Perspective*. New York: William Morrow and Co. Inc.

Stack, Jr., J. F.
1986 Ethnic Mobilization in World Politics: The Primordial Perspective. In *The Primordial Challenge: Ethnicity in the Contemporary World*. J. F. Stack, Jr. (ed.), pp. 1-11. Westport, CO: Greenwood Press.

Tambiah, S. J.
1988 Foreword. In *Ethnicities and Nations: Processes of Interethnic Relations in Latin America, Southeast Asia and the Pacific*. R. Guidieri, F. Pellizzi & S. J. Tambiah (eds.), pp. 1-6. Austin: University of Texas Press.

Thompson, R. H.
1989 *Theories of Ethnicity: A Critical Appraisal*. Westport, CO: Greenwood Press.

Toland, J. D.
1993 Introduction: Dialogue of Self and Other: Ethnicity and the Statehood Building Process. In *Ethnicity and the State*. Political and Legal Anthropology, Vol. 9. J. D. Toland (ed.), pp. 1-20. New Brunswick: Transaction Publishers.

Van den Berghe, P. L.
1970 *Race and Ethnicity: Essays in Comparative Sociology*. New York: Basic Books, Inc., Publishers.
1975 Ethnicity and Class in Highland Peru. In *Ethnicity and Resource Competition in Plural Societies*. L. A. Despres (ed.), pp. 71-85. The Hague: Mouton Publishers.
1981 *The Ethnic Phenomenon*. New York: Elsevier.

Van Horne, W. A., & W. W. Prange
1984 Introduction. In *Ethnicity and War*. W. A. Van Horne (ed.), pp. 1-20. Milwaukee: University of Wisconsin Press.

Vawter, B.
1977 Universalism in the New Testament. In *Ethnicity*. A. M. Greeley & G. Baum (eds.), pp. 78-84. New York: The Seabury Press.

Vincent, J.
1993 Ethnicity and the State in Northern Ireland. In *Ethnicity and the State*. Political and Legal Anthropology, Vol. 9. J. D. Toland (ed.), pp. 123-146. New Brunswick: Transaction Publishers.

Watson, J. L.
1977 Introduction: Immigration, Ethnicity, and Class in Britain. In *Between Two Cultures: Migrants and Minorities in Britain*. J. L. Watson (ed.), pp. 1-20. Oxford: Basil Blackwell.

Weber, M.
1964 *Wirtschaft und Gesellschaft: Grundriss der verstehenden Soziologie*. Köln - Berlin: Kiepenheuer & Witsch.
1978 *Economy and Society: An Outline of Interpretive Sociology*. G. Roth & C. Wittich (eds.). Berkeley: University of California Press.

Yinger, J. M.
1985 Ethnicity. *Am. Rev. of Sociology* 11: 151-180.
1994 *Ethnicity: Source of Strength: Source of Conflict?* New York: State University of New York Press.

Young, C.
1993 The Dialectics of Cultural Pluralism: Concept and Reality. In *The Rising Tide of Cultural Pluralism: The Nation-State at Bay?* C. Young (ed.), pp. 3-35. Milwaukee: The University of Wisconsin Press.

References in Part II

Adams, M., & M. Bradbury
1994 Organisational Adaptation in Conflict Situations. A Theme Paper for the 'Development in Conflict Workshop,' Birmingham, 1-2 November, 1994.

African Rights
1994 Humanitarianism unbound? Current dilemmas facing multi-mandate relief operations in political emergencies. Discussion paper No.5. *African Rights* November 1994.

Benthall, J.
1995 NGOs under the media regime. In *International NGO's and Complex Political Emergencies: Perspectives from Anthropology*. Exploratory workshop held at the London School of Economics, 9 January 1995. London: Royal Anthropological Institute.

Dodd, R.
1995 NGOs and the co-option of anthropology. In *International NGO's and Complex Political Emergencies: Perspectives from Anthropology*. Exploratory workshop held at the London School of Economics, 9 January 1995. London: Royal Anthropological Institute.

Duffield, M.
1995 NGO responses to complex political emergencies. In *International NGO's and Complex Political Emergencies: Perspectives from Anthropology*. Exploratory workshop held at the London School of Economics, 9 January 1995. London: Royal Anthropological Institute.

Hancock, G.
1989 *Lords of poverty: The free-wheeling lifestyles, power, prestige and corruption of the multi-billion dollar aid business*. London: Macmillan.

Harrell-Bond, B.
1986 *Imposing Aid: Emergency Assistance to Refugees*. Oxford: Oxford University Press.

International Peace Academy
1986 *Immediate Response: The Logistics of Disaster Relief.* Report of a conference held in London.

Lewis, I.
1995 Local level reconciliation versus Eurocentric "conflict resolution". In *International NGO's and Complex Political Emergencies: Perspectives from Anthropology.* Exploratory workshop held at the London School of Economics, 9 January 1995. London: Royal Anthropological Institute.

Minear, L., & T. G. Weiss
1995 *Mercy under Fire: War and the Global Humanitarian Community.* Boulder, CO: Westview Press

ODI
1994 NGOs and official donors. *Overseas Development Institute Briefing Paper* 1995 (4), August.

Seaman, J.
1995 The changing context for international NGOs. In *International NGO's and Complex Political Emergencies: Perspectives from Anthropology.* Exploratory workshop held at the London School of Economics, 9 January 1995. London: Royal Anthropological Institute.

Stockton, N.
1995 Aid under fire: relief and development in an unstable world. *DHA News.*

Summerfield, D. A.
1990 The Psychological Effects of Conflict in the Third World: A Short Study. Unpublished paper for Oxfam.

Templer, G.
1995 Discussion. In *International NGO's and Complex Political Emergencies: Perspectives from Anthropology.* Exploratory workshop held at the London School of Economics, 9 January 1995. London: Royal Anthropological Institute.

de Waal, A.
1989 *Famine that Kills.* Oxford: Clarendon Press.
1995 NGOs as institutions. In *International NGO's and Complex Political Emergencies: Perspectives from Anthropology.* Exploratory workshop held at the London School of Economics, 9 January 1995. London: Royal Anthropological Institute.

Walker, P.
1992 Foreign Military Resources for Disaster Relief: An NGO Perspective. *Disasters* 16 (2): 152-159.

Wallace, T.
1990 Refugee Women: Their Perspectives and Our Responses. Paper for the Institute of Social Studies, The Hague.

INDEX*

* *List of acronyms at end of Index*

List of acronyms:

BBC = British Broadcasting Corporation
CARE = Cooperative for Assistance and Relief Everywhere
CIS = Community of Independent States
COMECON = Council for Mutual Economic Assistance
CSCE = Conference for Security and Co-operation in Europe
EEC = European Economic Community
ECHO = European Community Humanitarian Office
EPLF = Eritrean People's Liberation Front
EPRDF = Ethiopian People's Revolutionary Democratic Front
ERA = Eritrean Relief Agency
EU = European Union
GATT = General Agreement on Tariffs and Trade
GNP = Gross National Product
ICRC = International Committee of the Red Cross
IFLO = Islamic Front for the Liberation of Oromiya
IGADD = Inter-governmental Authority on Drought and Development
IMF = International Monetary Fund
NATO = North Atlantic Treaty Organization
NGOs = Non governmental organizations
OALF = Oromo-Abbo Liberation Front
OAS = Organization of African States, Organization of American States
OAU = Organization of African Unity
ODI = Overseas Development Institute
OECD = Organization for Economic Cooperation and Development
OLF = Oromo Liberation Front
OPDO = Oromo People's Democratic Organization
PDO = People's Democratic Organizations
PVOs = Private Voluntary Organizations
RPF = Rwandan Patriotic Front
SALF = Somali-Abbo Liberation Front
SAM = Sanctions Assistance Mission
SNM = Somaliland National Movement
SSDF = Somali Salvation Democratic Front
TNC = Transitional National Council
TPLF = Tigray People's Liberation Front
UN = United Nations
UNDHA = United Nations Department of Humanitarian Affairs
UNDP = United Nations Development Program
UNESCO = United Nations Educational, Scientific and Cultural Organization
UNHCR = United Nations Hich Commissioner for Refugees
UNICEF = United Nations Children's Fund
UNITAF = Unified Task Force
UNOSOM = United Nations Operation in Somalia
UNPROFOR = United Nations Protection Force
UNRISD = United Nations Research Institute for Social Development
UOPLL = United Oromo People's Leadership for Liberation
USC = United Somali Congress
WEU = West European Union
WSLF = Western Somali Liberation Front

Page-setting: *Alta Qualità sas (Milano, Italy)*

Printers: *Studiostampa S.A. (R.S.M.)*